LEGEND

1 Emma Elizabeth Smith
2 Martha Tabram
3 Mary Ann Nichols
4 Annie Chapman
5 Elizabeth Stride
6 Catherine Eddowes
7 Mary Jane Kelly
8 Alice McKenzie
9 Female Torso
10 Frances Coles
XA The Goulston St. Graffiti
XB 22 Batty Street

The Lodger

THE LODGER

The Arrest and Escape of Jack the Ripper

Stewart P Evans and Paul Gainey

LONDON NEW YORK SYDNEY TORONTO

This edition published 1995 by BCA
by arrangement with Century

Copyright © Stewart Evans and Paul Gainey

CN 5835

Printed and bound in Great Britain by
Mackays of Chatham PLC, Chatham, Kent

FOR ERIC BARTON WHO MADE IT ALL POSSIBLE
AND
IN MEMORY OF RAY COLE – PARTNER IN CRIME

FOR MUM AND DAD
AND
MY GRANDPARENTS
WITH LOVE AND ADMIRATION

'The world needs to go through a process of purification in order to make it what it ought to be'

The Littlechild Suspect, 1889

Contents

Foreword

It gives me great pleasure to write this foreword to Stewart Evans and Paul Gainey's book, for Stewart's discovery was first reported in the April 1993 issue of *Ripperana*, a journal of Ripper research which I had founded in July of the previous year. The romance which continues to drive this research ever onward is invariably fuelled by but one dream: that somewhere must exist a yellowing document, in a forgotten corner, which will shed sensational new light on the great mystery of 1888. Rarely do such documents turn up, even more rarely do they prove to be of crucial importance to Ripper studies.

Although on the face of it straightforward enough, it was immediately apparent that Stewart's find was the most important since Dan Farson's discovery of a copy of Macnaghten's CID memorandum in 1959. What he had unearthed was a letter written on 23 September 1913 by Chief Inspector John Littlechild to the distinguished author and journalist G. R. Sims. Not only did this letter disabuse Sims of his belief that Macnaghten's favoured suspect, 'Dr D(ruitt)', was the most likely, it also stated that another senior CID officer, Sir Robert Anderson, 'only thought he knew' when he asserted that the killer had been definitely ascertained to be a Polish Jew.

Littlechild went on to outline his own suspect, a man previously unknown to modern researchers. What was immediately fascinating was that the Chief Inspector had worked for the Secret Department (Special Branch) at Scotland Yard, under the command of James Monro, rather than for the Criminal Investigation Department, which most people had long assumed to have had an exclusive interest in the Whitechapel murders. We soon realised that here, at last, was a potential solution to an intriguing mystery within a mystery – just what Home Secretary Henry Matthews was getting at in a private memo dated 22 September 1888, which read:

Stimulate the police about [the] Whitechapel Murders. Monro

might be willing to give a hint to the CID people if necessary.

Here is a clear indication that Monro's Secret Department suspected someone whose identity was unknown to the regular detective force, presumably because they had their own reasons for watching him. We do not know if the 'hint' was given, but the suspect was finally arrested and subsequently escaped the grasp of the police. If this had become known it would have caused an enormous number of red faces (or worse) at both Scotland Yard and the Home Office, with the Home Secretary's face undoubtedly the reddest of all. A smoke-screen was therefore put up by the most senior officers in the CID, Anderson and Macnaghten, as implied in the Littlechild letter. Monro himself in later life, remained reticent about the truth, but recognised that it was 'a very hot potato'.

Among the many firsts in the Ripper case was the pioneering use of crime-scene photography in Britain (at Miller's Court). The *British Journal of Photography*, on 16 November 1888, savoured the fact that their advice in this matter had been heeded by the Metropolitan Police, 'for we all know that our police authorities are credited with never being over-sanguine with any innovation which would necessitate a departure from any groove to which they are accustomed.' These photographs call to mind another sentence in the Littlechild letter, where the author states that his suspect was a 'Psychopathia Sexualis subject', a reference to a work published in 1887 by the Austrian Professor Richard von Krafft-Ebing. This book, for example, describes the case of a certain Andreas Bichel who confessed:

I opened her breast and with a knife cut through the fleshy parts of the body. Then I arranged the body as a butcher does beef . . . while opening the body [I] could have cut out a piece and eaten it.

The learned Professor commented that the case of Bichel points to 'the possibility that he had cut up the corpse and wallowed in the intestines'. Anyone looking at the Miller's Court photographs will be struck by the parallels – a 'Psychopathia Sexualis subject' indeed!

I am certain that research into the 'Littlechild Suspect' has tied up more loose ends in the case than ever before. Most notably, for the first time we can explain not only the sudden cessation of the killings, and the origin of the murderer's anatomical knowledge (as I myself practise as a surgeon, I am convinced of it), but also why the senior figures in the case were faced with a 'very hot potato'.

The CID apparently had seven serious suspects at one time, which they reduced to three (Druitt, Kosminski and Ostrog), largely on the basis of provable alibis. Over the years authors and researchers have come up with over a hundred pseudo-suspects, most of them patently absurd, like the Duke of Clarence (whose cast-iron alibi is a matter of historical record) and Sir William Gull (an elderly gentleman who had already suffered two strokes at the time!). The latest and most hyped of these is James Maybrick, a Liverpool cotton merchant whose candidacy as the Ripper has apparently survived Mike Barrett's admission that he composed the text of Maybrick's confessional 'diary' in 1991, dictating it to an accomplice. Mr Barrett has even cited the literary sources for his more purple prose, and pointed out transcription errors hidden under ink-blots.

The present book, by contrast, stems from a genuine document written by someone who may well have known the true story. Had John Littlechild not decided to write to Sims on that September day just before the First World War, the secret would almost certainly have died with him.

Nick Warren,
Winter 1994–5

Introduction

There are murder cases which are remembered throughout the generations, some because they remain unsolved, some because they were particularly gruesome, and others because they involved people who were already famous for other reasons.

A few fall into more than one of these categories. The most obvious example is that of Jack the Ripper, who operated over a hundred years ago and still makes the flesh creep, because he was especially vicious and was never caught or identified.

Fiction far outweighs fact in the volume of words used to describe the crimes, motives and character of Jack the Ripper. The facts are few, almost as few as the five murders he is believed to have committed. The fiction stems from the fact that despite mountains of theory and speculation, no one knows for certain who he was. No single writer has been able to establish the identity of the Whitechapel murderer, as he was originally called.

The atmosphere and lurid feel of this unique series of Victorian murders was succinctly summed up by the unknown journalist who wrote about the Whitechapel murders in the turn-of-the-century publication *Famous Crimes Past and Present*:

In the long catalogue of crimes which has been compiled in our modern days there is nothing to be found, perhaps, which has so darkened the horizon of humanity and shadowed the vista of man's better nature as the series of mysterious murders committed in Whitechapel during the latter part of the year 1888. From East to West, from North to South, the horror ran throughout the land. Men spoke of it with bated breath, and pale-lipped women shuddered as they read the dreadful details. A lurid pall rested over that densely populated district of London, and people, looking at it afar off, smelt blood. The superstitious said the skies had been of a deeper red that autumn, presaging desperate and direful deeds, and the aliens of the neighbourhood, filled with strange phantasies brought from foreign shores, whispered that evil spirits were abroad.

Significantly, the first full-length English work on the subject, *The Mystery of Jack the Ripper*, was not published until forty-one years, more than a generation, after the murders. It was written by an Australian-born journalist working in England, Leonard Matters. Since then many authors have confidently claimed that they have found the answer. They have not. They fail to convince, to provide conclusive proof, their causes and case histories being spoilt by misconception, misreporting, error, and the perpetuation of earlier imaginings, assumptions and fancy unsupported by fact. The identity of the Whitechapel murderer was and has remained an enigma.

It might have stayed that way had police officer and crime historian Stewart Evans not stumbled upon a curious and explosive disclosure which had remained hidden for over eighty years. A letter written twenty-four years after the Whitechapel murders by John George Littlechild, who had quickly risen to the rank of chief inspector at the head of the Secret Department, named a man who had been totally missed by historians and criminological researchers.

One of the most striking elements of the letter is that it shows the police were in fact closer to their prime suspect than anyone could possibly have imagined. The implication was that the suspect named had been arrested and subsequently lost. And yet, as we found, a cursory study of the details reproduced in the letter showed they were not the musings of a poorly informed ex-police officer. In fact, the opposite was the case. This particular detective, hugely admired at the time, was more informed than most about the twists and turns of the Whitechapel murders inquiry.

During the ensuing months the oddity of the name mentioned as that of the suspect and the possibility of further discoveries drew us back to the letter. The appeal was that of a more than usually intriguing crossword puzzle – with the added enigma of Scotland Yard's silence. We discovered that the man named in the letter flits like a phantom through history, lost in the dusty trails of the American West and the swirling fogs of Victorian London. He was in London in 1888, was being sought by the police in October at the height of the murders, and soon after was performing his well-established disappearing act.

And so, in the late spring of 1993, 105 years after the murders, we presented the details to the respected researcher, Keith Skinner, for further investigation. Keith saw the possibilities, and immediately began to study these intriguing new disclosures and to explore the prospects of the newly found suspect.

Stewart asked Keith the question which had been nagging at us both for several months: 'Is this Jack the Ripper?' His reply astounded us: 'He's looking good!'

At first it had seemed to us inconceivable that our suspect could have been missed by every researcher and writer on the subject for over one hundred years. Why were the senior officers investigating the murders so silent about this crucial lead? Was it pure embarrassment? Were they trying to protect the reputation of the Yard and disguise a mistake which would have dealt them a crippling blow? Could it be that certain officers feared they would be ridiculed, pilloried by the press or even dismissed had the escape become public knowledge?

As we studied the material unearthed by our research, we became convinced that any earlier explanations about the identity of the Whitechapel murderer were suspect, to say the least. We checked Scotland Yard, Special Branch and Home Office records, with no success.

We knew that our suspect was an American doctor who was believed to have been involved in a high-profile American crime before travelling to London in 1888. Contemporary newspapers on both sides of the Atlantic referred to a team of Scotland Yard detectives pursuing a Ripper suspect to the United States. Surely this was no mere coincidence.

Some days later more information arrived, and it became clear that the mystery had begun to assume unexpected dimensions. At this point Keith decided to abandon it, as he was involved in work on another project, leaving us to continue on our own.

By now the case had grown complex and far-reaching in its ramifications. There were many different leads to follow. The more we pursued one line of investigation, the more conscious we became of the mass of material being neglected. Our work at last brought us face to face with the foundations upon which the whole mystery of the new suspect had been built. Beneath the surface was something more startling, more significant and more immediately relevant than we could have believed possible when we began our work on the Littlechild letter.

At the start of our search we did not know precisely what we were looking for – or, for that matter, looking at. We had no theories and no hypotheses, we had set out to prove nothing. The conclusions we eventually reached were not postulated in advance. We were led to them, step by step, as if the evidence we accumulated had a mind of its own, was directing us of its own accord.

The letter indicated that Scotland Yard had compiled a large dossier on the Littlechild Suspect. This file has never been found. It appears that the police became involved in a conspiracy of silence. Any mention of the suspect is missing from the remaining police and Home Office files preserved at the Public Record Office. Without these missing documents, much of what has previously been written on the subject is no more than hype, hearsay and out-and-out lies. To quote retired antiquarian crime book dealer, Jack Hammond, 'There are liars, damned liars, and people who write books about Jack the Ripper.'

Much of our research has been overshadowed by the controversy surrounding the undoubtedly forged *Diary of Jack the Ripper*, of which James Maybrick, a famous alleged murder victim, is unconvincingly proposed as the author. The whole Maybrick debate has done no favours to the serious Ripper researcher.

Ripper author and expert Martin Fido believes that the Littlechild Suspect is the most significant find in Ripper research for many years:

> This seems the first line of enquiry proposed since my own original work on the Ripper that might just shake the current consensus of those who have most seriously examined the evidence.

It is our opinion that the evidence we have recorded is cogent and persuasive and that the Littlechild Suspect rates as the most likely person to have been the unknown killer awarded the chilling name Jack the Ripper. Here is a man who answers the description that our darkest imaginings supply, a man with an almost supernatural gift for vanishing, who has breezed through history without attracting the attention he certainly deserves.

Paul Gainey, Ipswich
Stewart Evans, Bury St Edmunds
1995

Authors' Notes

We have presented here what we hope is a readable account of the history of the Jack the Ripper murders of 1888, and a credible solution to the so far unanswered question, 'Who was Jack the Ripper?' In doing so we have unavoidably related the facts of each murder, essential to make this book complete in itself, and to correct some past errors.

However, the murders are looked at in a completely new context, and new interpretations are placed on many of the facts. The so-called 'Littlechild Suspect' is such an extraordinary character in himself that we are, indeed, fortunate to have thus been able to take a completely new look at the case without resorting to wild fantasy or fiction.

'Littlechild Suspect', as the reader will see, may be something of a misnomer, as he was also a Scotland Yard suspect – in fact their only real suspect. The credit for revealing this man is, however, Littlechild's, and hence the title may be felt appropriate.

It has been the fashion in recent academic works on the case to resort to voluminous footnoting. This is very evident in the excellent books *Jack the Ripper – The Uncensored Facts* by Paul Begg, and *The Complete History of Jack the Ripper* by Phil Sugden. These books are essentially reference works and this method of listing sources is very useful for the historian and researcher.

The present book, although entirely factual, is presented as a narrative of the murders and the hunt for the man suspected of being Jack the Ripper. In that sense it is not a reference work of the type mentioned, and constant resort to footnote references would, we feel, interrupt the story and confuse the casual reader. Realising the importance of listing references, however, we have included a source list to cater for this. In many cases where the reports or references are particularly important the sources are quoted in the text as part of the narrative. To prevent misinterpretation or loss of the contemporary mood we have reproduced several of the press reports verbatim.

All the quotes at the chapter heads are from the writings of the Littlechild Suspect himself, and although written in 1866 we have chosen those appropriate to the relevant chapter.

The photographs we have used are credited where possible, and the authors have made every effort to trace and acknowledge the source.

The authors have also made every effort to identify and acknowledge any ownership of copyright in references from which they have quoted at length. If any claimants to copyright have inadvertently been overlooked then the authors will be pleased to rectify the situation on notification of any such claim in writing.

Acknowledgements

This work owes its existence to many people but it was all made possible by Eric Barton, the antiquarian book dealer whose foresight and ability to find and preserve historical documents related to crime is without peer; and by Camille Wolff, whose help was indispensable.

A debt is also owed to Keith Skinner, the talented researcher who initially historically identified the Littlechild Suspect, and paved the way for further research.

Much of this book would not have been possible without the weighty contributions of that tireless researcher and student of psychology Jon Ogan; the maps would have been impossible without him.

To leading Ripper author and expert Phil Sugden, the authors also owe a debt of gratitude for his valuable advice in their first faltering steps in the world of authorship. Phil's help and guidance extended beyond this to include the contribution of valuable material for use in the present volume; also an objective and valuable appraisal of all the new material we present here.

We are grateful too to Nick Warren, whose backing and assistance is essential for anyone with the temerity to tackle the subject.

Thanks also to three distinguished American historians, who supplied valuable material on the assassination of President Lincoln and the involvement of the suspect: James O. Hall, Steven Miller and Michael Kauffman.

Richard and Molly Whittington-Egan's early encouragement and wise counsel lent valuable impetus.

Martin Fido and Paul Begg have been generous with their valued thoughts on a subject that few can claim to know more about. Melvin Harris, that veteran debunker of many a hoax, provided much useful information. D. Stuart Goffee's many hours at Colindale have cast much light on the suspect Michael Ostrog.

Jack Hammond provided a down-to-earth, if not slightly cynical, comment on a subject that can easily get out of hand.

We owe great thanks to Alan Littlechild and Professor Stephen Littlechild for much information supplied on their illustrious forebear, and for their interest in the project.

Peter Underwood has lent encouragement and assistance. Don Rumbelow's early advice on the finding of the letter guided Stewart on the path he was to follow.

Knowledge and information was also shared by American author and expert on classic British crimes, Al Borowitz. Oxford historian Deirdre Kincaid helped with information on Booth and the conspirators.

Generous assistance was afforded in America by Debbi Friedman, New York Public Library; Deborah Brown and Emily Miller, Missouri Historical Society; Cynthia Miller, St Louis Public Library; Cynthia Dixon, St Louis Vital Records Office; Joan Bova and, not least of all, Sheila Hayes of the St Louis Probate Court. Special thanks are due to Laurie Verge, of the Surratt Society, and to research historian Roger Hunt for his tireless efforts in the early stages of our research; also thanks to Deborah Richardson of Alvin H. Perlmutter Inc.

Once the path was embarked upon we were guided and helped by our editor, Mark Booth, Lindsay Symons and Elizabeth Rowlinson of Century.

Interest and encouragement was also received from Andy Ayliffe, Tony Ashworth, Jeremy Beadle, Clifford and Marie Elmer, Dave Froggatt, Mark Galloway, Jill and Malcolm Gibb, Jonathan Goodman, Val and Mike Hawkins, Allan Jones, Steve Kane, Roy King, Loretta Lay, Ray Luff, John Mayhew, Patrick Morley, Tim Powell, Neall Shelden, Louise and Ken Smith, Patterson Smith, Jim Tully, Stephen Wright, and that most gracious of hosts and veteran author Colin Wilson.

Thanks are also due to the staffs at the British Newspaper Library, Colindale; the Corporation of London Record Office; the Public Record Office, Kew, particularly Deirdre Allen; Suffolk Record Office, Ipswich; the Greater London Record Office; Guildhall Library; the British Library; Robin Gillis and the Metropolitan Police Museum; City of London Police; Suffolk Constabulary Force Museum; Tower Hamlets Bancroft Library; Missouri State Archives; Mid Manhattan Library; New York Public Library, National Archives, Washington DC; St Louis Public Library; Missouri Historical Society; St Louis Probate Court; St Louis Vital Records Division.

Extracts from Crown Copyright records in the Public Record

Office and the Corporation of London Record Office appear by permission of the Controller of Her Majesty's Stationery Office.

The thanks of any writer on this subject must be accorded to the unsung, unknown but diligent reporters of the many contemporary newspapers.

Finally, we cannot ignore the support and patience generously shown by our families and friends:

Steve Henry and Donovan Blake for their advice and guidance. Debbie and Andy Stuckes, and Chris Bull for their friendship.

Stewart thanks his family for their constant support and love, despite many hours of being subjected to talk on the Ripper: Dad, Doreen and Neill, Mum and Ron, Sharron and Rob Taylor, Michael and Pam Evans. His son Paul deserves special mention and the thanks of the authors for his excellent maps. His partner Rosemarie Howell is owed his eternal gratitude for making everything possible, and for all her constant support and expertise.

Paul thanks his parents and grandparents for their enthusiasm and nurturing spirit. Without their belief in a few pages written long ago, he would never have been involved in the writing of this book. And mostly he thanks Sarah, who never stops listening, believing and caring. Her encouragement and tolerance were beyond the call of duty.

Chapter 1

Assassination of a President

'I was also accused of complicity in the assassination of the President.'

Abraham Lincoln, President of the United States of America, died at 7.22 a.m. on Saturday 15 April 1865. He had been shot just over nine hours before at Ford's Theatre, in Washington, where he had gone with his wife and two guests for a performance of the English comedy *Our American Cousin*.

Amid the uproar of the terrified audience, the wounded President, unconscious from a shot in the head, was carried to a lodging house across the street from the theatre. The bullet had struck the most vulnerable part of his brain. Charles Sumner, the Massachusetts senator, who rushed to the scene, found Mrs Lincoln delirious in an adjoining room and the President, stretched diagonally on a bed too small for him, breathing heavily. Sitting at the head of the bed, he took Lincoln's hand and spoke to him.

'It is no use, Mr Sumner,' said one of the doctors. 'He can't hear you. He is dead.'

'But that cannot be,' the Senator protested; 'he is breathing.'

'It will never be anything more than this,' came the reply.

Sumner sat there all night, listening to the breathing. When in the cold, wet dawn it stopped, the Surgeon General, Joseph K. Barnes, crossed the dead man's hands over his breast.

Captain Robert Todd Lincoln, the President's elder son, sobbed uncontrollably on Sumner's shoulder, while the few friends and strangers still in the room knelt around the bed as the Reverend Phineas D. Gurley, the Lincolns' Washington pastor, uttered a prayer. Secretary of War Edwin M. Stanton, who had spoken contemptuously of Lincoln in the past, but in the last three years had worked with him in an ever more fruitful partnership, found immediate words which were not unworthy. From his vigil at the foot of the bed, with tears streaming down his cheeks, he declared, 'Now he belongs to the ages.'

The continent shook as the news of Lincoln's assassination sped over it. The first telegraphic despatches after the shooting were brief and tentative, but the details quickly unfolded: how the assassin had leapt from the President's theatre box to the stage, brandishing a dagger, and shouted, '*Sic semper tyrannis!*' before making his exit; how the actor John Wilkes Booth had been identified as the assassin; how William H. Seward, Secretary of State, had also been brutally attacked that night. The capital was wild with fear and rumour not knowing the extent of the conspiracy against the Government.

Booth, the brother and son of famous actors, had conceived the grandiose scheme of murdering the chief officers of the administration, and had reserved for himself the chief role. To others was delegated the duty of despatching the subordinates.

As with the Whitechapel murders of 1888, the Lincoln assassination is often distorted by faulty memory, and filtered through years of folklore. We have tried to discover the true facts and dispose of many wild theories and inaccuracies. It must first be said that Booth and Lincoln were products of an extraordinary age, whose deeds, like those of the Whitechapel murderer, cannot be explained outside the world as it was in 1865.

During early 1864 the American Civil War had raged more ferociously than ever. The promotion of General Ulysses S. Grant in March, to be commander of all Union forces, heralded a final offensive against the Confederates with dreadful resolve, Union forces pushed back confederate troops in bloody field-by-field combat. This in turn led to the raids and destruction of the Shenandoah the relentless frontal assaults of the Virginia campaign, and the burning of Atlanta. So began the unravelling of the old rules, and a willingness to retaliate for atrocities committed by the other army. The Confederates last major push had failed. Defeat was in sight.

In the second week of March 1864, Colonel Ulric Dahlgren, son of the Union admiral, was killed in an ambush while leading an aborted raid on Richmond. On his body were papers, in his own handwriting, indicating that his orders were to burn the Confederate capital and kill the Confederate president Jefferson Davis. Opponents of the Lincoln administration were outraged. News of the Dahlgren Raid reached John Wilkes Booth in New Orleans. He had always been outspoken in his hatred for Lincoln. But on the Dahlgren incident, he remained quiet. The wheels of revenge were already in motion, and Booth had no intention of drawing unwanted attention to himself.

The following year, 1865, started badly for the Confederacy. On 15 January, Union naval and land forces captured Fort Fisher guarding Wilmington, North Carolina. The last major Confederate port was closed. On 1 February, General Sherman began his invasion of South Carolina. A steel ring was being closed around the Confederate armies.

The previous day, in Washington, Congress had approved the Thirteenth Amendment abolishing slavery. The measure, which had already been passed by the Senate, required a two-thirds majority in the House. Lincoln worked hard behind the scenes to win the necessary support, and the amendment was passed by a margin of three votes, with the President's influence decisive. The promise of the Emancipation Proclamation had been carried out.

Between mid-April 1861 and mid-April 1865, some three million men in both North and South had seen service in the Civil War. Of these, 620,000 were killed, 360,000 from the North, 260,000 from the South. The most bloody and horrifying battles had seen thousands die at the human slaughterhouses of Antietam, Murfreesboro, Fredericksburg, Chancellorsville, the Wilderness, Spotsylvania and Cold Harbor. In the burned and blackened Shenandoah Valley were enough embers of barns and men to satisfy any prophet of doom. From Malvern Hill and Gettysburg down to Chickamauga, Chattanooga, Island Number 10, Vicksburg, the Red River and beyond, burying grounds deep and shallow held the soldiers who had fallen during the war.

Both sides had fought with honour; some had starved and suffered, from wounds or disease, and lost everything except a name for valour and endurance. When hostilities ceased, Lincoln's treatment of the vanquished was marked by a deep humanity. He ordered the immediate release of General Lee's two sons, whom some of his supporters wished to execute. Victory did not fill the President with exultation, but deepened his sense of responsibility and melancholy. Those who looked to him to impose harsh terms upon the defeated South were soon disillusioned. The close of his second inaugural address gave notice to the fanatical proponents of revenge upon the conquered that they must first reckon with his powerful opposition. The cabinet session of Friday 14 April 1865 came to an end with the expectation that on the following Tuesday they would again meet and resume discussion of how to bind up the nation's wounds.

John Wilkes Booth, one of ten children, had been born to Mr and Mrs Junius Brutus Booth in 1839 at their farm twenty-five miles from Baltimore. Writers have since called him a third-rate, frustrated and imbalanced actor. In reality, he was known for his extraordinary good looks, athletic prowess, and charismatic stage presence.

His first stage successes came in Southern cities. As the Southern states moved into secession, Booth moved North, where critic William Winter saw the young star's acting as 'raw, crude and much given to boisterous declamation'. Ironically, one of his fans was Abraham Lincoln, who once came to Ford's Theatre to see him play in *The Marble Heart*.

From 1861, as Booth travelled the North, he spoke openly for the Confederate cause. He often stopped to see his sister in Philadelphia. On one of these visits he revealed to her that he was smuggling quinine for the Confederacy. He started working for the Confederate 'underground' in February 1863. It was at that time, during a lull in his career, that Booth met David E. Herold, a clerk in a local drugstore. Herold's job gave him access to medicines that the Southern army desperately needed. If Booth was smuggling quinine to the South, it would be invaluable to have an acquaintance like Herold.

As an actor, Booth seemed to be respected and admired by high-ranking officers on both sides. General Grant himself was known to have supplied him with a pass which allowed him to move freely in Union army camps throughout the country. He told his sister Asia how General Grant's touring pass had given him 'freedom of range without knowing what a good turn he has done the South'.

Booth loved the South with a passion and yearned to perform some heroic deed that might atone for her impending defeat and his own failure to take up arms on her behalf. In 1864, when he was filling fewer engagements because of a failing voice, he seemed to have a deepening sense of guilt over keeping himself in safety and comfort while the war raged and the Southern cause sank lower. He had a restless and fiery nature, and he wanted to get into the action. But he had promised his mother he would not fight, and that was an oath he dared not break.

Until early 1864, captured soldiers were exchanged by Union and Confederate commissioners, but this practice ended when Federal authorities decided it was damaging the Union war effort. The impact of this decision was devastating.

The Confederate government had insufficient food to sustain prisons, but it did not want the stigma of starving these men. However, that was exactly what happened. Separated in contingents of varying size, facing ordeals that ranged from starvation to typhoid, dysentery to hypothermia, captive Union soldiers were dying by the thousands.

On 18 August 1864, the Union's Secretary of War, Edwin Stanton, issued the so-called 'retaliation order', which reduced the rations for Confederates in Union prisons to match those being given to Union men down South. By doing this, in effect Stanton had ordered the deaths of thousands. Estimates placed the death toll, in camps as well as in transit, as high as 10,000.

Booth himself had personal reasons for caring: Jesse Wharton, his best friend from school days, had been murdered by a guard at the Old Capitol Prison. In the summer of 1864, public anger rose with each side accusing the other of cruelty and murder. It was now that the Booth conspiracy began to take shape.

Booth devised a plan to capture President Lincoln and hold him hostage until the North's veto on exchanging prisoners was lifted. In August, he recruited to his cause Samuel Arnold, a childhood friend from his old school, St Timothy Hall, and Michael O'Laughlen, a Baltimore neighbour who had been a prisoner himself. He intended to kidnap Lincoln *en route* to the Soldiers' Home, where the President kept a summer residence.

In October Booth went to Canada to talk with officials. There he made contact with the Confederate government, and spoke with George Sanders, George P. Kane, who had been the police marshal of Baltimore back in 1861, and Patrick Martin. The plan appealed to them.

Martin arranged to transport Booth's theatrical wardrobe south, where the actor planned to resume acting. Unfortunately, the ship which was carrying Booth's trunk, the *Marie Victoria*, sank in the St Lawrence River. The whole crew was lost and Martin drowned in the accident.

Meanwhile, in Washington, Lincoln was preparing for the presidential election. He ran on a National Union ticket, with Andrew Johnson, a Democrat from Tennessee, as the candidate for the vice-presidency. His chief argument on his own behalf was that 'it is bad policy to swap horses while crossing a stream.' When advised that Grant might wish to take his place, he replied: 'If he takes Richmond, let him have it.' He also made plans to co-operate with his opponent, McClellan, if the other man should be nominated. But he need have had no misgivings about the result: only three Northern states – one of them Illinois – voted against him.

Aside from war measures, the history of Lincoln's presidency is not noteworthy for constructive policies. The tariff of 1864 was far above what everyone had predicted. Profiteers seem to have had a free rein and ran unchecked: the President appeared to neither know nor care. He openly used patronage to strengthen his position, and government advertising was placed in newspapers whose support was deemed advisable.

Lincoln was re-elected on 8 November 1864. Booth was incensed, saying that no president in his lifetime had ever served more than one term. On a trip to New York, Booth bought some Spencer carbines, some knives, a pair of handcuffs and a set of leg irons.

In mid-December, at Bryantown, Booth made an important new contact at the local tavern. Dr Samuel Mudd stopped by, bringing along his old friend Thomas H. Harbin, a Confederate agent. Mudd was to meet Booth again, in Washington, where the latter was introduced to John Surratt, a native of southern Maryland and an agent of the Confederate State Department. Surratt's mother, Mary, the widow of a Confederate informer, owned a tavern at Surrattsville, which Confederate couriers often used as a 'safe house' on their trips through the area. Recently she had rented the place out, and had set up a boarding house on H Street in Washington.

It was at Mary Surratt's boarding house that the plotters were to meet and compose their plan. Herold, carriage-maker George A. Atzerodt, and Private Lewis Thornton Powell (alias Paine) were among the key members of the team. Powell, a veteran of Antietam and Chancellorsville, wounded at Gettysburg, had deserted after nearly four years of fighting, adopted the name of Lewis Paine, and met Booth when he was penniless, in rags, without food.

Samuel Arnold was a farm hand who hated farm work; Michael O'Laughlen was a Baltimore livery-stable worker, fairly good at handling horses and even better at carrying liquor; Atzerodt was a German-born carriage painter who kept a shop in the town of Port Tobacco, Maryland. The crew filled the seven bedrooms of Mrs Surratt's boarding house.

On 4 March 1865, Abraham Lincoln was sworn in for his second term as President of the United States. On the steps of the Capitol he delivered the last major speech of his life.

General Lee surrendered on 9 April. The war was over, but Booth's desire to kidnap the President became even more intense, and soon his thoughts had turned to murder. Why should Booth want to kill Lincoln now that the war was winding down? Regardless of motive, he was about to play havoc with history.

By Tuesday 11 April, the Lincoln conspiracy had reached a pivotal point. For a number of reasons, including bad planning and unforeseen circumstances, Booth had failed to pull off the kidnap plan. But already preparation had begun on a second, more devastating crime. Unbeknown to his fellow conspirators, Booth had decided, apparently on his own, to change the plot from kidnap to murder.

Lewis Powell was checking out William H. Seward's house, where the Secretary was recovering from a broken jaw and arm, suffered in a recent carriage accident. Something was still going on, but it bore no relation to the scenario the plotters had talked over for hours in the Surratt house. It was left to a complete innocent to set the whole assassination chain into motion. H. Clay Harry Ford, who had known Booth for many years and admired him greatly, was in charge of the theatre on Good Friday, 14 April. Seeing Booth outside the theatre that morning, Ford told him that the President was going to attend that night's production of *Our American Cousin*.

This was exactly what Booth wanted to hear, and he immediately set about fine-tuning his latest plot, which called for co-ordinated attacks on President Lincoln, Secretary of State Seward and Vice-President Andrew Johnson. Lincoln was to be killed in the theatre, where Booth had access to the President's box.

Booth had known the Fords for years; they gave him free passes to their theatre at all times. That afternoon he was in and out of the place. He made a hole in the door to the President's box so he could look in to be sure Lincoln was there. He cut a niche in the hallway wall near the outside entrance. A metal bar placed in the niche could hold the door closed against any pressure from outside.

Booth called one last meeting at his lodgings at Herndon House, at 8 p.m. Atzerodt, Herold and Powell attended. According to George Atzerodt, it was at this meeting – two hours before the shooting – that Booth mentioned assassination for the first time. They arranged their timing: at the same hour and minute of the clock that night, Powell was to kill the Secretary of State and Booth the President. Atzerodt was to kill Vice-President Johnson. Herold would to guide Powell to the Seward home and then hurry to the support of Atzerodt.

A terrified Atzerodt, realising he was out of his depth, told Booth that he had enlisted purely to be involved in the abduction plan and not murder. Armed with a revolver he knew he could never use, Atzerodt disappeared into the night, never to see Booth again.

In the carriage into which the President and his wife stepped hours before Lincoln's assassination were Henry Reed Rathbone, assigned by Stanton to accompany the President, and his fiancée, Miss Clara Harris. Many sources have stated that the guard with Lincoln this evening was an 'inattentive policeman' called John Parker, one of the officers detailed from the Metropolitan Police Force of Washington for White House duty. Lincoln's close friend and faithful bodyguard, Ward Hill Lamon, was out of town and it has been argued that Parker had taken his place.

Writer and historian Michael Kauffman has shown conclusively that this is totally incorrect. On the night of 14 April Parker was assigned to protect the White House, not the President. He has been unfairly blamed for the lack of security surrounding Lincoln on the night of his assassination. Other historical experts have reviled Parker for many years for his apparent incompetence and lack of vigilance.

The Lincolns' valet, Charles Forbes, who took a chair outside the box at the theatre, seems to have been the only person who stood between the President and his assassin. No one can fully explain why there was no bodyguard with the President that night, allowing Booth to stand within feet of Lincoln before firing the fatal shot. Some witnesses have said the bodyguard was having a drink at the bar. Michael Kauffman believes theatre staff mistook Forbes for Parker.

The coachmen outside remembered 'Parker' talking and joking with them. Kauffman has a simple explanation for this obvious error. John Ford, the theatre owner, had struck a deal with the police, who regularly patrolled outside the theatre to ensure that no unsavoury characters gained access. It is likely that the coachmen thought the officer outside with them that night was the President's bodyguard. Indeed, Parker was later charged with deserting his post, but was acquitted.

Inside the theatre, at 9 p.m., the orchestra struck up 'Hail to the Chief' as the Lincolns and their guests were ushered through the dress circle to their private box at the right of the audience. Major Rathbone and Miss Harris sat towards the front, Mrs Lincoln sat further back and the President lay wearily in a rocking chair near the rear of the box. A few feet behind the President was the door, the only entry to the box. This door opened on to a narrow hallway that led to another door leading to the balcony of the theatre. The assassin had to pass through both these doors in order to enter the President's box.

At a stable near Ford's Theatre, at close to ten o'clock, Booth, Powell and Herold mounted their horses and parted, Booth to go to Ford's, Herold to guide Powell to the Seward house.

At the back door of Ford's, Booth called for the theatre carpenter, Edman Spangler, to hold his horse, then he entered and went down under the stage. He climbed the stairs leading to the dress circle, picked his way among chairs behind an outer row of seats, and reached the door of the passageway leading to the presidential box. Here he leant against the wall and took a cool survey of the house. He then opened the door into the narrow hallway leading to the box, stepped in, closed the door, fastened a metal bar into the mortised niche he had previously carved in the wall, and braced it against the door panel. Softly he swung the door back and with his brass derringer pistol in his right hand and a long dagger in the other, he stepped into the box.

Booth stood motionless within striking distance of the President. He raised the derringer, straightened his right arm, and levelling the barrel towards Lincoln, less than five feet away, pulled the trigger. A .44-calibre lead ball crashed into the left side of the President's head.

Major Rathbone, confused, sprang to his feet and threw himself at Booth. After a scuffle, Booth broke loose and slashed at the major's left arm with his knife. The blade went all the way to the bone. Mrs Lincoln saw her husband slump forward, and leapt towards him, stopping him tumbling to the floor. The killer mounted the box railing, and leapt for the stage eleven feet below. The spur of his riding boot caught in the flag which draped the box, causing him to land off-balance on the stage. Some sources have alleged that he landed on his left leg, breaking the shin bone a little above the instep.

Springing to his feet he shouted, '*Sic semper tyrannus!*' ('Thus always to tyrants'), the words attributed to Brutus when he killed Caesar, and, moreover, the motto of Virginia. The next instant he had disappeared backstage, and was gone. How Booth could possibly have made such an astonishing escape with a broken leg is a mystery which we will return to later.

While the audience sat totally stunned, Booth dashed out of an entrance and into the alley behind the theatre. There stood a fast bay horse, with a stable boy holding the reins. He pushed the boy away, mounted the mare, and made his escape.

Some two hundred soldiers quickly arrived to clear the theatre. The wailing and chaos that had begun inside soon spread to the street.

Four soldiers lifted Lincoln out of the box, and with the help of two others carried him to the nearest house, the Petersen residence at 453 Tenth Street. There they laid the body of the dying President, less than half an hour after the shot had been fired.

Lincoln's breath came hard, and his pulse was feeble. He was completely unconscious. Dr Robert Stone, the President's family physician, arrived, followed soon after by Surgeon General Joseph Barnes, who took charge, assisted by Dr Charles H. Crane. At 2 a.m., Dr Barnes tried to locate the bullet, but to no avail. He decided that any further attempts were pointless.

At about the same time that the President was shot, Lewis Powell rode up to the door of William Seward's house on Lafayette Square. He pushed past the servant at the door, saying he was a messenger from Seward's physician and had a package of medicine that must be personally delivered to his sickroom. Hearing the commotion, Frederick Seward, the Assistant Secretary of State, walked down the stairs and was confronted by the deranged stranger.

Powell, warming to his mission, levelled his revolver at Frederick Seward's head and pulled the trigger. The gun misfired. He immediately attacked Seward, beating him across the head with the pistol, tearing his scalp and fracturing his skull. The unstoppable Powell now burst into the Secretary's bedroom, where Private George Robinson, an army nurse, and Major Augustus Seward sprang from their chairs. The murder-bent intruder injured both with knife thrusts. Rushing to the bed where the Secretary of State had lain for nearly two weeks with a steel frame over his head and face, Powell stabbed over and over again at the throat of the sick man, delivering three ugly gashes to his cheek and neck. The steel frame foiled a death blow. In a desperate attempt to save himself, the Secretary of State rolled off the bed and wedged himself between the bed and the wall.

On his way down the stairs, Powell slashed at an attendant, then hurled himself out of the front door, leapt into the saddle and galloped away. Behind him he left five people bleeding from ghastly injuries: Augustus Seward had seven stab wounds, and Robinson four; Emerick Hansell, a messenger, suffered a serious wound in the back.

Before the attack, David Herold had been stationed in Lafayette Park but had fled to join Booth once Powell entered the house. His next task had been to find George Atzerodt to fulfil the final part of the plot, but Atzerodt was nowhere to be found.

The President never regained consciousness. Although there had been no chance of him surviving, the unconscious will to live was astounding. But 7.22 a.m. it was all over. An outburst of almost universal grief in the North acknowledged his passing. Most Southerners too were shocked and appalled at this tragic death. They had good reason to be. Ten years later Jefferson Davis said: 'Next to the destruction of the Confederacy, the death of Abraham Lincoln was the darkest day the South has ever known.'

There had never been a demonstration of grief in America such as that which followed. The tolling of the bells began in Washington. From New York, Boston, Chicago, Springfield, it spread to every town and village throughout the United States. Hour after hour, they tolled during that dark day, with flags flying at half-mast. Journalists employed extravagant language to describe the murder, turning all America into eyewitnesses of Lincoln's dreadful death.

In the parlour of the Petersen house on the day of Lincoln's death, Secretary of War Edwin Stanton took charge of the situation. Throughout the night he listened to statements. There was one priority: to find the killer.

Thousands of people joined troops and detectives in an all-out effort to track him down. They scoured the countryside in staggering numbers, patrolling all the waterways and searching every building. Some two thousand Union troops swarmed over southern Maryland. Steamships brought hundreds of soldiers down to Chapel Point, a docking area in southern Maryland. But still they could find nothing. From the night of Good Friday, 14 April 1865, until the morning of Wednesday, the killer of Abraham Lincoln remained at large.

While Booth and Herold hid, time was running out for the other conspirators. On Monday 17 April, Lewis Powell was arrested at the Surratt boarding house, and Mrs Surratt herself was taken into custody. On Thursday 20, troops captured George Atzerodt at the home of his cousin in Montgomery County, Maryland. Dr Mudd was arrested on Friday 21 April, when detectives searched his home and found Booth's boot in the upstairs bedroom.

Booth's injury would have been a vital clue in the search for the assassin. However, the authorities had no idea that he had broken his leg. Michael Kauffman has discovered, through detailed research of the original records, that not a single eyewitness reported seeing him limp as he fled across the stage at Ford's Theatre. People in the audience remembered that he had landed on the stage off-balance after jumping from the President's box. They stated that he landed on his *right* hand and knee, though it was the *left* leg that was broken.

A specific account by Charles Hamlin, a member of the audience that night, underlines one fact. Hamlin stated that Booth's body twisted in the air when he jumped from the box, and he landed facing the crowd with his right knee coming down first.

Kauffman has discovered that Booth told about a dozen people that he had broken his leg when his horse stumbled and fell on him during his escape. Herold backed up this version of events, adding that he himself was there and helped Booth mount up again after the accident. Kauffman says:

> When Booth mounted his horse in Baptist Alley and had trouble with the skittish mare, his left leg bore all the weight of his body, yet he indicated no pain at the time and, later, doctors did not report seeing signs of this trauma to the injury. If he had his left foot in the stirrup, he would have been putting his entire weight on his broken leg and the added torque of throwing his body over a moving horse. Even with the affects of adrenalin, this would have been impossible.

A Sergeant Cobb, who saw Booth at the Navy Yard Bridge twenty minutes after the shooting, noted that the assassin's voice was smooth and that he appeared at ease. Others remember, after the horse falling incident, that his voice was cracked in pain. Dr Mudd recalls that Booth's trousers were muddy when he arrived at his house on the morning of 15 April, and a farm hand told how Booth's horse had a badly swollen left front shoulder and a gash on its leg.

As Michael Kauffman has argued, there is no independent evidence to suggest that Booth broke his leg on the stage at Ford's Theatre. Only the actor's diary, found on his body, supports such a story. Kauffman suggests there is only one possible conclusion: 'When he penned in his diary that he broke his leg upon leaping from the presidential box, it was indeed more dramatic than writing that his horse fell on him. It sounds too much like the true John Wilkes Booth at his theatrical best.'

On the morning of 26 April, Booth and Herold were hiding out at a farm owned by Richard Garrett near Port Royal, Virginia. Lieutenant Edward Doherty and his twenty-five troopers from the 16th New York Cavalry had been trying to track the fugitives for several days. With them were Everton Conger, and Luther Byron Baker, two civilian detectives.

They arrived at the farm at about 2 a.m. on the morning of the 26th and cornered the fugitives in a tobacco barn. Although the building was surrounded, Herold and Booth refused to come out, leaving the detectives to talk over their options.

Herold cracked first and walked from the barn unarmed, but Booth remained inside, determined to fight his way out. Baker was getting impatient and Everton Conger decided to torch the barn. Within minutes the building was fully alight, the flames rolling up into the rafters and nearly engulfing Booth. He decided to make a break for the door.

Sergeant Thomas 'Boston' Corbett was watching Booth through the cracks in the barn. He had his revolver trained on the assassin, but until now had seen no reason to shoot. As Booth took five or six steps towards the door, a shot rang out and he fell forward on his face. Booth struggled to his feet and tried to run for it, just as Corbett fired another shot through a crack in the wall. The bullet went through Booth's neck, cutting the spinal cord. He was dragged away from the flames and up to the house, where he died two hours later.

Booth's death at the Garrett farm, twelve days after the assassination, brought an end to the manhunt. The investigations, however, were not over.

An estimated three hundred suspects were arrested for complicity in the assassination. A large number of them were guilty of working with Booth, but the War Department found it hard to make a case against them.

President Johnson appointed a military commission to try those accused of being Booth's accomplices. It announced its findings on 30 June. Arnold, O'Laughlen and Dr Samuel Mudd were all found guilty of conspiring with Booth. They were sentenced to life imprisonment. Dr Mudd had set Booth's broken leg, but otherwise was not linked directly to the crime. Arnold had provided vehicles for Booth and the other plotters. Edman 'Ned' Spangler, a sceneshifter at Ford's Theatre, was found guilty of aiding in Booth's escape, but was acquitted of conspiracy charges. He was to be imprisoned for six years. Four others of the accused – Powell, Herold, Atzerodt and Mrs Surratt – were found guilty and sentenced to hang. It was widely believed that Mrs Surratt was not one of the assassination plotters, and several members of the commission addressed a plea for mercy in her case to President Johnson. Johnson later declared that he had signed the order for the executions without any knowledge of such a mercy plea.

The condemned prisoners learned on 6 July that they were to be hanged the following day. The executions took place just outside the courtroom, in the prison yard. Herold squirmed for some time before expiring; Mary Surratt and George Atzerodt died quickly and quietly; but Lewis Powell kicked and struggled for twenty minutes.

America was obsessed with finding more accomplices and bringing them to justice. Rumours of a huge rebel conspiracy had spread like wildfire, as hysterical reports of terrorism made the rounds. Fear mingled with the outrage: nobody knew how many people were involved.

In Missouri, a thirty-two-year-old herb doctor was arrested, incarcerated and interrogated. Assistant War Secretary Charles Dana advised Judge Advocate General Joseph Holt that he felt the prisoner 'should be confined in the Penitentiary'. To this advice Dana added the suggestion: 'Let the Indian Doctor tell all he knows about Booth and Booth's associates.' What did the 'Indian Doctor' know? The files of the Bureau of Military Justice do not confide an answer to that question.

Eventually released from the Old Capitol, the doctor returned to his old haunts in Missouri and the furtherance of his renown as the 'curer of all ills'. No one seemed to notice his new bitterness or the fact that he was different from other men, though he had always hated women and was openly venomous about them. Eventually the eccentric doctor moved across the Atlantic to a new stamping ground – Liverpool, and then London – the killing field of Jack the Ripper.

Chapter 2
Time and Place

'Magnetic links that connected me with dear friends far away across the stormy Atlantic.'

So, from the battlefields of the American Civil War, we move to the cramped gas-lit streets of Victorian East End London, and a series of gruesome killings. What really happened? Who was responsible? To begin to answer these questions we must first return to the scene of the crimes: to the Whitechapel and Spitalfields area of London in the year 1888.

The previous year, Queen Victoria had celebrated the Golden Jubilee of her long reign; a decade earlier she had been proclaimed Empress of India, the brightest jewel in the Imperial Crown. Britain maintained her industrial supremacy and the Port of London was the biggest and busiest in the world. The edifice of Victorian society looked as enduring, dependable and solid as the Bank of England.

The unprecedented series of vicious and gruesome murders which began in the latter half of 1888 brought to the public consciousness the horrifying barbarity and harsh poverty of life within parts of the Imperial capital itself.

For many, crime was an economic necessity of life. One hundred years ago, in Westminster, Holborn and the East End, there were said to be no fewer than 100,000 people living by crime. Prostitution was rife. Nearly two million Londoners were officially classed as poor or very poor. Most of them lived in the East End. For centuries the City of London's stringent corporate and guild restrictions had forced new labour to live and work on the open marshland east of the City wall. Immigrants fleeing Continental persecutions, notably the seventeenth-century Huguenots, had settled here. Steadily the number of immigrants increased. By the end of the 1880s the brick-fields and the weavers' houses had become ghettos. Nearly fifty per cent of the workers paid from a quarter to half of their wages for one-room hovels for themselves and their families.

The East End gave an impression of constant activity. Pubs and clubs were open both early and late: drinking in the market areas would commence at 5 a.m. Drunken sailors from Limehouse and the Port of London penetrated as far as Whitechapel. The immigrant Jewish community was constantly threatened by the local Gentiles. And beneath the murky surface moved the plotting groups of alien anarchists fleeing persecution in their own countries.

From the 1870s the East End had begun to expand to the east and to the north. The railways brought growth to the villages on the periphery of London. The old main streets lined with half-timbered cottages and bow-fronted houses were rapidly filled out with two-storey homes, mostly jerry-built. These new areas soon degenerated into slums, with brawling, drunkenness and gaudy street markets familiar sights.

In a letter to the Secretary of State on 5 August 1889, the Commissioner at Scotland Yard, James Monro, described conditions in the East End:

Vice of a very low type exists in Whitechapel; such vice manifests itself in brawling and acts of violence which shock the feelings of respectable persons; these acts of violence are not repressed by action taken either before the Police or Magisterial Authorities. Clear out the slums and lodging houses to which vicious persons resort, and vice will disappear, respectability taking its place.

There is no doubt whatever that vice of a very low and degraded type is only too visible in Whitechapel. The facility with which the Whitechapel Murderer obtains victims has brought this prominently to notice, but to anyone who will take a walk late at night in the district where the recent atrocities have been committed, the only wonder is that his operations have been so restricted. There is no lack of victims ready to his hand, for scores of these unfortunate women may be seen any night muddled with drink in the streets and alleys, perfectly reckless as to their safety, and only anxious to meet with anyone who will keep them in plying their miserable trade.

There is no doubt that brawling and fighting do go on, repressed as far as possible by the Police; but it must be remembered that these women do not care to be protected against those who assault them, very seldom have recourse to the Station to complain, and still more seldom appear at any Police court to prosecute any charge which they may have laid before the Police. [Ref. HO144/220/A49301]

The few jobs available to women – as domestics, fur pullers, hawkers, or operatives in jam, pickle, or sweet factories – hardly provided appealing alternatives to prostitution. Large numbers of prostitutes, using cabmen to make contacts, would be found in the neighbourhood of pubs, music halls and major railway stations. And just as the costermongers lived in the shabby tenements of Whitechapel but picked up their wares in Covent Garden and Billingsgate and then sought their trade across London, so too the East End prostitutes spread their nets wide. The lucky might meet a generous client. The unlucky might find death.

The Irish Nationalist dynamite outrages were another serious problem in the capital. There was important backing for the Irish movement in America, and the Irish Republican Brotherhood, or Fenians, were a major threat to the British Government.

As early as 1867, one of the leaders of the movement, Captain T. J. Kelly, a veteran of the American Civil War, sailed from New York to Ireland with some compatriots to assist with the campaign. Kelly was one of many who were later arrested and imprisoned. In December 1867 an explosion at the Clerkenwell Prison proved to be an attempt to free Captain Richard O'Sullivan Burke, another Irish-American Civil War veteran and Kelly's second-in-command, who was being held on remand there.

The explosion demolished a section of the prison wall and several nearby houses. Twelve people were killed; another 120 suffered injury. The bomber, George Barrett, was arrested, and was hanged on 26 May 1868. The upshot was that the Government formed a special branch attached to the Home Office. It was headed by an Irish army intelligence officer, Colonel Fielding, who was assisted by a barrister, Robert Anderson, the later head of the Criminal Investigation Department (CID). In this former capacity Anderson became the 'handler' of Major Henri Le Caron (real name Thomas Miller Beach), an English adventurer and spy who had infiltrated the Fenian movement in America with great success.

The dynamite explosions continued and in January 1881 there was an explosion at Salford Barracks. On 6 May 1882 the Government was rocked by the murder of the new Chief Secretary for Northern Ireland, Lord Frederick Cavendish, and the Permanent Secretary in the Dublin civil service, Mr Thomas Burke. The murders took place in Phoenix Park, Dublin, and were committed by members of the Invincibles, a splinter group of the Fenian Society of Irish-Americans. The assassins used long surgical knives made by Weiss and purchased, especially for this use, in London. Five of the conspirators were later arrested, tried, found guilty and executed. Six others were imprisoned.

A direct result of this outrage was the formation of the first specialist department of the CID, the Irish Bureau. The Criminal Investigation Department itself had been formed only four years earlier, in 1878, from the detective branch. The Irish Bureau was headed by Superintendent Williamson, with reference to the head of CID, Vincent, Anderson, and ultimately the Home Secretary.

Fenian outrages continued in London throughout 1883, the work of Irish-American conspirators later known as the Dynamiters, or Dynamitards. On 15 March there was an explosion at the offices of *The Times*, and later the same day another at the Local Government Office in Whitehall. Similar attempts continued in 1884: on 30 May a constable discovered a device at the foot of Nelson's Column in Trafalgar Square. The sixteen sticks of dynamite were defused. Later the same day a wall at Scotland Yard itself was destroyed, wrecking the office of the then head of the Special Irish Branch, John G. Littlechild, by now a chief inspector. Fortunately, he was not in the office at the time.

The Special Irish Branch was brought into existence under Monro in 1883, and was directed by Littlechild until 1893. His chief assistant was Detective Inspector Sweeney, like many of the original members of this department an Irishman. The word 'Irish' was later dropped from the title, giving rise to the famous name 'Special Branch'. One of the more onerous of the department's tasks was the protection of some of London's most famous buildings, including Buckingham Palace, the Houses of Parliament, Government offices, the Law Courts and the Thames bridges. This strain on resources was partly redressed by some fifty men of the Royal Irish Constabulary who were brought over to assist with these duties.

Littlechild himself was very highly thought of, even by those outside the force. Thomas Beach, writing in 1892, said of him:

There are, I believe, some thirty men charged with the special duty of circumventing political crime in London. All praise and honour to them for the work they have done, and the sincerest of congratulations to Chief Inspector Littlechild, who so ably conducted the arrests of all the principals of the latter-day dynamite plots.

The bombings continued until the end of January 1885; there had been a total of thirteen in London since the extremists' campaign had begun in March 1883, at locations including St James's Square, Gower Street underground station, the crypt of the House of Commons and the White Tower at the Tower of London. Two of the conspirators – John Fleming and a former United States Army captain, Mackay Lomasney – had disappeared without trace when the boat they were in exploded as they attempted to place a bomb under the south-west end of London Bridge. The end of the campaign was heralded by the arrest of two dynamiters, Burton and Cunningham, who were tried and received life sentences.

In these early days the police had little or no technical equipment to assist them. The benefits of modern science, other than medicine, were only brought to bear upon criminal investigation, and then only experimentally, in 1894, some six years after the Ripper killings. The fingerprint identification system was not adopted until 1895. In fact it was not until 1901 that any real advance in technical aid to criminal investigation was to be seen.

Another problem plaguing the police and government of the late 1880s was the large number of processions and demonstrations by the unemployed and social reformers. In 1886 there were half a dozen demonstrations at Clerkenwell, Hyde Park and Trafalgar Square, requiring a large police presence to keep the peace. Up to 2,400 officers were used in this capacity. The explosive character of the East End was demonstrated in Jubilee year, just before the Ripper murders, when crowds of unemployed East Enders took to sleeping out in Trafalgar Square.

Commissioner Charles Warren had placed a ban on any rallies in the square. On Sunday 13 November 1887, a day which was to become known as Bloody Sunday, a large procession of socialists, radicals and Irish Home Rulers converged on the area in an attempt to defy the ban. Fights erupted in that part of the square cordoned off by the police. Warren's answer was the use of four thousand constables, three hundred Grenadiers and three hundred Life Guards, with a further seven thousand constables being held in reserve. Two people died and there were scores of casualties. The resentment generated by this use of military force against the civilian population lasted many years.

Further rioting occurred on the 17th, when several policemen were injured, and on the 23rd about 2,000 people were found brawling in Westminster Abbey. These scenes did not abate until the end of the month, and certain newspapers and politicians lent their support to the dissidents. There was now a total ban on meetings in Trafalgar Square and on all processions within a certain radius of it. The police and Government were lurching from one crisis to another.

And their most famous crisis was almost upon them.

Chapter 3
A Series Killer at Large?

'Dangerous man to widow or maid.'

Nobody knows for certain how many women were murdered by Jack the Ripper. It is generally accepted that there were only five victims, but this view varies depending on which expert you consult. In fact, a radical weeding process will leave the purist with only four murders definitely attributable to the Whitechapel murderer, 'Jack the Ripper'.

In 1888, over a period of approximately ten weeks, the savage killer roamed the mean East End streets, where he met and murdered several prostitutes between the hours of midnight and dawn. The victims were brutally slain and laid out, their throats cut, their abdomens ripped open and other mutilations inflicted.

Policemen regularly patrolled the streets where the Whitechapel murderer attacked his victims with such ferocity. Indeed, the number of officers was increased at the height of the outrages. But this did not seem to worry the unseen killer; he appeared to carry out his work with impunity. *The Times* remarked: 'The assassin, if not suffering from insanity, appears to be free from any fear of interruption while on his dreadful work.'

Jack the Ripper's killing field, the heart of the East End, comprising Whitechapel and Spitalfields, was an area of only a square mile or so. In the borough of Whitechapel there were ninety thousand people, of whom seventy thousand were women and children, mostly the unemployed poor who lived from hand to mouth. By 1880, there were estimated to be ten thousand prostitutes and three thousand brothels in London. Almost every room, nook or corridor in Whitechapel, Shadwell, Spitalfields and adjoining areas was at one time or another used for sexual purposes.

The horror and poignancy of the Jack the Ripper murders are intensified when we consider the degraded lives of his victims. Scorned by society, these women were defenceless, alienated and dispossessed. Their lives were limited to the goal of getting fourpence from a client, which would pay for a shot of gin, a glass of beer, or to rent a bed for the night in a common lodging house. Many of the 1,200 prostitutes who worked the area were badly mishandled by their clients, often beaten, disfigured and even murdered.

On the night of her murder, Bank Holiday Monday, 6 August 1888, thirty-nine-year-old Martha Tabram, also known as Turner, had been drinking in the White Swan pub on Whitechapel High Street with another prostitute, Mary Ann Connelly, also known as 'Pearly Poll', and two soldier clients. Evidence provided by Connelly showed that she and Tabram, in company with the two soldiers, had visited several public houses in Whitechapel between 10 p.m. and 11.45 p.m., at which time they separated, Connelly going up Angel Court with one of the soldiers and Tabram up George Yard with the other.

Tabram's body was found on the first-floor landing of George Yard Buildings, George Yard, Whitechapel, in a narrow thoroughfare off Whitechapel Road leading through to Wentworth Street. Thirty-nine stab wounds were noted by the police surgeon.

Certain characteristics set this case apart from routine murder: there was no apparent connection with a domestic quarrel, drunken affray or street robbery; the murderer had left no clue as to his identity; and the attack had been savagely violent. Deputy Coroner George Collier, sitting at the Tabram inquest in the absence of Mr Wynne E. Baxter, who was on holiday, spoke of the killing as 'one of the most brutal crimes that had occurred for some years ... almost beyond belief'.

The *Illustrated Police News* of 18 August reported:

The wound over the heart was alone sufficient to kill and death must have occurred as soon as that was inflicted. Unless the perpetrator was a madman, or suffering to an unusual extent from drink delirium, no tangible explanation can be given of the reason for inflicting the other thirty-eight stab wounds, some of which almost seem as if they were due to thrusts and cuts from a penknife.

Tabram was 5ft.3in. tall, with dark hair and complexion, and was wearing a black bonnet, long black jacket, green skirt and brown petticoat and stockings, with side-spring boots, all of which were old.

The night's events, as collated by the police, were as follows:

At 2 a.m. the beat policeman, PC 226H Thomas Barrett, had seen a soldier, a Grenadier, in Wentworth Street. He was aged between twenty-two and twenty-six years, 5ft.9 or 10in. tall, fair complexion, dark hair, small dark brown moustache turned up at the ends, and wearing one good conduct badge, no medals. Challenged by the constable, the soldier stated that he was waiting for a chum, who had gone with a girl.

Also at 2 a.m. Mrs Mahoney and her husband, of 47 George Yard Buildings, passed the spot where the body was afterwards found. There was nothing there. At 3.30 a.m. Alfred George Crow, a licensed cab-driver, another resident, stated that he had seen 'something' on the landing, but took no notice, and went to bed.

At 4.50 a.m., the body of the woman was found on the landing of George Yard Buildings by John Reeves of number 37 as he was coming down the stairs on his way to work. He called PC Barrett. PC Barrett noted that there was no blood on the stairs leading to the body, which was lying in a pool of blood. Dr Killeen of 68 Brick Lane was called to examine the body, and found thirty-nine puncture wounds on the body, neck, and private parts, inflicted with a knife or dagger. After Dr Killeen had pronounced life extinct the police ambulance litter arrived and the body was removed to Whitechapel mortuary.

Later that day Inspector Edmund Reid, of the local CID, took statements from the residents of George Yard Buildings. All the residents were found to be clear of suspicion, and the murdered woman was a stranger to them all.

The body was identified on 7 August by Henry Samuel Tabram of 6 River Terrace, East Greenwich, as that of his wife who had left him several years previously, and also by Mrs Mary Luckhurst, also known as Bousfield, of 4 Star Place, Commercial Road, Mrs Tabram's landlady until a month previously. The body was photographed the same day.

From the statements taken it was observed that the murder had taken place between 2 a.m. and 4.50 a.m. The soldier client was last seen with Tabram at 11.45 p.m., two and a quarter hours before the earliest estimated time of death. Inspector Reid believed that the 'something' which the cabman Alfred George Crow had seen was the body of Martha Tabram. Thorough enquiries failed to reveal that she had been seen with anyone other than the soldier, although given the lapse of time it was possible that she may have met someone else.

A further examination of the body identified thirty-nine puncture wounds, most of which were inflicted, according to the doctor, with a penknife, but one of which, on the sternum, had been caused by a stronger knife, possibly a dagger, which had gone through the bone.

The police pursued their enquiries with what information they had. On 7 August PC Barrett was taken to the Tower of London where he saw some soldiers in the guardroom, but failed to recognise any of them as the one he had spoken to. At 11 a.m. the next day the Grenadier Guards who had been on leave or absent on the night of the 6th were paraded in front of the policeman. PC Barrett picked out one with medals, then another, and both were taken to the orderly room. There the constable admitted a mistake in identifying the first, and his name was not taken. The second man was a John Leary, who gave an account of himself on the night of the murder which Private Law, to whom he referred in his statement, subsequently corroborated without communicating with Leary, thus clearing Leary.

At 11.30 p.m. on 9 August a Corporal Benjamin returned, having been absent without leave since 6 August. His clothing and bayonet were examined, but no marks of blood were found on them. He accounted for his time as having stayed with his father at the Canbury Hotel, Kingston, which was confirmed, on enquiry, by the police.

At 11 a.m. on 10 August a parade of soldiers was arranged at the Tower, for Connelly to identify the two soldiers she and Martha Tabram had been with, but she could not be found. At 11 a.m. on 13 August, Connelly having been located, a parade of soldiers was again held at the Tower. After she had watched this she said, 'They are not here. They had white bands round their caps,' indicating that they were Coldstream Guards and not Grenadiers.

The next day a parade of Coldstream Guards who were on leave or absent on the 6th was arranged, and on the 15th this parade took place at Wellington Barracks. Connelly picked out two men, one as being the corporal who had been with her, the other as the soldier who had gone with Tabram. The man she picked out as the corporal was in fact a private named George, who stated that he had been with his wife at 120 Hammersmith Road from 8 p.m. on the 6th until 6 a.m. the following morning. Enquiries by the police proved this to be correct. The other man, named Skipper, claimed that he had been in barracks on the night of the 6th, and the books confirmed that he had been there from 10.05 p.m. that night. The two were thus cleared of suspicion.

The enquiry was continued amongst the local prostitutes in the East End, but without any success. No soldier could be identified and the police suspected that 'Pearly Poll' was deliberately misidentifying men. It was also felt that the unfortunate PC Barrett had been totally mistaken in the man he had picked out.

Over the years the Martha Tabram murder has invariably been attributed to an unknown soldier, with the murder weapon often incorrectly identified as a bayonet. Some modern theorists now tend to claim that this killing was the first true 'Ripper' murder. They argue that the frenzied attack may have been an undeveloped version of his later methods.

There are several factors, however, that indicate that the offender may well have been a soldier. It was not unknown for drunken clients to commit such murders, very often after a dispute over payment or if the victim attempted to steal from them. Also, Wentworth Street, where PC Barrett checked the soldier who was loitering at 2 a.m. whilst waiting for a friend who had gone off with a female, was adjacent to George Yard, where the body was found. In fact, in a report dated 25 September 1888, Inspector Reid stated that Barrett had actually checked this soldier in George Yard itself. The medical evidence indicated that the murder had occurred at around 2.30 a.m., which tied in with the evidence of the other witnesses.

The whole situation may have been confused by the familiar soldiers' ploy of exchanging jackets, badges of rank and other identifying items when off duty, in case they should become involved in any trouble. As is evident from the police reports, the witnesses were indeed relying upon such items to identify the soldiers.

Much is often made of the time element. Could it be possible that Tabram would spend more than two hours with a client, albeit a soldier with money to pay for her services? One possibility is that while Connelly and her client had found a place to have sex relatively quickly, Tabram may have haggled over her price and had more difficulty in finding a location to complete their business. The unknown soldier checked by PC Barrett may, in fact, have been Pearly Poll's partner trying to find his friend.

It is clear that whoever her client was, Tabram settled on George

Yard Buildings, and it was here that she met her death. Perhaps there was a disagreement over payment and a furious dispute ensued between two people who were known to have been drinking for several hours. The killing did bear all the hallmarks of having been committed in a drunken fury. Did the soldier, in an alcoholic rage, repeatedly plunge a knife into Martha Tabram in the grim slums of the East End? There were only stab wounds on the body; no systematic mutilation was attempted and her throat was not cut.

The inquest into the Tabram murder was held at the Working Lads' Institute, Whitechapel Road, on the afternoon of 9 August. Various witnesses appeared but no further light was shed on the identity of her killer. The hearing was adjourned for two weeks, resuming on 23 August, when the verdict 'wilful murder against some person or persons unknown' was returned.

Most students of the subject agree that the Ripper killings actually began on the morning of Friday 31 August 1888, when Mary Ann Nichols was found dead in a secluded back street, Buck's Row, in Whitechapel. Under ordinary circumstances the death of a prostitute would cause no more than a momentary ripple in the dark pool of the East End. But these circumstances were far from ordinary. As an isolated event, Nichols' death should have faded in the public consciousness, but already the press had identified a 'series of murders'. Even though the Whitechapel of those days was one of the grimmest of all London slums, and life was cheap, here was something new: a 'fiend' was at work.

Nichols, known as 'Polly', the daughter of Edward Walker, a locksmith, and his wife Caroline, was born in Dean Street, off Fetter Lane, on 26 August 1845. After marrying William, a printer, on 16 January 1864, they went to live with Polly's father at 131 Trafalgar Street, Walworth, where they stayed for ten years. In 1874, they moved to their own home at 6D Peabody Buildings, Stamford Street, just off Blackfriars Road. There were five children: Edward John (1866), Percy George (1868), Alice Esther (1870), Eliza Sarah (1877) and Henry Alfred (1879). In 1881 the Nichols' marriage failed, an event that William blamed on his wife's heavy drinking. People who knew her said she would sell her body and soul for a drink.

Once she was free from all family restraints, Polly embarked upon the itinerant lifestyle which was eventually to lead to her death. She moved between various workhouses, and, on occasions, required unspecified medical attention in various infirmaries. Her husband continued to support her for several years until he found out that she had moved in with another man. Several times, she tried to make a fresh start, but her alcoholism always prevailed. In May of 1888 she left Lambeth Workhouse and entered the service of Mr Cowdry of Ingleside, Rose Hill Road, Wandsworth, remaining there until 12 July, when she absconded, stealing various items of clothing.

Within a day or two, she found lodgings at 18 Thrawl Street, Spitalfields, a common lodging house, and slept there and at another common lodging house at 56 Flower and Dean Street up to the night she died.

On the evening of Thursday 30 August 1888, at about 11 p.m. Nichols was seen walking the Whitechapel Road. At 12.30 a.m. she was seen to leave the Frying Pan public house, Brick Lane, Spitalfields. At 1.40 that morning she was in the kitchen at 18 Thrawl Street. She informed the deputy of the lodging house that she had no money to pay for her bed. She asked that a place might be kept for her, and left, stating that she would soon get the money. At this time she was drunk. She was next seen, alone, at 2.30 a.m. at the corner of Osborn Street and Whitechapel Road by Ellen Holland, a lodger in the same house who, seeing she was very drunk, asked her to return with her to Thrawl Street.

Nichols refused, remarking that she would soon be back, and walked away along Whitechapel Road in the direction of Buck's Row, which was about a hundred yards from the Jews' Cemetery, close by the Whitechapel railway station, at the same time crossing the invisible police boundary into J or Bethnal Green Division.

Ellen Holland was certain of her timing as she had heard the Whitechapel Church clock chime 2.30 and had drawn Nichols' attention to this fact. No other person, other than her killer, is known to have seen her alive after that. The distance from Osborn Street to Buck's Row was approximately half a mile.

At about 3.40 a.m., Nichols' body was discovered, on his way to work, by Charles Cross, a carman, at the entrance gates to a stable yard in Buck's Row. This spot was adjacent to number 2 Buck's Row and opposite Essex Wharf. Cross stopped to look at what he initially thought was a tarpaulin. Another carman, Robert Paul, also on his way to work, came along, and Cross approached to stop him, touching him on the shoulder and saying, 'Come and look at this woman here.' Paul then saw the body lying across the gateway.

After a brief examination the two men, unable to see properly in the dark, could not decide whether the woman was hurt, drunk, raped or dead. It was not, of course, uncommon to find alcoholics

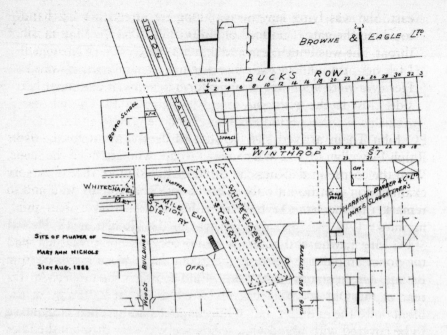

Location of Nichols' murder

lying around the streets of London. Cross felt one of her hands, which was very cold, and said, 'I believe she is dead.' Paul felt her face and hands. Her clothes were raised almost to her stomach. He knelt down to see if he could detect breathing but could not. It was very dark and he did not see any blood. He pulled her clothes down, at which point he fancied he felt a slight movement in her chest. 'I think she is breathing,' he said. As neither man wanted to be late for work, they went in search of a policeman without further examination of the woman.

They met PC Jonas Mizen at the corner of Hanbury Street and Old Montague Street and informed him of their find. Mizen immediately headed for Buck's Row where he found that PC John Neil, whose beat it was, had by now found the body and was calling for assistance. PC Neil had turned on his bull's-eye lantern and discovered that the woman's throat was severely cut. He later described the discovery of the body:

I was on the right-hand side of the street when I noticed a figure lying in the street. It was dark at the time. I went across and found deceased lying outside a gateway, her head towards the east. She was lying lengthways along the street, her left hand touching the gate. I noticed blood oozing from a wound in the throat. She was lying on her back, with her clothes disarranged. I felt her arm, which was quite warm from the joints upwards. Her eyes were wide open. Her bonnet was off and lying at her side, close to the left hand.

PC John Thain arrived shortly afterwards and went for Dr Rees Ralph Llewellyn of 152 Whitechapel Road, who attended the scene. With the corpse in darkness he could make no more than a cursory examination – sufficient only to pronounce the woman dead and to remark that he felt she had been dead for no more than thirty minutes.

PC Mizen, who had gone for reinforcements, now returned with the police ambulance – little more than a cart – and assistance from Bethnal Green station. The body was taken to the mortuary at the rear of the Old Montague Street Workhouse Infirmary. As it was lifted on to the ambulance PC Thain noticed that the back appeared to be covered with blood which, he thought, had run from the neck as far as the waist. There was a mass of congealed blood, about six inches in diameter, where the body had been lying, and this had run towards the gutter. It appeared to him to be a large quantity. There was also some blood where the victim's legs had been.

The body was accompanied to the mortuary by Sergeant Kerby, PC Neil and another officer. Police Inspector John Spratling, J Division, who arrived at Buck's Row after the body had been removed, also went to the mortuary, to compile notes for the coroner. There he had a look at the body, and found that the abdomen had been savagely cut in several places, exposing the intestines. Dr Llewellyn, who had returned home, was quickly called back. This time he made a more careful examination, declaring that the wounds in the abdomen were sufficient on their own to cause instant death.

An identification of the body was required, but enquiries were hampered by the East Enders' natural reluctance to become involved. Various people in the neighbourhood did wander into the mortuary to view the corpse but no one could identify the dead woman.

Polly's worldly possessions comprised the clothes in which she was dressed: a worn brown ulster overcoat, with seven large buttons, portraying a woman riding a horse and a man standing by the side; a brown linsey frock; a white chest flannel; white chemise; two flannel petticoats; a pair of brown stays; black ribbed woollen stockings; a black straw bonnet with black velvet trimming; and a pair of men's boots cut on the uppers. It was the underwear which revealed the secret of her identity: the petticoat bore the marks of Lambeth Workhouse which in turn led the authorities to William Nichols.

On 1 September William Nichols, of 37 Coburg Street, Old Kent Road, a printer employed by Messrs Perkins, Bacon and Co., Whitefriars Street, City, formally identified the body of the woman he had married. As he stood over the corpse he is reported to have uttered: 'I forgive you, as you are, for what you have been to me.' Polly's father was less forgiving. On viewing his daughter's body, he is claimed to have said, 'I knew she'd come to a bad end.'

It is clear that Polly Nichols was murdered and mutilated between 3.15 and 3.40 a.m. The eastern end of Buck's Row, where she was found, was badly lit, narrow and tenanted only on the south side. Dark and secluded, it was a regular resort of prostitutes, and a suitable location for a murder.

Dr Llewellyn found no marks of a struggle and no bloody trail as if the body had been dragged. He concluded that the cuts must have been caused by a moderately sharp, long-bladed knife wielded with violence. The murder had undoubtedly occurred where the body was found.

Inspector Spratling recorded details of the body's mortuary examination:

> ... her throat had been cut from left to right, two distinct cuts being on the left side. The windpipe, gullet and spinal cord having been cut through, a bruise apparently of a thumb being on the right lower jaw, also one on the left cheek. The abdomen had been cut open from centre of bottom of ribs on right side, under pelvis to left of stomach: there the wound was jagged. The omentum or coating of the stomach was also cut in several places, and two small stabs to private parts appeared done with a strong-bladed knife ...

The injuries inflicted upon Polly Nichols showed similar ferocity to that evinced in the murder of Martha Tabram. In two gashes the throat had been cut from ear to ear right back to the spinal column. Abdominal mutilations had laid the belly open from a point just below the breastbone to the lower abdomen. Although no organs had been removed, the violence of her death was chilling. Contemporary press referred to the injuries as 'rips'. It is probable that Polly was throttled before her throat was cut and her body mutilated, thus effectively silencing her.

The killer had disappeared into the night, the probability being that whilst carrying out his horrific work on Nichols' corpse he had become disturbed by the approach of the first witnesses, Cross and Paul. They had arrived along Buck's Row from the direction of Brady Street and the killer would undoubtedly have fled at their approach, past the board school and out on to the Whitechapel Road, either through Wood's Buildings or Court Street. Many experts speculate that had he not been disturbed, the mutilations to the body, would have been very much more extensive.

The inquest on Polly Nichols was held on 3 September. Coroner Wynne Baxter, freshly returned from a Scandinavian tour, was resplendent in a pair of white and black checked trousers, dazzling white waistcoat, crimson scarf, and dark coat. He criticised the police for failing to detect the mutilations before the body was undressed at the mortuary, forgetting the difficulties accompanying the finding of the body. Baxter also criticised the police for allowing the body to be washed before Dr Llewellyn could examine it. This caused an argument, with James Hatfield, one of the elderly paupers who had assisted in washing the corpse, denying that the police had instructed that the body should not be touched, while the police said the opposite; this contretemps was closed without any satisfactory outcome. The coroner then presided over a rigorous examination of the case.

The occupants of the cottages adjoining the murder site were questioned. Mrs Emma Green, who lived in the house next door to the stable yard, number 2 Buck's Row, had been sleeping in a front room, which she shared with her daughter. This front room almost overlooked the site of the murder. Mrs Green had had a poor night's sleep on the night Polly was butchered: but she had not heard a single sound.

The manager of Essex Wharf, Walter Purkiss, and his wife had spent the night in their bedroom opposite the murder site; they had not been disturbed. What sort of killer could carry out such a horrific attack and then disappear with mystifying silence and eerie invisibility?

The motive for the killing was clearly not robbery, since Nichols had owned nothing worth stealing. The attack seemed to have no purpose except as an expression of violence or perverted sexual gratification. For the first time police began to speak of a chilling possibility – that the streets of Whitechapel harboured a deranged killer who would strike again.

That the press were already identifying the fact that they were witnessing a series of killings by the same hand or hands is evidenced by a report that appeared in the *East Anglian Daily Times* of Saturday 1 September 1888, headlined, 'Horrible Murder of a Woman – Another Whitechapel Mystery'.

This article began by referring to the 'horror and sensation' of the Tabram murder and continued with the facts relating to the finding of Nichols' body. This murder was described as more ferocious and brutal than that of Tabram, and Nichols' injuries were listed in great detail. The article also highlighted the fact that the Tabram murder had occurred on a Bank Holiday, and that another murder had occurred on the Bank Holiday previous to that. This reference was to the killing of forty-five-year-old Emma Smith, on the night of Easter Monday, 2–3 April 1888. Smith, in fact, had been attacked and robbed by a group of youths who had beaten her and thrust a stick into her vagina. Two days later she died from peritonitis in the London Hospital. However, rightly or wrongly, a series of murders had been identified and connected. The article concluded, 'All this leads to the conclusion, that the police have now formed, that there is a maniac haunting Whitechapel, and the three women were all victims of his murderous frenzy.'

The popular opinion, then, was that the murderer was a maniac with hate distorting his face; his manner had to be menacing and evil. The police began to hunt for a man known as 'Leather Apron', a prostitute-beater named John Pizer, whose name had been brought to their attention in the course of their investigations.

In a report dated 7 September 1888 by Inspector Joseph H. Helson, head of J Division CID and the local inspector in charge of the case, appeared the following:

The enquiry has revealed the fact that a man named Jack Pizer, alias Leather Apron, has, for some considerable period, been in the habit of ill using prostitutes in this, and other parts of the Metropolis, and careful search has been, and is continued to be made to find this man in order that his movements may be accounted on the night in question, although, at present, there is no evidence whatever against him.

Leather Apron's victims were kicked and punched but not cut. Pizer apparently carried a sharp knife, the kind used to trim leather, and he frequently menaced women with it. He was, according to the *Star*, 'a Jewish slipper-maker who has abandoned his trade in favour of bullying prostitutes. The distinguishing feature of his costume is a leather apron, which he always wears, and from which he gets his nickname.'

In the early hours of Monday the 10th, John Pizer was tracked down to 22 Mulberry Street and arrested by Detective Sergeant William Thick. The police found five long-bladed knives in his lodgings, of a sort thought to have been used by the murderer. Pizer said that he used them in his boot-making trade. He protested his innocence, and his story that he had been in hiding in the Mulberry Street house for four days, since Thursday, was backed up by his stepmother and brother, who lived there. He also had an alibi for the night Polly Nichols was murdered – he was in a lodging house in Holloway Road.

On the 11th Pizer was put before an identification parade at Leman Street police station. A vagrant, Emanuel Delbast Violenia, identified him as the man whom he heard threaten a woman on the night of the murder. But after being cross-examined, Violenia's evidence was so discredited that the police set Pizer free.

At this point the name of the most famous Ripper hunter is introduced to the police inquiry. According to Inspector Helson:

> The enquiry is being carefully continued, by Inspector Abberline, from CO [Central Office, Scotland Yard] and myself and every effort is used to obtain information that may lead to arrest of the murderer. [Ref. MEPO3/140ff.235–8]

In a report dated 19 September 1888, Abberline gave details of the extensive police enquiries into the murders:

> Inquiries were made in every conceivable quarter with a view to trace the murderer but not the slightest clue can at present be obtained. In the course of our inquiries amongst the numerous women of the same class as the deceased it was ascertained that a feeling of terror existed against a man known as Leather Apron who it appeared has for a considerable time past been levying blackmail and ill using them if his demands were not complied with, although there was no evidence to connect him

with the murder. It was however thought desirable to find him and interrogate him as to his movements on the night in question, and with that view searching inquiries were made at all common lodging houses in various parts of the Metropolis, but through the publicity given in the 'Star' and other newspapers the man was made acquainted with the fact that he was being sought for and it was not until the 10th Inst. that he was discovered when it was found he had been concealed by his relatives. On his being interrogated, he was able however to give such a satisfactory account of his movements as to prove conclusively that the suspicions were groundless. Suspicion was also attached to three men employed during the night of the murder by Messrs Barber and Co., 'Horse Slaughterers', Winthrop Street, which is about 30 yards from where the body was found. They have however been seen separately and lengthy statements taken from them as to how they spent their time during the night, and the explanations given by them were confirmed by the police, who saw them at work, and no grounds appeared to exist to suspect them of the murder. [Ref. MEPO3/ 140 ff.242–256]

Further details of the investigation are included in a report of the same date by Chief Inspector Swanson:

The absence of the motives which lead to violence, and of any scrap of evidence either direct or circumstantial, left the police without the slightest shadow of a trace, consequently enquiries were made into the history and accounts given of themselves of persons, respecting whose character & surroundings suspicion was cast in statements made to police. [Ref. HO144/221/ A49301C ff.129–134]

Amongst these were the three slaughtermen, Henry Tomkins, Charles Britton and James Mumford, employed by night at Messrs Harrison, Barber & Company's premises in Winthrop Street. Their statements, taken separately without any means of communicating with each other, satisfactorily accounted for their time, and were even corroborated in part by the police on night duty near the premises.

The funeral of Mary Ann Nichols took place on Thursday 6 September, and the simple arrangements were kept secret in order to avoid scenes with crowds. A two-horse closed hearse made its way down Hanbury Street, with a large crowd, numbered in thousands, watching its progress in the direction of the Old Montague Street mortuary. The hearse went via Whitechapel Road, doubling back to the rear entrance of the mortuary, situated in Chapman's Court. The polished elm coffin, bearing a plate inscribed with the legend, 'Mary Ann Nichols, aged 42 [she was actually 43], died August 31st, 1888', was removed by the undertaker and his men and driven to a rendez-vous point on Hanbury Street. The mourners were late arriving, which gave time for the news to spread, and a large crowd flocked to see the coffin. A body of police under Inspector Allisdon of H Division surrounded the beleaguered hearse and prevented people from getting too close.

The cortège finally set off for Ilford with Mary's father, two of her children, and another of her father's grandsons in the procession. They travelled along Baker's Row, passing the corner of Buck's Row, and into the main road where a line of uniformed police were stationed, one every few yards. And so the first victim of the White-chapel murderer was laid to rest.

All the police enquiries had proved fruitless in providing any indication as to the identity of the murderer. The inquest was resumed on Monday 17 September with four detective inspectors – Abberline, Helson, Spratling and Chandler – present. After the evidence was heard the inquest was adjourned again until the following Saturday, the 22nd, when the coroner summed up and reached the usual verdict of murder against person or persons unknown.

Thus this most famous of unknown killers had embarked upon his bloody career; the legend that was to become Jack the Ripper had begun, and the name of Whitechapel would hereafter never be free of its stain.

Chapter 4

The Ripper Hunters

'... gentlemen of the most unimpeachable veracity.'

It was decided that the local police investigating the murders would benefit from the assistance of the Central Office at Scotland Yard. From the early days of the CID it had been the practice to send more experienced detective officers to assist the divisional detectives in complex or important cases.

It was also a difficult time for the Yard hierarchy, with the resignation of James Monro, the assistant commissioner heading the CID, effective as of 31 August, following a long period of disagreement with the Commissioner, Charles Warren. Monro's replacement was Dr Robert Anderson, who was not to take command immediately as he had insisted on a month's holiday on his doctor's orders. He did not return from Switzerland to assume overall supervision of the CID until 6 October 1888.

In the belief that here was no ordinary series of murders, extraordinary means of capturing the unknown miscreant were decided upon. The surviving, incomplete, police files tell us little of Scotland Yard's deployment of officers to assist the local CID. In fact the assignment of three Central Office detective inspectors to Whitechapel to hunt the murderer is best described in ex-Chief Inspector Walter Dew's book, *I Caught Crippen*. A young detective officer in H Division, Whitechapel, at the time of the murders, Dew was actively engaged in the investigation and devotes no less than a third of his book to 'The Hunt for Jack the Ripper'. Speaking with the knowledgeable insight of an 'insider', he sheds considerable light on the police side of the story and conveys the true atmosphere of those fraught times.

Dew had joined the Metropolitan Police in 1882. He wrote:

In the early part of 1887 I was transferred to the 'H' or Whitechapel Division of the Metropolitan Police, and attached to

Commercial Street Police Station. I had attained my first ambition as a police officer, being now a member of the famous Criminal Investigation Department – a detective officer. Whitechapel, Spitalfields and Shoreditch were now my hunting ground, with hundreds of criminals of the worst type as my quarry. I knew Whitechapel pretty well by the time the first of the atrocious murders, afterwards attributed to Jack the Ripper, took place. And I remained there until his orgy of motiveless killing came to an end.

Dew is an excellent source of information on the senior policemen investigating the murders. Writing mainly from his very good memory, as did so many retired police officers, he says

Let us take a quick look at the men upon whom the responsibilities of the great man-hunt chiefly fell. The officers sent from Scotland Yard were Chief Inspector Moore, Inspector Abberline and Inspector Andrews, assisted, of course, by a large number of officers of subordinate rank.

This is important, for here Dew identifies the fact that three detective inspectors were assigned to the task, on the ground, of hunting the Ripper. At this time Moore was only a detective inspector, and the senior man of the three was Abberline, a detective inspector first-class. Dew adds: 'In addition to them was Detective Inspector Reid, the local chief, who worked under the direction of his colleagues from the Yard.' So here we have, clearly defined, the leaders of the team engaged in the great Ripper hunt.

Frederick George Abberline, forty-five years old at this time, had joined the Metropolitan Police in 1863. He was a Dorset man, born in Blandford, and was promoted to inspector in 1873 when he was posted to H Division Whitechapel, where he spent fourteen years. In 1887 he moved to Central Office at Scotland Yard, and by 1888 was an inspector first-class. His rank was enhanced by the years of experience he had spent as the H Division local inspector.

Abberline was the most prominent of the policemen on the ground, and was repeatedly described as being in charge of the Ripper enquiry. With regard to the active investigation this was undoubtedly true, but a Chief Inspector at Scotland Yard, Donald Sutherland Swanson, was given overall charge. He collated the information received from the investigating officers and reported directly to the head of CID, Dr Robert Anderson.

Police records describe Abberline as a fresh-complexioned man, 5ft.9½in. tall, with dark brown hair and hazel eyes. By 1888 he was overweight and balding, and wore a thick moustache and bushy side-whiskers. Dew recalls:

> [He] was portly and gentle speaking. The type of police officer – and there have been many – who might easily have been mistaken for the manager of a bank or a solicitor. He also was a man who had proved himself in many previous big cases. His strong suit was his knowledge of crime and criminals in the East End, for he had been for many years the detective inspector of the Whitechapel Division, or as it was called then the 'local inspector'. Inspector Abberline was my chief when I first went to Whitechapel. He left only on promotion to the Yard, to the great regret of myself and others who had served under him. No question at all of Inspector Abberline's abilities as a criminal hunter.

Although modest and softly spoken, there is no doubt that Abberline's track record befitted his rank. During his years as H Division's inspector he had accumulated an unrivalled knowledge of the area and its villains. His even-handed and meticulous methods of working had won him the admiration and affection of his colleagues.

Inspector Henry Moore had joined the Metropolitan Police in 1869 and was forty years old in 1888. After serving at Clapham (W Division), Holloway (Y Division) and Peckham (P Division), he was promoted to inspector in 1878, and moved to Scotland Yard in 1888. Dew describes him as 'a huge figure of a man, as strong-minded as he was powerful physically. He had much experience behind him, and was in every way a thoroughly reliable and pains-taking officer.' According to Sir Melville Macnaghten, later Assistant Commissioner CID, Moore was 'one of the smartest officers I ever had the honour of being associated with'.

In early September 1889 Moore was interviewed by an American journalist from Philadelphia, R. Harding Davis, and the story was published in some American papers. The intrepid reporter attended Leman Street police station at 9 p.m. and experienced unexpected difficulty in entering because of 'red tape', a far cry from the easy-going American police stations he was used to. He was introduced by the superintendent to 'a well-dressed gentleman of athletic build' who introduced himself as Inspector Moore. Moore then took the reporter on a tour of the Ripper's hunting grounds.

Davis was led through a network of narrow passageways 'as dark and loathsome as the great network of sewers that stretches underneath them a few feet below'. Remarking on the complexity of the local streets, Moore told the journalist:

> Now, you know, I might put two regiments of police in this half-mile of district and half of them would be as completely out of sight and hearing of the others as though they were in separate cells of a prison. To give you an idea of it, my men formed a circle around the spot where one of the murders took place, guarding, they thought, every entrance and approach, and within a few minutes they found fifty people inside the lines. They had come in through two passageways which my men could not find. And then, you know, these people never lock their doors, and the murderer has only to lift the latch of the nearest house and walk through it and out the back way.

Thus Moore described the problems faced by the Ripper hunters.

Davis was then shown through a well-known common lodging house, where he asked the inspector if he felt nervous of the area. In reply Moore handed him the cane he was carrying. It looked fairly innocuous and was painted to look like maple, but on taking hold of it the American found it was made of iron. 'And then they wouldn't attack me, it's only those who don't know me that I carry the cane for,' said Moore.

During the walk the reporter noticed several men loafing about the streets dressed as locals but 'with a straight bearing that told of discipline, and with the regulation shoe with which Scotland Yard marks its men'. Whispered words were passed between them and Moore.

Of the murderer, Moore commented:

> What makes it so easy for him is that the women lead him of their own free will to the spot where they know interruption is least likely. It is not as if he had to wait for his chance; they make the chance for him. And then they are so miserable and so hopeless, so utterly lost to all that makes a person want to live, that for the sake of fourpence, enough to get drunk on,

they will go in any man's company, and run the risk that it is not him. I tell many of them to go home, but they say that they have no home, and when I try to frighten them and speak of the danger they run, they'll laugh and say, 'Oh, I know what you mean. I ain't afraid of him. It's the Ripper or the bridge [suicide] with me. What's the odds?' and it's true; that's the worst of it.

Stopping in Pinchin Street, Moore pointed to the dark recesses under some railway arches. 'Now, what a place for a murder that would be,' he said. When Davis' article was finally published, it ended thus:

A week later, while I was in mid-ocean on my way back, the body of the ninth victim was found just under those very arches, and not three minutes' walk from the police station. I don't know whether Jack the Ripper was lurking near us that night and had acted on the inspector's suggestion, or whether the inspector is Jack the Ripper himself, but the coincidence is certainly suspicious. As for myself, although I assented to its being a good place for murder at the time, I can prove my alibi by the ship's captain.

After his retirement Moore's career was summed up in a Great Eastern Railway [he was a superintendent with the Railway Police on retiring from the Metropolitan Police] report as follows:

A glance at his Scotland Yard record shows that he specialised in murder cases, and once on the track he seldom failed to bring the offender to justice. The most notable exception to this was the Whitechapel killer. He captured the Frenchman, Ravellot, in Toulon, who murdered Father Sequi in Old Compton Street in 1894. A year later he arrested Guiseppi Ravetti near Turin for the murder of Antoine Brosetti in Long Acre. He also figured largely in the arrest of Dr Collins, who was charged with causing the death of Mrs Uzielli.

It is the third, and perhaps least known, of the Ripper hunters who is of particular interest to us. Walter Simon Andrews, forty-one years old at the time of the murders, could be referred to as 'the forgotten detective'. However, he plays a significant part in our story. He was assigned to the case right at the start with Abberline and Moore, but unlike them, his name disappears from the record, and was subsequently mentioned only once, in a newspaper report at the end of the year. It does not appear at all in the surviving official reports of the case. A strange omission, but the authors believe that Andrews was tasked solely with the apprehension of one known suspect, which would explain his absence from the records.

Andrews was born on 27 April 1847 at Boulge, near Woodbridge, Suffolk, to William and Sarah Andrews. He joined the Metropolitan Police on 15 November 1869, at the age of twenty-two, and was promoted to detective sergeant on 18 November 1875. He was transferred to a division on promotion to inspector on 6 July 1878.

Dew described him as 'a jovial, gentlemanly man, with a fine personality and a sound knowledge of his job'. Author Guy B. H. Logan referred to him as 'One of the Yard's best men'. He had a distinguished career and was respected by his fellow officers and villains alike.

Andrews retired on 31 August 1889, at the age of forty-two, on the grounds of ill-health. He was suffering from thrombosis in the veins of a thigh. He received a pension of £76. His pension book describes him as 5ft.8in. tall, with brown hair turning grey, hazel eyes and a fresh complexion. He had scars on his left groin and thigh, no doubt from operations, and the little finger of his left hand was crooked. His retirement records were signed by the executive superintendent, Charles Cutbush, and they show that he was never injured during his years of service.

The local inspector, Reid, was a veteran of sixteen years' Metropolitan Police service, including time at Scotland Yard. At forty-two he was another capable and experienced officer and had succeeded Abberline at Whitechapel. Other H Division men involved in the hunt were Inspector Joseph Chandler, and Detective Sergeants Thick and Leach.

As previously stated, the overall office task of supervising the enquiry and collating all the information fell to Chief Inspector Swanson. A Scot by birth, he had joined the Metropolitan Police in 1868. As an academic he was well suited to the desk duties he was tasked with in 1888. In this sense he had, perhaps, a better overview of the whole investigation than any other officer. Edwin T. Woodhall, an ex-police officer himself, states in his book, *Secrets of Scotland Yard*:

Swanson in 1888 is best recalled for the work he undertook in the general inquiries, supervision, investigation and reports upon the Whitechapel murder(s) committed by the blood-lust maniac Jack the Ripper. At 40 years of age, Swanson was the highest-ranking career police officer actively involved in the investigation.

In summing up the overall police investigation of the murders we turn again to Walter Dew. Although his opinion may be considered biased, it does seem to be a fair and objective one in the light of modern knowledge:

I feel I must say a few words in defence of the police – of whom I was one – who were severely criticised for their failure to hunt down the wholesale murderer. There are still those who look upon the Whitechapel murders as one of the most ignominious police failures of all time. Failure it certainly was, but I have never regarded it other than an honourable failure.

Dew firmly believed that everything possible had been done to locate the murderer:

Looking back to that period, and assisted in my judgement by the wideness of my own experience since, I am satisfied that no better or more efficient men could have been chosen. These three men did everything humanly possible to free Whitechapel of its Terror. They failed because they were up against a problem the like of which the world had never known, and I fervently hope, will never know again.

There was criticism, too, of the Chief of the Criminal Investigation Department, Sir Robert Anderson, and the Chief Commissioner, Sir Charles Warren, later of Spion Kop fame. This was equally undeserved.

In the light of the more recent investigation into the 'Yorkshire Ripper' murders, it can be argued that a modern police force would have fared no better. Recent investigations have also involved the killer being arrested and questioned, only to be released again. What we want to show in the course of this book is that the Victorian police came a great deal closer to bringing the miscreant to justice than has before been generally realised.

So, briefly, these were the men assigned to investigate the most horrific and baffling series of murders that Scotland Yard had ever been tasked with tackling. They were about to witness the true horror of the nature of their quarry. Just over a week after the Nichols murder the police were summoned to a small, dirty yard at the rear of some terraced houses in Hanbury Street, Spitalfields. The nightmare had just begun.

Chapter 5

Horror in Hanbury Street

'At such times I feel the hot blood tingling to my finger ends.'

While talk of 'Leather Apron' still raged, the real killer struck again on the morning of Saturday 8 September 1888, in the back yard of number 29 Hanbury Street, Spitalfields, leaving another prostitute, Annie Chapman, with her throat cut and her body severely mutilated.

Forty-five-year-old Annie, a short, stout, unattractive woman, had married John Chapman, a coachman to a farm bailiff in Windsor, in 1869, but they separated in 1882. Inspector Frederick Abberline reported that the split had been caused by Annie's drinking habits, but John died in 1886 from cirrhosis of the liver, which indicates that he was also a heavy drinker.

Annie, destitute and ill, had no family from whom she could seek help. Although there were three children from the marriage, one daughter had died, the second was reputed to be living in France in an unnamed institution, and the son was said to have been placed in a home for cripples. It was believed that Annie had a sister. Shortly before her death, she mentioned her intention of trying to borrow boots from her so that she could go hop-picking, an event that did not materialise. She also had a brother, Fountain Smith, who attended both the inquest and the funeral. He testified that he had seen Annie shortly before her death and had given her two shillings.

On the night of her murder Annie had been to an infirmary, probably the outpatients' department at St Bartholomew's Hospital near Newgate Street, East London, which was within walking distance of her usual lodgings.

After drinking in a nearby pub she returned to Crossingham's Lodging House at 35 Dorset Street, where the deputy, Timothy Donovan, demanded money for a bed, which she was unable to pay. Donovan, observing the strict rule of payment in advance and

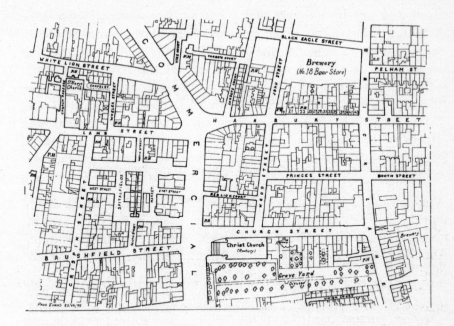

Location of 29 Hanbury Street

ignoring her unwell and undernourished state, turned Annie Chapman out of the doss-house and into the hands of her murderer.

Annie left the house at 2 a.m. in search of a client willing to pay a few pence for her sexual favours. Nightwatchman John Evans saw her leave Dorset Street. Nearby Hanbury Street, approximately ten minutes' walk from Buck's Row, was another typical East End street, dirty and lined with neglected, overpopulated terraced houses. It was here that Annie Chapman was destined to meet the Ripper and her death.

The salient details of the Chapman murder are preserved in a report by Chief Inspector Swanson to the Home Office, dated 19 October 1888. In view of past controversies over the exact details of this murder, mainly arising from inaccurate and conflicting early newspaper reports and later embellishment by sensationalist authors, we draw our information from this important document. [Ref. HO144/221/A49301C]

At 6 a.m. on 8 September, the body of the unfortunate woman was discovered in the back yard of 29 Hanbury Street, Spitalfields, by John Davis, an elderly resident of that address. Too terrified to examine the body, Davis ran into the street and summoned help from two nearby workers and a passing box-maker, Henry John Holland. James Kent, of 20 B Block, King David Lane, Shadwell, working as a packing-case-maker at 23a Hanbury Street, stated that he went to work at 6 a.m. on the day of the murder. At about 6.10 he was waiting for his fellow workers to arrive. It was then that he was approached by the elderly Davis, belt in hand, who said, 'Men, come here.' Kent and a companion, James Green, went with Davis to where the body was lying in the yard. They did not go down the steps into the yard. Kent stated that the woman's face was visible, her clothes disarranged, and the apron she was wearing appeared to have been thrown over the clothes. He could not see any blood apart from that smeared over her hands and face as if she had been struggling. She had a handkerchief of some kind round her throat. Her hands were raised and bent, with the palms towards the upper portion of her body as if she had fought to protect her throat. There were smears of blood about her legs but he did not notice her injuries as he was too frightened to examine her closely. On returning to the front of the house, seeking the police, he had to have a brandy.

At 6.10 a.m. Inspector Joseph Chandler was on duty in Commercial Street near the corner of Hanbury Street when he saw several men running towards him. After hearing that another body had been found, Chandler hurried to number 29 and was the first to inspect the body closely. He at once sent for Dr George Bagster Phillips, the divisional police surgeon, and to the police station for more men and an ambulance.

Examination of the body showed that the throat had been severed deeply by a jagged incision. Removed from but attached to the body, and placed above the right shoulder of the corpse, were a flap of the wall of the belly, and the whole of the small intestine and attachments. Two other portions of belly wall and the pubes were placed above the left shoulder in a large quantity of blood. There was an abrasion of the head of the first phalanx of the ring finger, and the distinct marking of a ring or rings, probably the latter, on the proximal phalanx of the same finger. The following parts were missing: part of the belly wall including the navel, the womb, the upper part of the vagina and the greater part of the bladder. The doctor gave it as his opinion that the murderer was possessed of anatomical knowledge, from the manner of the removal of the viscera, and that the knife used was not an ordinary one, but was such as a small amputating knife, or a well-ground slaughterman's knife, narrow and thin, with a sharp blade six to eight inches in length.

Dr Phillips was not the first to indicate that the murderer might possess some anatomical skill, indicating to the press and populace a doctor or someone with medical knowledge. Dr Llewellyn, at the Nichols inquest, had already put on record that the killer could have 'some rough anatomical knowledge'.

This opinion was underlined by Dr Phillips. The killer had removed the uterus intact, and divided the vagina low enough to avoid damage to the cervix uteri. He obviously recognised the organs and knew how to extract them. In Phillips' opinion, the knowledge and skill involved were impressive given the speed and frenzy with which the murderer carried out his barbarous work. These observations are particularly significant when we look at the Littlechild Suspect: he was a qualified doctor with surgical knowledge.

Phillips thought that the woman had been dead at least two hours, probably longer, and gave instructions for her to be conveyed to the Whitechapel Mortuary. There is little doubt, from the evidence of eyewitnesses, that his initial estimate of the time of death was seriously adrift, and he later admitted as much at the inquest.

The doctor and Inspector Chandler then searched the yard itself. A portion of an envelope was found containing two pills, and bearing a Sussex Regiment seal in blue. On the front was a handwritten letter 'M' and, lower down, 'Sp', as if someone had written 'Spitalfields'. The rest of the envelope was torn away. It had no postage stamp but the red postmark read: 'London, Aug 23, 1888'. The address appeared to commence with '2'.

A number of other items were found in the yard – an empty nail box, a piece of flat steel and, about two feet from a water tap and saturated with water, a leather apron.

Robbery could not stand as a credible motive for a crime distinguished by such 'a rage of cruelty, a fantastic brutality'. If Annie had been attacked by a common thief the abdominal mutilations would have been quite pointless, since death had already resulted from either strangulation or loss of blood from the throat wounds.

The timing of the Chapman killing – it must have been committed between 5.30 and 6 a.m. – meant that the murderer had walked through the streets in almost broad daylight without attracting attention. This strengthened the belief of the police that he must live nearby. The leather apron in the yard was dismissed as having any connection with the murderer: Mrs Amelia Richardson, a resident of 29 Hanbury Street, told the inquest that it belonged to her son, and that two days before the murder she had found it in the cellar and put it under the water tap in the yard and left it there. She also identified the nail box and the piece of steel as her property.

The day after the murder, 9 September, the body was identified as that of Annie Chapman by John Evans, of 35 Dorset Street, Spital-fields, the nightwatchman of the lodging house where she had resided, and also by her brother, Mr Fountain Smith, of 44 Bartholo-mew Close, EC.

Amelia Richardson rented two floors at 29 Hanbury Street, and sub-let some of the rooms. At 4.45 on the morning of the murder, her son John had gone into the yard at the rear of the house with two tasks in mind. He wanted to check that the cellar entrance was secure, and he needed to attend to his boots, which were hurting him. After looking over the premises and finding everything in order, he sat on the rear steps and trimmed some leather from his boots before leaving the yard. Nothing was amiss. Had the body been there at that time he would surely have seen it.

At some point during the next hour the unfortunate Annie led her killer down the dark and no doubt smelly passageway into the yard, where he rapidly despatched her.

At 5.25 a.m. Albert Cadosch of 27 Hanbury Street, on the west side of number 29, had occasion to go into the yard at the rear of number 27, which was separated from that of its neighbour only by a wooden fence about five feet high. He heard conversation pass between some persons apparently in the yard of 29 Hanbury Street, but the only word he could catch was 'no'. There is a note in the margin of the police report, 'Was the voice of the man that of a foreigner?' but this question does not appear to have been answered. At 5.28 a.m., Cadosch returned to his yard and heard a noise as of something falling against the fence, but he did not take any further notice.

At 5.30 a.m. a Mrs Elizabeth Long, 'alias Durrell' according to the index in the police file, of 32 Church Street stated that she saw a man and woman talking near to 29 Hanbury Street. She heard the man say, 'Will you?' and the woman reply, 'Yes,' before she passed along. She saw only his back, and stated she would be unable to know him again. She described him as apparently over forty years of age. He appeared to be a little taller than the woman and in her opinion looked like a foreigner. She thought he had a dark coat on. Later, at the inquest, she also stated he was wearing a brown deerstalker. On viewing the body at the mortuary, she positively identified the woman as the deceased.

It is important to draw attention to Mrs Long's description of the man in the dark coat and brown deerstalker hat. Her evidence was the first real indication that the murderer may have been a foreigner. Although she did not see his face, something – possibly his accent – had given her that impression.

Was Mrs Long the first person to see the unknown killer? At the time, the police felt it 'unfortunate' that her evidence was weakened by Phillips' evidence indicating an earlier time of death. However, there is no doubt that the doctor's estimate was totally inaccurate, and Mrs Long was supported by the other evidence, especially that of Cadosch, whose time estimate was very close to hers, regarding the time of the murder. The inevitable conclusion must be that here was the first genuine sighting of the Whitechapel murderer, and the first description of him, albeit rather lacking in detail.

The inquest into the death of Annie Chapman was opened by Wynne Baxter on Monday 10 September, for evidence of the discovery, by John Davis, and identification of the body, by Timothy Donovan, John Evans, and Amelia Farmer, a friend of the deceased. Farmer gave details of Chapman's past history, as well as evidence of Chapman feeling unwell recently. She stated that Chapman was not very particular about what she did to earn a living and used to stay out very late at night. She often visited Stratford.

The hearing continued on the 12th when Fountain Smith gave evidence of identification. Kent and Green then testified and stated that they saw no one go out to the body before Inspector Chandler arrived. John Pizer also appeared, agreeing that he was known as 'Leather Apron', and accounting for his whereabouts at the time of the murder. Henry John Holland, of 4 Aden Yard, Mile End Road, gave evidence of answering Davis' summons at about 6.08 a.m., seeing the body, and running to get a police officer. The inquest was adjourned until the next day.

On the afternoon of Thursday the 13th Inspector Joseph Chandler gave his evidence. Inspectors Abberline, Helson and Beck were present, as was Sergeant Thick. Dr Phillips revealed that he had been called to the scene of the murder, arriving at 6.20 a.m. He stated that the deceased was lying in the yard, on her back, on the left-hand side of the steps leading from the passage of the house into the yard. The head was about six inches in front of the level of the bottom step, and her feet were pointing towards a shed at the bottom of the yard. The left arm was placed across the left breast, and the legs were drawn up, the feet resting on the ground and the knees turned outwards. The face was swollen and turned on the left side. The tongue, much swollen, protruded between the front teeth, but not beyond the lips. The front teeth were perfect so far as the first molar, and 'very fine teeth they were'. Phillips then described the abdominal injuries as previously detailed.

He continued, stating that he had searched the yard and had found a small piece of coarse muslin, a small-tooth comb, and a pocket comb in a paper case. These items had 'apparently been placed there in order – that is to say arranged there'. The body was cold, but there was some heat under the intestines that remained in the body. There was no marked stiffness of the corpse but it was evidently commencing. He noticed that the throat was dissevered completely, and the incisions of the skin were jagged and reached right down the neck. On the back wall of the house, between the steps and the drain on the left side, approximately eighteen inches from the ground, there were about six patches of blood, varying in size from a sixpenny piece to a small point, and on the wooden paling between the two yards were smears of blood corresponding to where the head of the woman lay. This was about fourteen inches from the body. Immediately above the part where the blood had flowed from the neck the blood was well clotted.

Soon after 2 p.m. the same day the doctor had gone to the labour yard of the Whitechapel Union to further examine the body. He found that it had been attended to since its arrival at the mortuary, probably partially washed. The same protrusion of the tongue was still present and there was a bruise over the right malar (cheek) bone. There was also a bruise over the temple, and two distinct bruises, each the size of the top of a man's thumb, on the forepart of the chest. There were bruises on other parts of the body. There was an old scar over the left frontal bone. The doctor noted the abrasions on the knuckle of the ring finger, and the distinct mark of a ring, or more probably rings, having been worn. There were two cuts on the neck from left to right. He formed the opinion that the incisions to the other parts of the body were made after death, and that the absence of blood was due to the large escape of blood from the neck. Phillips then made the interesting observation that the appearance of the body indicated that breathing had been interfered with prior to death – indicating strangulation or partial strangulation – death resulting from syncope or failure of the heart's action in consequence of the loss of blood, caused by the severance of the throat.

When asked what type of instrument had caused the wounds, he replied, 'Probably the same sort of instrument was used at the throat and the other parts of the body. It must have been a very sharp knife with a very thin, narrow blade, and must have been at least six to eight inches in length – probably longer.'

'Was it an instrument that a slaughterer would use?' he was asked.

'Yes, well ground down. I think the blade of the knife used in the shoe trade would not be long enough.'

Then came the important question; 'Was any anatomical knowledge displayed?'

He replied, 'I think there was; there were indications of it. I think the anatomical knowledge was only less displayed or indicated by being hindered in consequence of haste.'

'Was the whole of the body there?'

'No. The absent portions were from the abdomen. I think the mode in which they were extracted did show some anatomical knowledge. I am positive there were indications of a struggle in the yard. I am convinced there had been no strong alcohol taken immediately before death. The marks of bruises on the face were evidently recent, especially about the chin and the sides of the jaws. The bruises about the chest were of long standing, probably of days. I am of opinion that the person who cut the deceased's throat took hold of her by the chin, and then commenced the incision from left to right.'

The evidence of Dr Phillips gives a good indication of the nature of the killer's mode of attack. There were indications of strangulation, or partial throttling, prior to any cut being made, and signs that the throat cutting had been accomplished whilst the victim was lying on the ground with her killer to her right and over her. The older bruises on Annie's body were the result of a fight with a fellow lodger, Eliza Cooper, around the beginning of the month. It was a typical lodging house squabble over the loan of a piece of soap which Annie had failed to return.

The inquest was resumed once more on the afternoon of Wednesday 19 September, when Eliza Cooper, a hawker, gave her evidence stating that she had last seen the deceased alive on the previous Wednesday and that Chapman wore three brass rings on her left hand. Chapman was known to associate with two men known as

'Stanley' and 'Harry the Hawker', but she also brought other men casually to her lodgings.

Dr Phillips was re-called, and told by Wynne Baxter that the post-mortem results should be placed on the depositions, and read out loud to the court and public. The doctor expressed 'regret' that the coroner should have reached this decision, as he felt that it would 'thwart the ends of justice', this feeling being entirely in line with the police philosophy of withholding as much information regarding their enquiries as possible. Unmoved, Wynne Baxter stated that justice had already had 'a long time in which to avenge itself'. He was obviously disdainful of the police failure to effect an arrest.

Now the coroner had the court cleared of females and boys, and reluctantly Dr Phillips revealed more detailed information about the injuries inflicted. He gave evidence of the excised portions of the body, stating that it was his belief that the mutilation was performed in order to obtain possession of the womb. This idea was to lead to much speculation and theorising. He also stated that the mode of removal of the abdominal wall indicated a certain amount of anatomical skill. In the doctor's opinion he himself could not have accomplished the dissection, even without a struggle, in under a quarter of an hour. If he had performed the cuts and incisions in a deliberate way, as would a surgeon, he estimated that it would have taken him the best part of an hour.

There were also signs of strangulation on the body: about one and a half to two inches below the left ear were three scratches, with a corresponding bruise on the right side of the neck. Together with the swollen tongue and signs of cyanosis in the face and lips, the indications of strangulation are persuasive.

Elizabeth Long gave her evidence next. The reports of the inquest in the newspapers of 22 September add a little to the information contained in the police report. She stated that she was making her way along Hanbury Street on her way to Spitalfields Market, and that she fixed the time at half past five by the striking of a neighbouring clock. She saw a man come to a woman and stand and talk with her near number 29, reported the *Suffolk Chronicle*. She saw the woman's face, and although she had never seen her before, she recognised her as the same woman when she saw her in the mortuary. She did not see the man's face and would not recognise him again. He was, however, dark-complexioned, and was wearing a brown deerstalker hat. She thought he was wearing a dark coat, but could not be sure. He was over forty, as far as she could tell, and was of 'shabby genteel' appearance. She repeated the conversation she had overheard. She left them standing there and went to her work.

As with other witnesses, it is very difficult to assess Mrs Long from this distance in time. In her favour, her evidence seems simple and straightforward, and the fact that she was willing to come forward as a witness is in itself a good sign. Her interest in the couple is probably attributable to the fact that she was witnessing a prostitute in the act of picking up a client. It appears that she actually witnessed the initial approach of the killer to his victim, and her evidence ties in neatly with the other testimony given.

Edward Stanley, a bricklayer's labourer, known as 'the Pensioner', gave evidence of knowing Chapman and of sometimes visiting her. He denied that he had stayed with her, as claimed by the lodging house keeper, and said he had voluntarily attended Commercial Street police station and offered to give evidence. Other witnesses were then examined, and a discussion took place regarding the offering of a reward, several of the jury agreeing that the Government should come forward in that direction. The inquest was adjourned for another week.

The police investigation into the murder may be summarised from the contemporary reports as follows: the inhabitants of 29 Hanbury Street were seen and their rooms searched. Their statements were taken, as were those of the inhabitants of the adjoining houses.

An 'immediate and searching' enquiry was made at all common lodging houses to ascertain if anyone had entered that morning with blood on his hands, face or clothes, or under any suspicious circumstances.

A special enquiry to find the missing rings was made at all pawn-brokers, jewellers and dealers. Enquiries were also made into the antecedent history of the murdered woman. She was the widow of a coachman named Chapman who had died about eighteen months previously, and from whom she had been separated for eight years, on account of her drunken and immoral ways. He had allowed her ten shillings per week up to the time of his death. She was then occasionally visited by the man named Stanley, who had come forward and accounted for his time.

Several persons were detained pending enquiries into their movements covering the dates of 7 and 31 August and 8 September. The particulars of other persons seen in different parts of the metropolis, under apparently suspicious circumstances to the persons giving the information, were circulated. Enquiries were also undertaken to trace suspected persons whose address or particulars were supplied in correspondence.

Other prostitutes and women of similar circumstances were seen and questioned, and enquiries were made at public houses in the locality.

These combined enquiries did not supply the police 'with the slightest clue to the murderer'. Officers felt that:

> the only indication of the direction to find the murderer lay in the evidence of Dr Phillips, which was in substance that the individual possessed some skill and anatomical knowledge – and that the instrument with which the injuries were inflicted was probably a small amputating knife, or a well-ground butcher's knife, narrow and thin, sharp with a blade from six to eight inches long.

They reasoned:

> If the evidence of Dr Phillips is correct as to the time of death, it is difficult to understand how it was that [John] Richardson did not see the body when he went into the yard at 4.45 a.m. but as his clothes were examined, the house searched and his statement taken in which there was not a shred of evidence, suspicion could not rest upon him, although police specially directed their attention to him. Richardson is a market porter. Again if the evidence of Mrs Long is correct and she saw the deceased at 5.30 a.m., then the evidence of Dr Phillips as to probable time of death is incorrect. He was called and saw the body at 6.20 a.m. and he then gives it as his opinion that death occurred about two hours earlier, viz. 4.20 a.m., hence the evidence of Mrs Long which appeared to be so important to the Coroner must be looked upon with some amount of doubt, which is to be regretted.

Thus the enquiries were summed up.

The piece of envelope found near the body was accounted for by the evidence of a witness, William Stevens, who had seen Chapman in the kitchen of 35 Dorset Street with a box of pills and medicine obtained from the hospital. The box fell to pieces and she picked up a piece of paper from the kitchen floor and wrapped two pills in it. He thought that the piece of envelope bearing the Royal Sussex

Regiment seal was identical with the piece of paper she had picked up.

The newspapers theorised in search of an adequate explanation for the apparently motiveless murders. Was the killer a religious maniac bent upon the extirpation of sin by the slaying of prostitutes? Or were his crimes revenge for some real or fancied injury suffered at the hands of such women?

A report in the *Suffolk Chronicle* of 15 September 1888 warned darkly:

> The police believe that the murder has been committed by the same person who perpetrated the three previous ones in the district, and that only one person is concerned in it. This person, whoever he might be, is doubtless labouring under some terrible form of insanity, as each of the crimes has been of a most fiendish character, and it is feared that unless he can speedily be captured more outrages of a similar class will be committed.

The *Chronicle* reported that neighbours on either side of the most recent murder site were charging people to view the yard where the killing had taken place. It continued:

> On Saturday a rumour got about that the murderer had been caught, but the only ground for such a statement was that a blind man had been arrested in Spitalfields Market on a warrant to answer a charge of stabbing. Later in the day this man was charged at the Worship Street Police Court, and sentenced to three months' hard labour.

A little girl called the attention of the police to marks in the yard behind number 25 Hanbury Street, next door but one to the scene of the murder. Bloodstains were found which indicated that the murderer had crossed two fences and ultimately made his escape through number 25, but this evidence was discounted when the stains were found to be urine.

Another story uncovered by the press was that 'Dark Annie', as Chapman was known, was seen drinking at a tavern in Brick Lane with the man supposed to be her murderer. The barmaid of the hostelry told a reporter that she opened the place at 5 a.m. as usual on a Saturday morning, because of Spitalfields Market being in the vicinity. She was too busy to notice who was in there and she might have served the woman but had no recollection of it. She most certainly could not say whether the 'unfortunate creature' was accompanied by a man or not. This was typical of the stories that abounded after the murders.

The mood of the day was typified by a newspaper report as follows:

> The terror and excitement were somewhat abating when, at about 11 o'clock, the people who had congregated in Commercial Street were thrown into a fresh state of alarm. It was rumoured that about a quarter of an hour previously the man who was supposed to be the murderer, or connected with the murder, had been in the locality, but this statement, owing to the want of previous success in detecting the perpetrators of the other murders, was received with incredulity. A short time afterwards, however, a young man, apparently about 25 years of age, was seen running down Commercial Street at full speed, followed by a large body of policemen with drawn batons, and a large crowd of persons. The man was gradually gaining on his pursuers [*sic*], but owing to the cries of the policemen a large body of men and women blocked the street. The man at once grasped the situation, and rushed down a side street. The excitement at this time became intense, as it was thought that the man, who was supposed to be the murderer, would escape. After an interval of about two minutes, however, a cheer was raised, and shortly afterwards the man was seen between five or six policemen. It would be almost impossible to describe his appearance; he was the picture of terror, the colour of his face being between a ghastly white and yellow. He is about the medium height and was fairly dressed. When the police arrived in Commercial Street the people crowded round, in order to look at the captured man, but they were kept at a distance by a body of policemen. The man was taken to the Commercial Street police station. It is thought that in consequence of this arrest a clue will be obtained as to the perpetrators of the dastardly crimes which have thrown the inhabitants of the district into the greatest state of alarm during the last few weeks.

Of course, this was just another of many arrests that had no connection at all with the real murderer. However, it does show the state of public unrest and excitement in the area.

This same article also reported that the local chief constable of the district, Colonel Monsell, had visited the locality in the 'early forenoon' of the day of the murder and inspected the body of the victim.

Hanbury Street was almost impassable because of the crowds that had assembled near the scene of the murder. Thousands of people passed through the locality and extra constables were drafted in from other divisions to keep order. On the Sunday night after the killing the excitement was undiminished, with large crowds of the 'poorer classes' loitering in the vicinity. Added to this, a number of the 'more well-to-do' were to be seen either gazing with 'awe-stricken' faces at 29 Hanbury Street, or endeavouring to glean additional information on the circumstances of the tragedy.

According to a newspaper report:

> The police authorities at Scotland Yard and Whitechapel are fully conscious of the difficult nature of the task they have before them in identifying any particular individual with the series of appalling crimes. 'God knows,' said an official to our reporter, 'but we may have another tonight, though we have men patrolling the whole region of Whitechapel and Spital-fields.' That the police are putting forth every possible effort there can be no doubt. On Sunday night there was a large force on duty. One-third of the men are in plain clothes, and even those entitled to leave are retained.

The officers at Commercial Street at this stage had no fewer than fifty witness statements relating to the possible identity of the offender. The police did not, of course, make public the nature of any evidence provided in these statements, although it was believed that they were of little value.

One investigative reporter, whilst at the police station, did hear a statement which he felt worthy of note. A young woman named Lyons, 'of the class commonly known as "unfortunate" ', stated that at three o'clock on the afternoon of Sunday 9 September, the day after the murder, she met a strange man in Flower and Dean Street, described as one of the worst streets in the East End. He asked her to go to the Queen's Head public house at half past six and drink with him. Having obtained her agreement to do so, he disappeared, but was at the pub at the appointed time. Whilst conversing, Lyons noticed a large knife in the man's right-hand trouser pocket, and called another woman's attention to this fact. Lyons was then startled by the man's remark, 'You are about the same style of woman as the one that's murdered.' Lyons replied, 'What do you know about her?' and he replied cryptically, 'You are beginning to smell rats; foxes hunt geese, but don't always find them.' Having uttered these words the stranger hurriedly left. Lyons followed him until near Spitalfields Church where he turned around and saw her behind him. He then ran at a swift pace into Church Street and was lost to view. The report stated that the man's description fitted that published of 'Leather Apron'.

In the twenty-four hours after the murder, the police visited over two hundred common lodging houses in their search for the killer, and had rounded up a number of suspects. The *Suffolk Chronicle and County Express* tells us that on the night of 9 September William Piggott, a fifty-three-year-old ship's cook, was arrested in Gravesend. One of Piggott's hands was injured but he is said to have initially drawn attention to himself in the Pope's Head Tavern by noisily expressing a hatred of women. A report of 15 September stated:

He is still an inmate of the workhouse infirmary, and it is stated that his mental condition has not materially improved. The idea that he was connected in some way with the recent terrible crimes has not been entirely abandoned, and he is still kept under surveillance, while diligent enquiries are being made into his previous history.

A report, dated 19 September, by Charles Warren outlines the police's major suspects at this point:

No progress has as yet been made in obtaining any definite clue to the Whitechapel murderers. A great number of clues have been examined and exhausted without finding anything suspicious. A large staff of men are employed and every point is being examined which seems to offer any prospect of a discovery.

There are at present three cases of suspicion.

1. The lunatic Isensmith [*sic*], a Swiss arrested at Holloway who is now in an Asylum at Bow and arrangements are being made to ascertain whether he is the man who was seen on the morning of the murder in a public house by Mrs Fiddymont.

2. A man called Puckeridge was released from an asylum on

4 August. He was educated as a surgeon and has threatened to rip people up with a long knife. He is being looked for but cannot be found as yet.

3. A Brothel Keeper who will not give her address or name writes to say that a man living in her house was seen with blood on him on morning of murder. She described his appearance and said where he might be seen. When the detectives came near he bolted, got away and there is no clue to the writer of the letter.

All these three cases are being followed up and no doubt will be exhausted in a few days – the first seems a very suspicious case, but the man is at present a violent lunatic. [Ref. HO/144/221/A49301C ff.90–1]

The first man mentioned was Jacob or Joseph Isenschmid, a mentally disturbed pork butcher. The second man, identified by author and historian Phil Sugden as Oswald Puckridge, was released from Hoxton House Lunatic Asylum three days before the George Yard murder. He had been admitted to the asylum on 6 January 1888, was entered into the register as a pauper, and was discharged on 4 August.

It is very difficult to assess Puckridge as a suspect, because there is little information on him. He was born on 13 June 1838 at Burpham, Sussex; he described himself as a chemist; and he married Ellen Puddle when he was thirty. On 28 May 1900, he was admitted to the Holborn Workhouse in City Road and died on 1 June of 'broncho pneumonia'. There is no evidence to connect him with the crimes.

Also being investigated by the police after Annie Chapman's murder were three insane medical students who had attended London Hospital. Two were found, interviewed and eliminated, while a third, John Sanders, of Maida Vale, was thought to have disappeared abroad. In fact, during the period of the murders he was confined at West Malling Place, a private asylum in Kent. He died, aged thirty-nine, in the Heavitree Asylum, Exeter, in 1901.

An itinerant pedlar, Edward McKenna, was arrested and released after witnesses failed to recognise him. John Fitzgerald, a plasterer or bricklayer's labourer, was arrested after he confessed to the Chapman murder, but was released when his statement was found to be false. But it was Joseph Isenschmid who was the leading suspect at this stage. His first name, as revealed by Phil Sugden's research, was actually Jacob, but as all the official police reports refer to him as Joseph, we can only assume that this was the name he went by.

Inspector Abberline wrote on 18 September:

> Although at present we are unable to procure any evidence to connect him with the murders he appears to be the most likely person that has come under our notice to have committed the crimes.

Swiss-born Isenschmid was first brought to the attention of the police by two doctors, Dr Cowan and Dr Crabb, who alleged that he was an insane butcher who left his lodgings at strange times in the middle of the night. He was arrested on 12 September and taken to Holloway police station. He was then transferred to the Islington Workhouse, and later to Grove Hall Lunatic Asylum, Bow. Sergeant Thick examined the clothing in which he had been arrested but could find no traces of bloodstains.

According to the *Star*, his behaviour during his periods of insanity was frequently violent, and people were cautioned to keep away from him. He was frequently seen sharpening a long knife.

Isenschmid has been linked with an incident which occurred on the morning of the Chapman murder and which was reported in the *Star of the East* of Monday evening, 10 September. Mrs Fiddymont, who was mentioned in Charles Warren's report, was the wife of the proprietor of the Prince Albert public house, better known as the Clean House, situated at the north-east corner of the junction of Brushfield and Steward Streets, only half a mile from the scene of the murder.

She stated that at 7 a.m. on the morning of 8 September she was standing in the first compartment of the bar talking with a friend, Mrs Mary Chappell of 28 Steward Street. A man appeared in the middle compartment whose rough appearance alarmed the women. He was rather thin, about 5ft.8in. tall, aged between forty and fifty years, with a ginger-coloured moustache and short sandy hair. He had a 'shabby genteel' look and was wearing pepper-and-salt-coloured trousers, which fitted badly, a torn light blue check shirt with no waistcoat, a dark-coloured coat and a brown stiff hat topping off the ensemble. To enhance his sinister appearance the hat was pulled down over his eyes, partially concealing his face. He asked for a half a pint of four ale, which she drew, at the same time scrutinising him in the mirror at the back of the bar.

The man noticed Mrs Chappell also watching him and he immediately turned his back, putting the partition between himself and her. What particularly set Mrs Fiddymont ill at ease were the blood spots she noticed on the back of his right hand. She also noted the torn shirt. There was a narrow streak of blood under his right ear, parallel to the edge of his shirt, and dried blood between his fingers. Mrs Chappell confirmed Mrs Fiddymont's story. The man's eyes were 'startling and terrifying' and Mrs Fiddymont was so frightened that she asked her friend to stay.

The man swallowed his ale 'at a gulp' and went out. Mrs Chappell slipped out of the other door to watch him. He went towards Bishopsgate Street and she called the attention of another witness, Joseph Taylor, a local builder, to him. As soon as his attention had been drawn to the man, Taylor followed him. He walked rapidly and came alongside the man but did not speak to him. The man glanced at Taylor, who noticed that 'his eyes were wild as a hawk's'. He walked holding his coat together at the top and had a nervous and frightened way about him. Taylor stopped following him but watched him as far as Halfmoon Street where he lost sight of him. Taylor was described as a 'perfectly reliable man, well known throughout the neighbourhood'. Mrs Fiddymont and Taylor were subsequently called by the police to Commercial Street police station to see if they could identify the other suspect, Piggott as the man they had seen, but they did not think he was.

Abberline conceded on 18 September that the police were unable to 'procure any evidence to connect him [Isenschmid] with the murders'. What is apparent is that they considered insanity and medical knowledge to have been important factors in a suspect, but in this case they had little else to go on. On 21 September, the *Star* reported that Isenschmid's brother had satisfactorily accounted for his movements on the morning of the Chapman murder. His innocence was confirmed when the murderer struck again while he was still confined at Grove Hall.

In the early hours of 18 September another suspect made his dramatic appearance. He was Charles Ludwig, aged forty, a German hairdresser. At about 3 a.m. Alexander Finlay, or Feinberg, was standing at a coffee stall in Whitechapel when the respectably dressed but drunken Ludwig approached and was refused service by the stall-holder. Ludwig, much annoyed, noticed that Finlay was watching. He asked him, 'What are you looking at?', pulled out a knife and tried to stab him. He followed Finlay round the stall, making several lunges at him. A constable came on the scene and Ludwig was arrested.

On the way to the police station Ludwig, no doubt trying to dispose of the evidence, dropped a long-bladed penknife. On being searched at the station he was found to have a razor and a long-bladed pair of scissors on him. Another constable gave evidence at the Thames police court the following morning stating that in the early hours he heard loud screams of 'Murder!' proceeding from a dark court off the Minories called Three Kings' Court, although it was no longer really a court as all the houses had been pulled down to make way for the railway, leaving a twelve-yard-long alley with a walled-in space about forty feet square at the end. The court led to some railway arches, and was well known as a dangerous locality. On entering the court the constable found Ludwig with a prostitute. She appeared very agitated and said, 'Oh, policeman, do take me out of this!' She was, apparently, so frightened that she could offer no further statement and the constable led the two of them out of the court, sending Ludwig on his way.

As we know, prostitute–client disputes were all too common and the police invariably dealt with them in this fashion if there was no obvious serious offence involved. The constable walked the woman to the end of his beat where she then said, 'Dear me, he frightened me very much when he pulled a big knife out.' The astounded policeman said, 'Why didn't you tell me that at the time?' to which she replied, 'I was much too frightened.'

Realising the implications of what she had said, the constable immediately set off in search of Ludwig, but could not find him. He warned several fellow officers what had happened. He had failed to ascertain the identity of the woman but felt he would recognise her again; this would have been made fairly simple by the fact that she had only one arm! She was, in fact, Elizabeth Burns.

Ludwig claimed he could not speak English and it was ascertained that he had arrived in England from Hamburg about fifteen months previously. He had entered the employment of Mr C. A. Partridge, hairdresser, in the Minories two weeks prior to the last Saturday. They had met in a German club in Houndsditch which was a house of call for German hairdressers. About a week after meeting Partridge, Ludwig had asked if he could sleep in his house, to which the other man consented. Ludwig gave as his reason for this request the fact that there was a man lying dead in the house in which he was then staying, and he did not like to stop there. He made another move on the night of Sunday 16 September, going to stay with a German tailor named Johannes in Church Street, Minories, and leaving his scanty worldly goods at his employer's. Johannes soon changed his mind about having Ludwig at his house because of his 'dirty habits', and told him that he must leave on Monday morning. This accounted for Ludwig wandering about on the night of his arrest.

Mr Partridge stated that his employee was fond of drink but ridiculed any idea of him being the Whitechapel murderer. Ludwig was still in custody when the killer next struck.

On Wednesday 26 September the final hearing of the Chapman inquest took place, and Wynne Baxter summed up the evidence. A flamboyant and somewhat controversial character, his comments were held in some esteem by the press and were reported in great detail to a public avidly consuming every available titbit. An important aspect of Baxter's summing-up was the fact that he ventured into the realms of theorising. He referred to the 'reckless daring' of the murderer, and the silence of the killing in a well-populated area. 'The brute who committed the offence did not even take the trouble to cover up his ghastly work, but left the body exposed to view,' he continued. 'Probably as daylight broke he hurried away in fear.' He observed the absence of the rings wrenched from Chapman's fingers, and the missing uterus. He noted that the injuries had been inflicted by someone with 'considerable anatomical knowledge and skill. There are no meaningless cuts. The organ has been taken away by one who knew where to find it, what difficulties he would have to contend against, and how he should use his knife so as to abstract the organ without any injury to it. No unskilled person could know where to find it, or have recognised it when it was found.' He continued along similar lines, dismissing robbery as a motive.

Then came the part of his oration that was to have a profound effect on many aspects of the story of the Whitechapel murders. In seeking a motive he declared, '... for it is clear that there is a market for the missing organ'. He pointed out the value of press publicity in the detection of crime, a view that the police officials, and the doctor, did not share. As a result of the press reports of the last hearing, he claimed, he had received a communication from 'an officer of one of our great medical schools'. He stated that this man had information which might have a bearing on the investigation:

I attended at the first opportunity, and was informed by the sub-curator of the Pathological Museum that some months ago an American had called on him, and asked him to procure a number of specimens of the organ that was missing in the deceased. He stated his willingness to give £20 for each specimen, and said his object was to issue an actual specimen with each copy of a publication on which he was then engaged. He was told that his request was impossible to be complied with, but he still urged it, saying he wished them preserved, not in spirits of wine, the usual medium, but in glycerine, in order to preserve them in a flaccid condition, and he wished them sent to America direct. It is known that this request was repeated to another institution of a similar character. Now, is it not possible that the knowledge of this demand incited some abandoned wretch to possess himself of specimens?

Baxter stated that he had immediately communicated his findings to Scotland Yard.

He next referred back to the earlier murders of Smith and Tabram, as well as mentioning the two recent ones he had been enquiring into. 'It is, therefore, a great misfortune that nearly three weeks have elapsed without the chief actor in this awful tragedy having been discovered.' Enlarging on his own profile of the unknown killer, Baxter added:

His anatomical knowledge carries him out of the category of common criminals, for that knowledge could only have been obtained by assisting at post-mortems, or by frequenting the post-mortem room. Thus the class in which search must be made, although a large one, is limited. Moreover, it must be a man who was from home, if not all night, at least during the early hours of the 8th September. His hands were undoubtedly bloodstained, for he did not stop to use the tap in the yard, as the pan of clean water under it shows. If the theory of lunacy be correct, which I very much doubt, the class is still further limited, while if Mrs Long's memory does not fail, and the assumption be correct that the man who was talking to the deceased at half past five was the culprit, then he is even more clearly defined. He was a foreigner of dark complexion, over 40 years of age, a little taller than the deceased, of shabby-genteel appearance, with brown deerstalker hat on his head, and dark coat on his back.

The jury returned the inevitable verdict of 'Wilful murder against some person or persons unknown'. Dr Phillips had arrived late for the inquest and was apprised by a press reporter of Wynne Baxter's 'startling statement' made in his summing-up. The doctor replied that he considered it a very important communication, and that the public would now see his reason for not wishing in the first place to give a description of the injuries. He attached great importance to the application which had been made to the Pathological Museum, and to the advisability of following up this information as a possible clue.

Wynne Baxter's story of the American seeking specimens was controversial and must have aroused the displeasure of the staid medical institutions when they were subsequently pestered by reporters for confirmation. They claimed that the incident referred to had occurred well over a year previously and related to a respectable foreign physician, staying in London, who had been enquiring as to the possibility of obtaining specimens of wombs. The story, however, is not that easily disposed of.

Two medical schools, those attached to University College and Middlesex Hospitals, strangely refused to clarify the matter, unlike others who stated that there had been no such application. Phil Sugden suggests that there was certainly more to this story than met the eye, especially in the light of a statement, appearing in the *Daily Telegraph*, from an official hospital spokesman, who said that they 'indignantly repudiate the suggestion that it was a hoax or that the matter was of no importance' and who talked enigmatically of 'the interests of justice' being imperilled by any disclosure. Had the hospital, in fact, already identified the American to the police?

As a result of Wynne Baxter's well-publicised statement, several important new elements were introduced into the story: the anatomical knowledge of the killer; an American stranger seeking specimens of the missing organ; and the murderer being rather more than an ordinary common criminal. The Whitechapel murderer's status and reputation were now enhanced.

While the police pursued their enquiries, becoming tied up with numerous false leads and unlikely suspects, the real killer was soon to emerge again from his unknown lair. In another of the twists that were only too common in this case, he chose a night on which a second killer also claimed a victim.

Chapter 6

Stride Out?

'The knife is a source of immense mischief to the human family.'

At 10.30 p.m. on Saturday 29 September, a man aged about thirty-three entered the Red Lion public house at 24 Batty Street, Whitechapel, a road immediately to the east of Berner Street, off Commercial Road. Whilst the men in the pub were talking of the recent murders, the stranger interrupted, saying that he knew the murderer, and that they would hear about him in the morning. He then turned and left. This unexplained incident has been ignored in earlier books, but in the light of our present knowledge it now assumes a strange significance. To the north of the Red Lion, separated only by a narrow alley, was a lodging house, number 22 Batty Street.

At 11.53 p.m. the same night, Albert Backert of 13 Newnham Street, Whitechapel, spoke to a stranger in the Three Tuns Hotel, Aldgate. After Backert had been approached by a woman selling matches, the stranger remarked that these people were a nuisance and enquired how old the women were who were in the habit of waiting outside. Backert said he thought that some of them who looked about twenty-five were in fact over thirty-five, but used powder and paint to make themselves look younger. The man then asked where these women normally went, to which Backert replied that he heard that some went to Oxford Street, Whitechapel, others to some houses in the Whitechapel Road, and others to Bishopsgate Street. The man asked Backert whether he thought that they would go with him down Northumberland Alley, a dark and lonely court in Fenchurch Street. Backert said he did not know, but supposed they would.

The man went outside and spoke to the woman who was selling matches and gave her something. He then returned to the bar, and Backert bade him good night at 12.10 a.m. Backert thought the woman was waiting for the man outside. Backert did not believe he would be able to identify the woman again, because he did not take particular notice of her, but he felt he would know the man again. He described him as dark, about thirty-eight years old, 5ft.6 or 7in. tall, wearing a black felt hat, dark clothes, morning coat and black tie, and carrying a shiny black bag. This incident was to assume more importance in Backert's mind the following morning when he learnt of the double murder.

The first killing took place at Dutfield's Yard, Berner Street, just before 1 a.m. on Sunday 30 September, when forty-four-year-old prostitute Elizabeth Stride, also known as Long Liz, was murdered but not mutilated.

Long Liz was born in Torslanda, Sweden, the daughter of a farmer. She had one sister and two brothers. She left home in 1860, aged sixteen, and after settling in Gothenburg worked as a domestic servant. By 1865 the Swedish police had registered her as a prostitute. It is not known why, in 1866, she decided to leave Sweden and move to England. Perhaps the death of her parents and the fact that she had given birth to a stillborn baby drove her away from home.

In 1869 she married John Stride, a carpenter, but they soon separated, and by 1877 she had fallen on hard times and was living in an East End workhouse. She was frequently arrested for being drunk and disorderly. Although it is difficult to say categorically, it would seem that John Stride died of heart failure in 1884, in an east London workhouse.

Long Liz's body was discovered at 1 a.m. by a hawker, Louis Diemschutz, who worked as a steward in a Jewish socialist club that sided on to Dutfield's Yard. As he drove into the yard in a pony and trap, returning from a day's hawking of cheap jewellery at Crystal Palace, the horse shied twice to the left, drawing Diemschutz's attention to what appeared to be a heap of clothes on the ground. He poked at it with his whip, then lit a match, which was snuffed out by the wind.

He had seen enough and fetched help from the club, where members, including Isaac Kozebrodski, were singing and dancing. Diemschutz and Kozebrodski set off in search of a policeman. They raced as far as Grove Street, shouting 'Police!' at the top of their voices. Edward Spooner, a horse-keeper, heard their cries and returned with them to Dutfield's Yard where a small crowd had already begun to gather. Spooner lifted the woman's head and saw blood still flowing from her throat.

Long Liz lay on her muddy left side, her right arm over her

stomach, her left arm extended from the elbow, the hand clutching a packet of cachous, a breath sweetener often used by prostitutes. Some of the cachous had spilled into the gutter. According to Dr Blackwell, the doctor called to the scene, the packet had lodged between the thumb and fourth finger and had become almost hidden. Her right hand was bloody, and her mouth was slightly open. The back of her right hand and the inner surface of that wrist were dotted with blood.

The legs were drawn up, knees fixed and feet close to the wall. The body was still warm. The bow of a checked silk scarf around her throat had pulled tight and turned to the left of her neck. The scarf's lower edge was frayed, as if by a very sharp knife. The throat was deeply gashed and below the angle of the right jaw there was an apparent abrasion of the skin about an inch and a quarter in diameter. The windpipe was severed. Bruises on the victim's shoulders and chest indicated that she had been seized and forced down on to the ground before the wound had been inflicted. There were no other injuries or mutilations. She was wearing a black crêpe bonnet, a long black jacket trimmed with fur, an old black skirt, a dark brown velvet bodice, two petticoats, a white chemise, white stockings, and side-spring boots. There was a red rose with maiden-hair fern on her jacket.

Like Nichols and Chapman, Stride was married but was separated from her husband. Like them, she was something of an alcoholic, who worked as an East End prostitute. However, there the similarities end. She was in better health and better looking than the other two women, and had not been turned away from lodging houses in the small hours. On the eve of her murder Liz had been working as a cleaning woman in Flower and Dean Street.

At the time of Diemschutz's discovery of the body, most of the members remaining on the premises of the International Working Men's Club were still upstairs, singing. PC Henry Lamb and another constable were found patrolling in Commercial Road, and ran to the scene of the murder. Lamb urged the crowd to keep back, then sent his fellow constable for the nearest doctor and asked another man to fetch help from Leman Street police station.

Dr Frederick William Blackwell, of 100 Commercial Road, and his assistant, Edward Johnston, went to Berner Street after being contacted by PC Lamb's colleague. Dr Blackwell later told the inquest that the woman's clothing had not been disturbed by her killer, and although her hands were cold, there was some warmth in her face, and her neck, chest and legs were quite warm. Her clothes were not wet with rain, indicating that she had not been lying in the yard long. It was Blackwell's opinion that Liz Stride had not been dead more than twenty minutes and at the most half an hour. If Blackwell reached Dutfield's Yard at 1.16 a.m., then the murder took place after 12.46 a.m. and very possibly after 12.56 a.m. The timing is very important because of the sequence of events on that unforgettable night, when a second victim was to fall under the knife.

At 1.25 a.m., Inspector Reid received a telegram at Commercial Street police station and immediately went to the scene of the murder, where he found Chief Inspector West, Inspector Pinhorn, and several sergeants and constables. Dr George Bagster Phillips the H Division Police Surgeon, was also called out and arrived at the scene at about 2.00 a.m. Superintendent Arnold arrived a short time later. At about 4.30 a.m. the body was conveyed to St George's Mortuary, Cable Street, where Inspector Reid noted her details.

Evidence of events preceding the murder began to emerge. A labourer, William Marshall, of 64 Berner Street, had seen a woman, whom he later identified as Stride, opposite his house at about 11.45 p.m. with a stout and decently dressed middle-aged man, about 5ft.6in. tall and wearing a black cutaway coat. He had looked like a clerk to Marshall: he wore no gloves, carried no stick or anything else in his hands, and on his head was a 'round cap with a small peak to it' like a sailor's hat. He kissed Long Liz and said: 'You would say anything but your prayers.' Then they walked down the street in the direction of Dutfield's Yard, by which time it was about 11.55 p.m. The nearest gas lamp was about twenty feet away, which meant that the couple were not standing in good light. They walked past Marshall in the middle of the road but he was unable to describe the man any better.

A police officer saw a woman he was sure was Stride in Berner Street at about 12.30 a.m. PC William Smith said she was talking to a man opposite the scene of the murder. The woman was wearing a red rose. He described Stride's companion as of respectable appearance, holding a parcel done up in newspaper about 18in. long and 6 to 8in. broad. The man was about 5ft.7in. in height, wore an overcoat and dark trousers and had a dark, hard felt deerstalker on his head. Smith gave the man's age as 'about twenty-eight'. The *Police Gazette* later expanded this to: 'complexion dark, small dark moustache; dress, black diagonal coat, hard felt hat, white collar and tie'.

At about 12.40 a.m., Morris Eagle, a member of the Jewish club, had returned to Dutfield's Yard after taking his young lady home, and the body had not been there then.

A Hungarian Jew, Israel Schwartz, who spoke little or no English, stated that at 12.45 he saw a man stop and speak to a woman who was standing in the gateway where the murder was committed. The man tried to pull the woman into the street, then turned her round and threw her down on the footpath, at which the woman screamed three times, though not very loudly. On crossing to the opposite side of the street, Schwartz saw a second man standing lighting his pipe. The man who had thrown the woman down called out, apparently to the man on the opposite side of the road, 'Lipski!' At that point Schwartz ran away, and was followed by the second man, who, however, did not follow Schwartz as far as the railway arch, at the end of the street.

It may be useful for us to digress a moment here to explain the significance of the name 'Lipski'. Israel Lipski, real name Lobulsk, was a twenty-two-year-old Jewish immigrant who had been tried for the murder by poisoning of one Miriam Angel on 28 June 1887, at 16 Batty Street, a three-storey lodging house run by a Mr and Mrs Lipski (no relation). It is interesting to note that Batty Street ran parallel to Berner Street, just to the east. Lipski lived in the attic of the lodging house, and the pregnant Mrs Angel on the second floor. Lipski had been found hiding under the poisoned woman's bed and had also swallowed some nitric acid. He claimed the woman had been assaulted by two workmen who had then attacked him. The motive was believed to be sexual, there being indications of necrophilia. One of the officers investigating the case was Sergeant Thick. Lipski was tried in July 1887 before Mr Justice James Fitz-james Stephen, and found guilty. He was hanged on 22 August 1887, having confessed to the murder the day before.

Schwartz could not say whether the two men were together or known to each other. He described the first man, who threw the woman down, as aged about thirty, 5ft.5in. tall, with dark hair and a small brown moustache, full-faced and broad-shouldered, and wearing a dark jacket and trousers, and a black cap with a peak. The second man was aged thirty-five, 5ft.11in. with light brown hair, wearing a dark overcoat and an old black hard felt hat with a wide brim, and carrying a clay pipe in his hand.

Chief Inspector John George Littlechild of Scotland Yard: has he finally exposed the identity of Jack the Ripper?

(*Below*) Damage to the Scotland Yard building caused by a Fenian bomb in May 1884.

President Abraham Lincoln: Tumblety was suspected of involvement in the assassination conspiracy.

Dr Luke Pryor Blackburn of Kentucky: Tumblety's assumption of the alias 'Dr Blackburn' contributed to his arrest.

Dr Francis Tumblety at the time of his arrest in America in 1865.

The Old Capitol Prison, Washington D.C., where Tumblety was held prisoner.

The discovery of the body of
Martha Tabram, as depicted on the
cover of a popular turn-of-the-
century publication.

Annie Chapman's row with a fellow
lodger days before she was murdered.

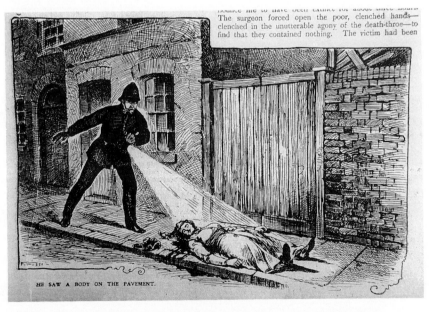

The surgeon forced open the poor, clenched hands—
clenched in the unutterable agony of the death-throe—to
find that they contained nothing. The victim had been

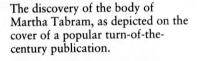

HE SAW A BODY ON THE PAVEMENT.

The discovery of Mary Ann Nichols' body on the footpath in Buck's Row.

"HE TURNED AND LOOKED AT ME."

Mary Kelly with the Ripper on the night of her murder.

Contemporary cartoon (1889) depicting how the satirical press saw the police in relation to the Ripper crimes.

George Yard Buildings, scene of the Martha Tabram murder of 7 August 1888.

Gunthorpe Street, formerly George Yard. Martha Tabram was murdered at the top of the road on the left.

The body of Mary Ann Nichols, the first identifiable Ripper victim, murdered on 31 August 1888.

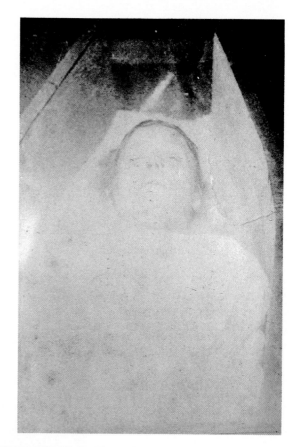

Durward Street, formerly Buck's Row. Mary Ann Nichols' body was found under the two windows before the beginning of the houses on the right.

Annie Chapman, murdered on
8 September 1888.

The front view of
29 Hanbury Street,
Spitalfields, scene of the
Annie Chapman murder.

Chief Inspector Swanson pointed out that fifteen minutes separated the incident Schwartz witnessed and the finding of Stride's body, ample time for Long Liz to have escaped and met her murderer; although two separate attacks on the same woman at the same location within such a short space of time must be regarded as unlikely.

Inspector Abberline stated in a report dated 1 November that since the Lipski case 'the name has very frequently been used by persons as a mere ejaculation by way of endeavouring to insult the Jew to whom it has been addressed, and as Schwartz has a very strong Jewish appearance I am of opinion it was addressed to him as he stopped to look at the man he saw apparently ill-using the deceased woman.' (Ref. MEPO3/140ff.204–6)

Enquiries were made in the neighbourhood but no one by the name of Lipski could be traced. The murder house at 16 Batty Street had been demolished earlier in 1888 to make way for a new tenement, and it would thus appear that the Lipskis living there must have moved away.

Another witness, a dock labourer named James Brown, crossed Berner Street at about 12.45 a.m. and noticed a couple standing by a wall, opposite the murder site. The man was bending over the woman with his arm resting on the wall above her head. He heard the woman say, 'Not tonight. Some other night.' He noticed that the man was wearing a long dark overcoat, nearly down to his heels. If it was the same couple that Schwartz and Brown saw, one of them must be mistaken as to time. On seeing Stride's body at the mortuary, Brown was only 'almost certain' she was the woman he had witnessed in Berner Street. Discrepancies in his description also raise doubts as to the identity of the woman he saw.

Mrs Fanny Mortimer, standing outside her house at 36 Berner Street, saw a 'young man and his sweetheart' at the corner, twenty yards away, around the time of the murder. This was possibly the same couple as seen by Brown, and was not Stride and her companion. Mrs Mortimer also spoke of having seen a man with a black bag walk past her along Berner Street from the direction of Commercial Road and into the east side of Fairclough Street. The man, Leon Goldstein of 22 Christian Street, later went into Leman Street police station to identify himself. The black bag had contained empty cigarette boxes.

Another alleged witness, Matthew Packer, a fruiterer of 44 Berner Street, was seen by Sergeant Stephen White at 9 a.m. on 30 September during the course of that officer and PC Dolden visiting every house in the street. Packer stated that he had closed his shop at 12.30 a.m. on the night of the murder because of the rain, which was no good for business. In answer to the officer's question as to whether he had seen a man or a woman going into Dutfield's Yard, or anyone standing in the street about the time he was closing his shop, Packer replied, 'No, I saw no one standing about neither did I see anyone go up the yard. I never saw anything suspicious or heard the slightest noise, and knew nothing about the murder until I heard of it this morning.' White also spoke with Mrs Packer, Sarah Harris and Harry Douglas, all residing at the same house. None of them could give the slightest information.

This is significant in the light of subsequent events when Packer claimed in the *Evening News* of 4 October to have sold some grapes to a man who was with Stride. Inspector Moore directed White to re-interview Packer, but on returning to the address White discovered that Packer had gone to the mortuary with two private detectives, employed by the Whitechapel Vigilance Committee, in order to identify the body. White followed Packer to the mortuary, where the fruiterer told him that he had seen the body and believed it to be that of the woman accompanying the man who had bought some grapes on the Saturday night. At this point the private detectives 'induced' Packer to leave with them. At 4 p.m. White returned to Packer's address, but while talking with him the two private detectives arrived and again 'induced' Packer away, saying they were taking him to Scotland Yard to see Sir Charles Warren.

At the Yard, Warren took a statement from Packer. To reinforce the statement the two detectives, of Le Grand & Co., Strand, claimed that they had been to Dutfield's Yard on the 2nd and had found a grape stalk in a drain where the yard had been washed down by the police. In his statement Packer claimed to have sold half a pound of black grapes at 3d. to a young man, aged between twenty-five and thirty, about 5ft.7in. tall, with a long black coat buttoned up, a soft felt hat, rather broad shoulders and a quick, rough voice. A woman had come up with him from the Back Church end of the street. She was dressed in a black frock and jacket, with fur round the bottom of the jacket, and a black crêpe bonnet, and was playing with a flower like a geranium, white outside and red inside. He confirmed that the woman was the same as the body he had seen in St George's mortuary. The couple had passed by in the direction of Commercial Road, but then crossed the road to a point outside the board school where they talked for about half an hour. They appeared to be listening to the music coming from the Jewish club. After this Packer had shut up shop for the night. Packer claimed in his statement to Warren that he had sold the grapes at about 11.00 p.m. and saw them still standing by the school at 11.30 p.m. when he closed, which did not agree with the time that he had first told White he had closed, i.e. 12.30 a.m. He further added that he had put the man down to be a young clerk, wearing a frock coat and no gloves, and two or three inches taller than the woman.

Packer's story contained many inconsistencies and it is difficult to assess its value, if any. The report of the incident in the *Evening News* was rather fuller, contained conversations, and seemed altogether more embellished than that made to the police. Packer also denied that he had been seen by the police, which must cast considerable doubt on anything he may have had to say. In a description given by him to the *Daily Telegraph* of 6 October, there were even more details. From this description, the newspaper had some sketches made of the man, and Packer chose one wearing an 'American-type hat'. The newspaper then published this and another sketch as supposed likenesses of the murderer, a move which further confused the issue and even caused the detention of a 'suspect' in Boulogne! In the light of subsequent variations, modifications and discrepancies in his statements we must entirely dispose of Packer as a reliable witness. He was, in fact, probably telling the truth when he was first seen by Sergeant White.

The description of the man seen by PC Smith was circulated by wire 'amongst police', and, by the authority of the Commissioner, was also given to the press. The description of the man seen by Schwartz fifteen minutes later was also circulated by wire. Swanson commented:

> It will be observed that allowing for differences of opinion between the PC & Schwartz as to apparent age & height of the man each saw with the woman whose body they both identified there are serious differences in the description of dress: thus the PC describes the dress of the man whom he saw as black diagonal coat, hard felt hat, while Schwartz describes the dress of the man he saw as dark jacket, black cap with peak, so that at least it is rendered doubtful whether they are describing the same man.

Swanson expanded on this by saying that there was no doubt cast on the truth of Schwartz's statement and that if they were describing different men then it was more probable that the one seen by Schwartz was the murderer, 'for a quarter of an hour afterwards the body is found murdered'. Swanson still allowed that the man seen by Schwartz may not have been the murderer, reasoning that, if she was soliciting, there was still time for her to have met yet another man, 'reached an agreement' and then for the 'murderous action' to have taken place. Clearly if Stride was soliciting different men it would have further confused matters, especially since men are not generally ready to come forward to admit that they have been solicited.

It does, however, seem unlikely that Stride would have been subjected to two attacks within fifteen minutes, and Schwartz most definitely did witness an attack on her, at the very scene of the murder. This places the initial attack and probably her murder, around fifteen minutes before her body was found. It was noted that 'The Police apparently do not suspect the 2nd man whom Schwartz saw on the other side of the street & who followed Schwartz.' Swanson then pointed out the similarity between the description given by Schwartz and that of a man seen near to Mitre Square just before the second murder of the night, supplied by another witness. He noted that 'for purposes of comparison, this description is nearer to that given by Schwartz than to that given by the PC.'

The inquest on Stride was opened on 1 October, continued on 3 October and resumed two days later. At the resumed inquest on 5 October Dr Phillips, the police surgeon, was re-called and was questioned about the wound and the weapon used. He did not think that a long knife had been used to inflict the throat wound. Wynne Baxter asked him: 'Was there any other similarity between this and Chapman's case?' To this Phillips replied, 'There is a great dissimilarity. In Chapman's case the neck was severed all round down to the vertebral column, the vertical bone being marked, and there had been an evident attempt to separate the bones.'

The evidence surrounding the Stride murder is very problematical, and extremely confusing when read in full. The lasting impression is of a domestic dispute-related murder. On the Tuesday before her death, Stride had walked out of the home she shared with Michael Kidney, a brutal, heavy-drinking labourer, who was known to have frequently assaulted her. The case does not bear the distinctive stamp of a Ripper killing.

The police carried out extensive enquiries, issued 80,000 pamphlets to occupiers, and interviewed over 2,000 lodgers in common lodging houses. The Thames Police investigated sailors on board ships in the docks and river, and made extended enquiries as to Asiatics present in London. About eighty people were detained at police stations and their statements taken and verified. As a result of communications received the police made enquiries into the movements of upwards of three hundred more. Seventy-six butchers' and slaughterers' premises were visited and the characters of the employees enquired into, including all who had been employed during the previous six months. Three 'of the persons calling themselves Cowboys' from 'the American Exhibition', a Wild West show put on by touring Americans, were traced but gave satisfactory stories. Swanson ended his report, 'There are now 994 Dockets besides police reports.'

Amid all the clutter of the Stride case, one question stands out: did the man who had killed Long Liz at about 1 a.m., on being disturbed by the pony and trap flee westwards towards Aldgate to there meet the second victim of that night, Catherine Eddowes? This is the contention of the majority of Ripper authors.

Chapter 7
A Double Event?

'... will still go on blood-letting and sowing a profitable harvest for the undertaker and sexton.'

At the time of her death Catherine Eddowes was forty-six years old. She had been born on 14 April 1842 in Wolverhampton, the daughter of a metal-worker. She lived for a time with a man called Thomas Conway, an army pensioner and father of her three children, but for seven years had dwelt at 6 Fashion Street with another man, John Kelly. According to the custom of the time she adopted the name of her common-law husband, and called herself Kate Kelly.

Although Catherine was described as a prostitute, both John Kelly and her lodging-house keeper stated that she did not walk the streets like a common whore. It should be remembered, however, that it was in their own interests to deny that she was a common prostitute: from Kelly's point of view so that he should not be seen as a pimp, and from that of the lodging-house keeper so that he should not be accused of running a brothel.

That Saturday night at about 8.30 p.m. she had been arrested by PC Louis Robinson of the City Police outside 29 Aldgate High Street for being drunk and disorderly. She was unable to answer the PC's questions and he picked her up and carried her to the side of the road, where she fell sideways. She smelt strongly of drink and was wearing an apron. He summoned assistance and she was taken to Bishopsgate police station. She was left to sober up in a cell and was discharged at 1 a.m. – about the same time that Elizabeth Stride was being murdered in the yard off Berner Street.

PC George Henry Hutt, the gaoler, saw her out and asked her to pull the door to. She replied, 'All right, good night, old cock.' She was still wearing her apron. She set off southwards, along Houndsditch towards Aldgate High Street and Mitre Square, an eight-minute walk away.

PC Edward Watkins of the City Police, a veteran of seventeen years' service, had commenced duty that night at quarter to ten. His beat took him from Duke Street, Aldgate, through Heneage Lane, part of Bury Street, then into Creechurch Lane and Leadenhall Street. From Leadenhall Street he walked into Mitre Street and Mitre Square, then round the square, back into Mitre Street and into and along King Street to St James Place. After walking round St James Place, he returned to Duke Street to start again. This perambulation took him between twelve and fourteen minutes, and he had been thus occupied since 10 p.m. without seeing anything suspicious. If he had not stopped for a cup of tea with a nightwatchman somewhere, as patrolling PCs often did, he would have passed through the top part of Duke Street at some time around 1.35 a.m. It was about this time that three Jews were leaving the Imperial Club at 16–17 Duke Street.

The Jews, Joseph Lawende, of 79 Fenchurch Street, Aldgate (possibly a business address as his address in the inquest papers is shown as 45 Norfolk Road, Dalston), Joseph Hyam Levy, of 1 Hutchinson Street, Aldgate, and Harry Harris, of Castle Street, found on leaving the Club that it was raining, and Lawende, a commercial traveller, walked a little way away from the others. They saw a man talking to a woman at the corner of Church Passage, which led into Mitre Square. The woman was standing with her face towards the man, and her back towards Lawende. She had her hand on the man's chest and was wearing a black jacket and black bonnet. She appeared to be short.

The man was taller, and was wearing a cloth cap with a cloth peak. Lawende's full description of the man was withheld at the inquest but may be found in a Scotland Yard report of 19 October by Swanson (Ref. HO144/221/A49301C): aged thirty, 5ft.7 or 8in. tall, with a fair complexion and fair moustache, of medium build, wearing a pepper-and-salt-coloured loose jacket, a grey cloth cap with a peak of the same colour, a reddish handkerchief tied in a knot round the neck, having the appearance of a sailor. Swanson adds an interesting rider, saying that Lawende's identification of Eddowes was by her clothing only, 'which is a serious drawback to the value of the description of the man. Ten minutes afterwards the body is found horribly mutilated and it is therefore reasonable to believe that the man he saw was the murderer.' Lawende himself added, 'I doubt whether I should know him again.' The couple were a distance of about fifteen feet from the club and Lawende heard no speech, although they appeared to be conversing very quietly, not

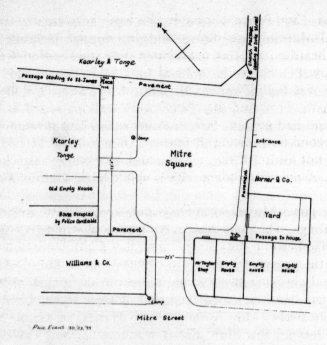

Mitre Square – scene of Eddowes' murder

quarrelling. Having passed them, Lawende did not look back, indicating that he had taken little interest in them.

His companions saw even less. Levy, a butcher, stated that they had passed the couple and he did not take any notice of them. The man was about three inches taller than the woman, but he could furnish no description of either of them. He added, rather cryptically, 'I said when I came out to Mr Harris, "Look there, I don't like going home by myself when I see those characters about," ' although he saw nothing about them which caused him to fear them. A juror at the inquest questioned Levy as to how well lit the spot was where the couple were standing, and he replied that it was badly lighted. He walked on into Aldgate leaving the couple still talking together, although he had heard no words.

At 1.30 a.m., PC Watkins had walked his usual beat through Mitre Square where all was quiet. At 1.45 a.m. Catherine Eddowes' body was discovered when PC Watkins' beat took him back to Mitre Square. She lay on her back in the south-western corner outside an empty house, illuminated by his square bull's-eye lamp. Watkins stated, 'I have been in the force a long while but I never saw such a sight. The body had been ripped open, like a pig in the market.'

Another City Police constable, Richard Pearce, who lived at number 3 Mitre Square, had gone to bed at 12.30 a.m. that night and had heard no noise or disturbance until called out at 2.20 a.m. by a fellow PC. His window faced the square and the spot where the body was found was visible from it. He was the only tenant in the square. However, there was a caretaker at number 5, George Clapp, who had gone to bed, with his wife, at 11 p.m. in a room on the second floor facing the square. He too had heard no sound and was not aware of the murder until between 5 and 6 the next morning. A nurse attending Mrs Clapp was sleeping on the third floor.

George James Morris, aged forty-four, watchman to Messrs Kearley and Tonge, wholesale grocers with warehouse premises in Mitre Square, had been on duty since 7 p.m. that night, but had heard no noise in the square. He had spent most of the night cleaning the offices and checking the warehouse. The door leading into Mitre Square had been ajar for about two minutes when PC Watkins knocked or pushed at it. At this time Morris was sweeping the stairs in the counting house area facing the square, about two yards from the door. He turned and opened the door wide to be confronted by Watkins, who said, 'For God's sake, mate, come to my assistance.' Morris, surprised, said, 'Stop till I get my lamp,' and immediately went outside, asking, 'What's the matter?' Watkins said, 'Oh dear, here's another woman cut up to pieces.' Morris said, 'Where is she?' to which the troubled PC replied, 'In the corner.'

Morris went over to the corner and shone his lamp on the mutilated body. His reaction was to immediately blow his whistle and run up Mitre Street into Aldgate. He saw no suspicious persons about. He stated that he had been in the warehouse between 11 p.m. and 1 a.m. and that he had not seen Watkins previously that night.

PC James Harvey had started duty at the same time as Watkins. His beat was from Bevis Marks to Duke Street, Church Passage, and Aldgate. From there he went to Mitre Street, back to Houndsditch, along Goring Street and back to Bevis Marks to commence again. He stated that at 1.40 a.m. he went down Duke Street and Church Passage as far as Mitre Square, where he saw no one and heard no noise. He did not enter the square as that was part of Watkins' beat. He left Church Passage and went into Aldgate. Returning to Duke Street, he heard a whistle blown and saw George Morris with a lamp. PC Harvey asked Morris what was the matter, to which Morris replied, 'A woman has been ripped up in Mitre Square.' Harvey then saw another constable, PC Holland, on the other side of the street and said to him, 'Come with me.' They went into Mitre Square where they found Watkins standing with the body. Morris then returned to his duties in the warehouse. PC Holland immediately went to call out Dr Sequeira, and private individuals who were present were sent for other constables, who arrived almost immediately. Harvey remained with Watkins and the Inspector was sent for.

Harvey had timed events by the post office clock, which he had passed between 1.28 and 1.29 a.m. He stated that he was at the end of Church Passage at about 1.38 or 1.39 a.m. All timings are dependent upon the constables adhering rigidly to their allocated beat duties and not taking any unofficial breaks or detours, which, of course, they would not have admitted.

Dr Sequeira, the first medical man on the scene, arrived at 1.55 a.m. He stated that the locality was familiar to him and the spot where the body was found was 'the darkest portion of the square', although 'there would have been sufficient light to enable the perpetrator of the deed to have committed the deed without the addition of any extra light.' Life had not been extinct for more than fifteen minutes and he did not think the murderer would necessarily have been spattered with blood. He thought that the killer had no particular design on any particular organ and that he was not possessed of any great anatomical skill.

The full horror of the mutilations is best described in the evidence of Dr Frederick Gordon Brown, the City of London Police surgeon, given at the subsequent inquest. Stating that he had arrived at the scene shortly after 2 a.m., he described what he found as follows:

The body was on its back, the head turned to the left shoulder, the arms by the sides of the body as if they had fallen there, both palms upwards, the fingers slightly bent. A thimble was lying off the finger on the right side. The clothes [were] drawn up above the abdomen, the thighs were naked, left leg extended in a line with the body, the abdomen was exposed, right leg bent at the thigh and knee. The bonnet was at the back of the head, great disfigurement of [the] face, the throat cut across, beneath the cut was a neckerchief. The upper part of the dress was pulled open a little way, the abdomen was all exposed.

The intestines were drawn out to a large extent and placed

over the right shoulder – they were smeared over with some feculent matter, a piece [of] about two feet was quite detached from the body and placed between the body and the left arm, apparently by design. The lobe and auricle of the right ear was cut obliquely through. There was a quantity of clotted blood on the pavement on the left side of the neck, round the shoulder and upper part of arm, and fluid blood-coloured serum which had flowed under the neck to the right shoulder, the pavement sloping in the direction. [The] body was quite warm, no death stiffening had taken place.

She must have been dead most likely within the half-hour. We looked for superficial bruises and saw none, no blood on the skin of the abdomen or secretion of any kind on the thighs. No spurting of blood on the bricks or pavement around. No marks of blood below the middle of the body – several buttons were found in the clotted blood after the body was removed. There was no blood on the front of the clothes. There were no traces of recent connection.

Eddowes was wearing a black straw bonnet trimmed with green and black velvet and black beads, and with black strings. The bonnet was loosely tied, and had partially fallen from the back of her head. There was no blood on the front of the bonnet but the back was lying in a pool of blood which had run from the neck.

Her black cloth jacket had an imitation fur edging to the collar and sleeves, with two outside pockets trimmed with black silk braid and imitation fur. The jacket had no blood on the front outside but there was a large quantity of blood inside and on the outside of the back.

She was wearing a chintz skirt with three flounces and a brown button on the waistband, and there was a jagged cut 6½in. long from the waistband on the left side of the front, the edges of which were slightly bloodstained. There was blood on the bottom, back and front of the skirt.

She had a brown linsey dress bodice, with black velvet collar and brown metal buttons down the front. This had blood inside and outside the back of the neck and shoulders and a 5in. clean cut at the bottom of the left side from left to right.

She was wearing all the clothes she possessed and also had on a grey stuff petticoat with white waistband, with a cut 1½in. long at the front bearing bloodstains to the edges. There were also blood-stains on the front at the bottom of the petticoat.

A very old green alpaca skirt bore a jagged downward cut 10½in. long in front of the waistband, bloodstained inside the front under the cut. Another very old ragged blue skirt with a red flounce and light twill lining bore a similar cut through the waistband, blood-stained both inside and outside the back and front.

Her white calico chemise was very much bloodstained all over and torn in the middle of the front. She had on a man's white vest, buttoned down the front with two outside pockets. This was torn at the back and very bloodstained at the back. There were blood and other stains on the front.

She wore no drawers or stays. Her boots were men's lace-ups with mohair laces, and the right one was repaired with red thread. There were six blood marks on the right boot.

Her other possessions and apparel were a piece of red silk gauze, bearing cuts, on her neck, and a large white handkerchief, blood-stained; two unbleached calico pockets, tape strings cut through, also top left-hand corner cut off one; a blue striped bed ticking pocket, waistband and strings cut through; a white cotton pocket handkerchief with red and white bird's-eye border; twelve pieces of white rag, some slightly bloodstained; a piece of coarse white linen; a three-cornered piece of blue and white shirting; two small blue bed ticking bags; two short black clay pipes; a tin box containing tea and another containing sugar; a piece of flannel and six pieces of soap; a small-tooth comb, a white-handled table knife and a metal teaspoon; a red leather cigarette case with white metal fittings; an empty tin match box; a piece of red flannel containing pins and needles; a ball of hemp and a piece of old white apron.

It is interesting to note how destitute itinerants such as Eddowes carried everything they valued on their person. With nowhere safe to store these cherished items, her only option was take them every-where with her.

When the body arrived at the Golden Lane mortuary, some of the blood had become dispersed. The clothes were taken off carefully from the body, and a piece of her ear dropped from the clothing.

Later the same day Dr Brown conducted his post-mortem examin-ation, in the presence of Dr George William Sequeira, of 34 Jewry Street, Aldgate, the surgeon first on the scene of the murder, and Dr William Sedgwick Saunders, of 13 Queen Street, Cheapside, the

Public Analyst for the City of London. Dr Brown's report was as follows:

I made a post-mortem examination at half past two on Sunday afternoon, rigor mortis was well marked, body not quite cold, green discolouration over the abdomen. After washing the left hand carefully a bruise the size of a sixpence, recent and red, was discovered on the back of the left hand between the thumb and first finger, a few small bruises on right shin of older date. The hands and arms were bronzed, no bruises on the scalp, the back of the body, or the elbows.

The face was very much mutilated. There was a cut about quarter of an inch through the lower left eyelid dividing the structures completely through. The upper eyelid on that side, there was a scratch through the skin on the left upper eyelid near to the angle of the nose. The right eyelid was cut through to about half an inch. There was a deep cut over the bridge of the nose extending from the left border of the nasal bone down near to the angle of the jaw on the right side across the cheek, this cut went into the bone and divided all the structures of the cheek except the mucous membrane of the mouth. The tip of the nose was quite detached from the [rest of] the nose by an oblique cut from the bottom of the nasal bone to where the wings of the nose join on to the face. A cut from this divided the upper lip and extended through the substance of the gum over the right upper lateral incisor tooth. About half an inch from the top of the nose was another oblique cut. There was a cut on the right angle of the mouth as if by the cut of a point of a knife, the cut extended an inch and a half parallel with [the] lower lip. There was on each side of cheek [sic] a cut which peeled up the skin forming a triangular flap about an inch and a half. On the left cheek were two abrasions of the epithelium, there was a little mud on the left cheek – two slight abrasions of the epithelium under the left ear.

The throat was cut across to the extent of about six or seven inches, a superficial cut commenced about an inch and a half below the lobe and about two and a half inches below and behind the left ear, and extended across the throat to about three inches below the lobe of the right ear. The muscle across the throat was divided through on the left side, the large vessels on the left side of the neck were severed. The larynx was severed below the vocal cords, all the deep structures were severed to the bone, the knife marking intervertebral cartilages. The sheath of the vessels on the right side was just opened. The carotid artery had a fine hole opening. The internal jugular vein was opened an inch and a half, not divided. The blood vessels contained clot. All these injuries were performed by a sharp instrument like a knife, and pointed.

The cause of death was haemorrhage from the left common carotid artery. The death was immediate and the mutilations were inflicted after death.

We examined the abdomen, the front walls were laid open from the breast bone to the pubes. The cut commenced opposite the ensiform cartilage, the incision went upwards not penetrating the skin that was over the sternum, it then divided the ensiform cartilage. The knife must have cut obliquely at the expense of the front surface of that cartilage. Behind this the liver was stabbed as if by the front of a sharp instrument. Below this was another incision into the liver of about two and a half inches, and below this the left lobe of the liver was slit through by a vertical cut. Two cuts were shewn by a jagging of the skin on the left side. The abdominal walls were divided in the middle line to within a quarter of an inch of the navel, the cut then took a horizontal course for two inches and a half towards the right side. It then divided round the navel on the left side and made a parallel incision to the former horizontal incision leaving the navel on a tongue of skin. Attached to the navel was two and a half inches of the lower part of the rectus muscle on the left side of the abdomen. The incision then took an oblique direction to the right and was shelving. The incision went down the right side of the vagina and rectum for half an inch behind the rectum. There was a stab of about an inch on the left groin, this was done by a pointed instrument, below this was a cut of three inches going through all tissues making a wound of the peritoneum about the same extent. An inch below the crease of the thigh was a cut extending from the anterior spine of the ilium obliquely down the inner side of the left thigh and separating the left labium forming a flap of skin up to the groin. The left rectus muscle was not detached. There was a flap of skin formed from the right thigh attaching the right labium and extending up to the spine of the ilium. The muscles on the right side inserted into the pouparts ligament were cut through. The skin was retracted through the whole of the cut in the abdomen but the vessels were not clotted – nor had there been any appreciable bleeding from the vessel. I draw the conclusion that the cut was made after death and there would not be much blood on the murderer. The cut was made by someone on [the] right side of the body, kneeling below the middle of the body. I removed the contents of the stomach and placed it in a jar for further examination. There seemed very little in it in the way of food or fluid but from the cut end partly digested farinaceous food escaped. The intestines had been detached to a large extent from the mesentery. About two feet of the colon was cut away. The sigmoid flexure was invaginated into the rectum very tightly. The right kidney [was] pale and bloodless with slight congestion of the base of the pyramids. There was a cut from the upper part of the slit in the under surface of the liver to the left side and another cut at right angles to this which were about an inch and a half deep and two and a half inches long. The liver itself was healthy. The gall bladder contained bile. The pancreas was cut but not through on the left side of the spinal column, three and a half inches of the lower border of the spleen by half an inch was attached only to the peritoneum.

The peritoneal lining was cut through on the left side and the left kidney carefully taken out and removed – the left renal artery was cut through. I should say that someone who knew the position of the kidney must have done it. The lining membrane over the uterus was cut through. The womb was cut through horizontally leaving a stump of three quarters of an inch, the rest of the womb had been taken away with some of the ligaments. The vagina and cervix of the womb was uninjured. The bladder was healthy and uninjured and contained three or four ounces of water. There was a tongue-like cut through the anterior wall of the abdominal aorta. The other organs were healthy.

There were no indications of connection. I believe the wound in the throat was [the] first inflicted, I believe she must have been lying on the ground. The wounds on the face and abdomen prove that they were inflicted by a sharp pointed knife and that in the abdomen by one six inches long. I believe the perpetrator of the act must have had considerable knowledge of the position of the organs in the abdominal cavity and the way of removing them. The parts removed would be of no use for any professional purpose. It required a great deal of knowledge to have removed the kidney and to know where it was placed, such a knowledge might be possessed by someone in the habit of cutting up animals. I think the perpetrator of this act had sufficient time or he would not have nicked the lower eyelids. It would take at least five minutes. I cannot assign any reason for these parts being taken away. I feel sure there was no struggle. I believe it was the act of one person. The throat had been so instantly severed that no noise could have been emitted. I should not expect much blood to have been found on the person who had inflicted these wounds. The wounds could not have been self-inflicted.

My attention was called to the apron. It was the corner of the apron with a string attached. The blood spots were of recent origin. I have seen a portion of an apron produced by Dr Phillips and stated to have been found in Goulston Street. It is impossible to say it is human blood. I fitted the piece of apron which had a new piece of material on it which had evidently been sewn on to the piece I have, the seams of the borders of the two actually corresponding. Some blood and apparently faecal matter was found on the portion found in Goulston Street. I believe the wounds on the face to have been done to disfigure the corpse.

The idea propounded at the time by some doctors, that the victims had voluntarily lain on the ground, is in reality not very likely. For despite their dirty clothes and drunken state, they are unlikely to have stretched out on the filthy ground to have sex. This service would most likely have been provided standing up against a wall, either with their backs to it or facing it. It is probable, as we have seen, that the women were strangled and laid on the ground before their throats were cut. In each case bruises were found on their necks where pressure in strangulation would have been applied.

It would appear that all the victims were taken by surprise. Despite the fact that people were awake within a few yards of the murders, there was evidently little resistance or any sound. The indications are that the killer first subdued them with a throttling grip on the throat, then laid them on the ground to inflict the awful throat wounds and mutilations.

The possible, even likely, sighting of the murderer by Joseph

Lawende is considered by most Ripper students to provide the best description of 'Jack the Ripper', but it must be treated with great caution for a number of reasons:

a. Only Lawende, of the three Jews, could furnish any description of the man, and he qualified this by saying that 'I doubt whether I should know him again.'
b. The spot was badly lit, and the sighting was from a distance of at least fifteen feet.
c. The witnesses were taking no particular notice of the couple.
d. The only identification of the woman as Eddowes, by Lawende, who saw only her back, was by clothing, and he stated merely that he 'believed' they were the same. This is far from positive bearing in mind (b) and (c) above, and the fact that the clothing was black.
e. The area was a favourite resort for prostitutes to pick up clients and the possibility must remain that the couple may not have been Eddowes and her murderer.

When compared with Mrs Long's sighting of the probable murderer in Hanbury Street, the latter's must be the more reliable, even though she only saw the man from behind. Her sighting was in virtual daylight, she passed the couple on the path, and she was taking notice of them, even overhearing a conversation.

PC Alfred Long, of Westminster Division, had been drafted in to H Division to supplement the patrols in that beleaguered area in a vain attempt to apprehend the unknown killer. At 2.55 a.m., eighty minutes after the discovery of the mutilated corpse of Catherine Eddowes in Mitre Square, Long was patrolling nearby Goulston Street, aware of the murder in Berner Street.

In the passage of the doorway leading to numbers 108–119 Model Dwellings, Goulston Street, on the east side of the road halfway between Wentworth Street and New Goulston Street, Long found part of a woman's apron covered in blood, one portion being wet. Above the apron, on the wall, had been written in chalk:

The Juwes are
The men that
Will not
be Blamed
for nothing

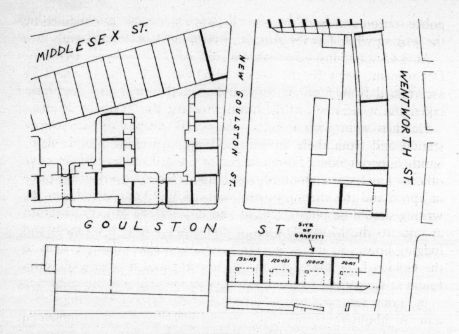

Location of graffiti in Goulston Street

Long could not tell if the lettering was recent. He immediately called the PC on the adjoining beat and searched the staircases, of which there were six or seven, and other areas of the building, but found nothing else. He did not make any enquiries in the tenements. At the inquest Long was asked about the exact wording on the wall, as DC Halse claimed that the word 'not' was in a different position, so that the message read, 'The Juwes are not the men . . .' Long faltered under cross-examination and the coroner sent to the PC's station for the PC's pocket book. However, Long confirmed the wording he had originally given, and the layout of the message used here is taken directly from the copy in the police files.

PC Long left the other officer at the entrance to watch for anyone entering or leaving the building, and took the portion of apron to Commercial Street police station, arriving at five or ten past three. The inspector on duty then went with Long to Goulston Street and inspected the writing. Long later claimed that when he had previously passed the spot where he later found the apron, at about 2.20 a.m., it had not been there.

On hearing that the piece of apron had been found, City detectives, DC Halse, with DS Lawley and DC Hunt, went to Leman Street police station and from there to Goulston Street. Halse remained by the writing while Lawley and Hunt returned to Mitre Square.

At 3.45 a.m., Inspector McWilliam, head of the City Detective Department, went to the Detective Office, Old Jewry, where he ascertained from Station Sergeant Izzard the steps that had been taken and wired news of the murder to Scotland Yard.

He then went with Detective Sergeant Downes to Bishopsgate station and from there to Mitre Square, where he found Major Smith, Superintendent Foster, Inspector Collard and several detective officers. Lawley and Hunt informed him of the discovery of the piece of apron and the writing on the wall. McWilliam ordered that the writing should be photographed and directed the officers to return at once to the Model Dwellings and make a search of them and lodging houses in the neighbourhood. McWilliam himself went to the Golden Lane mortuary where he compared the piece of apron found in Goulston Street with the apron worn by the deceased.

PC Long returned to the entrance of the Model Dwellings at 5 a.m. At about the same time, having already visited Commercial Street police station, Sir Charles Warren arrived at Leman Street. There he ascertained from Superintendent Arnold all that was known of the two murders. He immediately decided that the most pressing question was the writing on the wall, which he felt had been written with the intention of inflaming the public mind against the Jews. Mr Arnold, with a view to preventing serious disorder, decided to obliterate the message.

The story is best continued in Warren's own words:

I considered it desirable that I should decide this matter myself, as it was one involving so great a responsibility whether any action was taken or not. I accordingly went down to Goulston Street at once, before going to the scene of the murder, it was just getting light, the public would be in the streets in a few minutes, in a neighbourhood very much crowded on Sunday mornings by Jewish vendors and Christian purchasers from all parts of London.

There were several Police around the spot when I arrived, both Metropolitan and City. The writing was on the joint of the open archway or doorway visible to anybody in the street and could not be covered up without the danger of the covering being torn off at once. A discussion took place whether the writing could be left for an hour until it could be photographed, but after taking into consideration the excited state of the population in London generally at the time, the strong feeling which had been excited against the Jews (the suspect Pizer was Jewish), and the fact that in a short time there would be a large concourse of the people in the streets and having before me the report that if it was left there the house was likely to be wrecked (in which from my own observation I entirely concurred) I considered it desirable to obliterate the writing at once, having taken a copy of which I enclose a duplicate.

The chalked message was rubbed out at approximately 5.30 a.m. in the presence of PC Long, who did not hear anyone object to its removal. Sir Charles Warren then left the scene, satisfied that he had averted a riot, and went to the site of the murder, although he does not state which: Berner Street, which was in his own territory, or Mitre Square, on the City ground. A careful reading of various reports leads us to favour Mitre Square.

By way of further explanation to the Home Office Warren reported:

I may mention that so great was the feeling with regard to the Jews that on the 13th ulto, the acting Chief Rabbi wrote to me on the subject of the spelling of the word 'Juewes' on account of a newspaper asserting that this was Jewish spelling in the Yiddish dialect. He added, 'In the present state of excitement it is dangerous to the safety of the poor Jews in the East End to allow such an assertion to remain uncontradicted. My community keenly appreciates your humane and vigilant action during this critical time.' It may be realised therefore if the safety of the Jews in Whitechapel could be considered to be jeopardised 13 days after the murder by the question of the spelling of the word Jews, what might have happened to the Jews in that quarter had that writing had been left there would have been an onslaught upon the Jews, property would have been wrecked, and lives would probably have been lost, and I was much gratified with the promptitude with which Superintendent Arnold was prepared to act in the matter if I had not been there.

Warren leaves us in no doubt as to the circumstances of the removal of the message. However, he does raise a question as to the spelling of the word 'Jews' in the message. The spelling has no relevance to the case unless the words were written by the murderer. This has been the subject of much debate in the past, and there is still no agreement on the matter. The police themselves did not know, and even disagreed with each other. Another point of contention was how recent the message was. Swanson refers to it being blurred, whilst Halse thought that it looked recent. However, as recent writing can still be blurred by someone brushing past it, and since one would not expect ostensibly anti-Semitic messages to survive long in such a location, it most probably was recent. But that does not necessarily equate with it being written by the murderer. Graffiti was common then, as it is today. It is difficult to imagine that the killer stopped, in pitch darkness, to write a cryptic message on a wall. More likely he simply threw the bloodstained rag into the doorway as he passed.

There is absolutely no doubt that the piece of bloody apron was from the one belonging to Eddowes, stained as it was with blood and faeces, and had been used by the murderer to wipe his hands and knife. Bearing in mind that Eddowes' body had been found at 1.45 a.m., and that the murderer would have fled through Goulston Street only minutes after the deed, the bloodstained apron would have been deposited in the doorway before 2 a.m. This, as we have seen, does not tie in with PC Long's statement of events which, if it is to be believed, indicates that the murderer returned and left the apron after 2.20 a.m. This, clearly, is an unthinkable course of action for a killer fleeing the scene of his crime. What is far more likely is that the apron and the writing on the wall were indeed there when PC Long passed at 2.20 a.m. but that he did not spot them. No doubt part of his brief for patrol was to check all doorways, recesses, and courts as he passed and he would not have been able to admit that he had failed in his duty without getting into serious trouble.

The fact that police officers were only too aware of the punitive measures they were subject to was highlighted in an article in the *Star of the East* of Monday 1 October 1888. The writer, displaying unusual insight into police practices, stated:

In view of the mystery which surrounds the whereabouts of the murderer or murderers, it might be suggested that the police authorities should take the constables into their confidence, and, for the time being, considering the exceptional circumstances attending the murders, put aside a very stringent rule of the service, the enforcement of which under ordinary conditions is absolutely necessary. For instance, it is by no means unusual, doing duty in the streets, to have suspicious incidents come under his observation of which he takes no notice until after he learns of a crime such as has just rekindled public indignation. Under existing circumstances, an officer who made known such 'negligence' would undoubtedly be dismissed the service, and in view of this it cannot be expected that any officer would knowingly bring about his own discharge. Information which might be of the greatest importance as regards a case such as the present is possibly withheld for the very reason that, unless the authorities relax their severity, the man would be bringing about his own downfall.

The so-called 'double event' of 30 September was generally accepted by the police, press and most writers since to have been the work of the same killer. This is illustrated by a report in the *East Anglian Daily Times*, on Monday 1 October, the day after the murders:

The Whitechapel fiend has emerged from the lair in which he has lain concealed for three weeks, and his track is marked by two murders. There can be no doubt that they are by the same hand, though one of the two is of a common-place character. The second, however, is distinguished, and in fact individualised by a repetition of the atrocious complements which marked that of the 8th of the month. The police are without a clue to the assassin, and are quite baffled, though the interest of Scotland Yard was shown in an unusual form by the arrival at the scene of the tragedy of Sir Charles Warren himself. Not, however, that our Sirdar of police was able, or, so far as I have learnt, has been able to offer any practicable or productive advice. As your readers may imagine, this extraordinary recurrence of crime in their neighbourhood has driven the inhabitants of Whitechapel into a frenzy of horror and alarm. In fact, the entire metropolis shares tonight the indignation which prevails throughout the East End. Philosophy is helpless. There is still an utter absence of conventional motive for the crime. We are constantly driven back to the old theory that the butcheries are the work of a madman with homicidal propensities. In this latest case the murderer was within an ace of detection, as he is known to have despatched his second victim during the fifteen minutes' beat of the policeman, who immediately afterwards came upon the woman. The scene which presented itself to the eye of that policeman appears to have since incapacitated him for duty. The immediate consequence of the renewal of the Whitechapel horrors – this, I may remark, being the fourth murder committed within a half-mile radius – has been to arouse popular feeling against the foreign inhabitants of the parish, and the police, as I learn officially, fear an outbreak against the Jews in particular, and are actually taking precautionary measures accordingly.

The killer was recognised by his *modus operandi* of murdering prostitutes in the East End by cutting their throats. Put this simply, and taking Eddowes' murder into account, it is easy to see how Liz Stride would, logically, fall into the pattern. The lack of mutilation in the Stride case could be explained by claiming that the Ripper was disturbed at his work and was unable to complete his ghastly purpose.

From the available evidence, however, a much simpler explanation can be offered: Long Liz was not a Ripper victim; rather she was murdered after a domestic quarrel. Her boyfriend, Michael Kidney, claimed that the last time he had seen her was on 25 September when she left their shared room at 35 Devonshire Street, and that he fully expected to find her at home when he returned from work that evening.

However, giving evidence at the inquest, a friend of Stride's, Catherine Lane, claimed that Long Liz had told her that she had in fact left Kidney after a row. He strongly denied this, but it is obvious that they had had a stormy relationship. He estimated that out of the three years they had been living together, she had actually lived apart from him for at least five months.

Kidney, a drunken brawler with a violent streak, had been jailed for his unruly behaviour in July 1888, and had assaulted Long Liz in the past. On one occasion, in 1887, she even went to the extent of having him arrested, but when he was charged in court she failed to appear against him and the case was dismissed. It is likely that she feared retribution from Kidney more than he feared the punishment of the court.

When Stride's body was discovered she was still clutching the small packet of cachous pastilles. Surely, if she was being attacked by an unknown assailant, she would want her hands free to fight him off? This indicates that she knew her attacker. Although she expected to be beaten, she did not believe that her life was in danger.

All the genuine Ripper murders show an unmistakable pattern: the victim accompanied to a quiet and lonely spot and then murdered and mutilated with incredible swiftness and savagery.

The *Star of the East* of 1 October, reporting the Stride murder, observed:

> The people residing in the cottages on the side of the court were all indoors, and most of them in bed, by midnight. Several of these persons remember lying awake and listening to the singing, and they also remember the concert coming to an abrupt termination, but during the whole of the time, from retiring to rest until the body was discovered, no one heard anything in the nature of a scream or woman's cry of distress.

The scene of the murder does not fit a typical Ripper murder site. The courtyard was illuminated by the windows of the club, which occupied the whole length of the court on the right. Between twenty and thirty people were in the club at the time of the murder.

It would also appear that a different sort of knife – round-ended, not pointed – had been used to despatch Stride. No signs of prior strangulation were found either.

The conclusion to be drawn from all this is that there were two killers at work on the night of 30 September – Catherine Eddowes was butchered by the Ripper, while Long Liz Stride was murdered by a different assailant, perhaps even her own lover.

The 'double event' of the murders of Eddowes and Stride provided the press with even more sensational and lurid headlines and reports, and added further fuel to the clamour for the resignation of Sir Charles Warren and the Home Secretary. It was felt that not enough was being done to identify and apprehend the murderer, and the police were strongly criticised. Vigilance committees were formed, petitions signed and demonstrations held. Thousands of letters about the murders and the murderer's identity were sent to the police and the press, exhibiting every kind of social, sexual and racial prejudice.

The Eddowes murder also saw the City Police introduced into the investigation in a major way. Although they were to work closely with the Metropolitan Police, the indications are that they had some definite ideas of their own. Right from the start of their involvement, it would seem, they felt that Eddowes' killer was not the same miscreant who had earlier murdered Elizabeth Stride in Berner Street.

Chapter 8

Mysterious Communications

'After I had laid down my pen, I unfolded a morning paper that, as usual, was placed upon my table and there read the startling intelligence.'

Without doubt the most famous nickname ever bestowed upon a murderer is that of Jack the Ripper. But who awarded him this unforgettable appellation? There are three possible answers to this conundrum: first, the killer himself; second, an unknown hoaxer; and third, an enterprising journalist.

The Central News Agency, established in January 1870, collected news by telegraph from correspondents throughout the United Kingdom and abroad. It telegraphed important events, Parliamentary reports, Stock Exchange and market reports, law cases, results of races, etc., to newspapers, exchanges, clubs and newsrooms. It also telegraphed brief messages of important events to private persons. Communications intended for general publication were forwarded to the Central News by messenger or telegraph. Its premises were at 5 New Bridge Street, Ludgate Circus.

The name 'Jack the Ripper' originated from a letter contained in an envelope addressed to 'The Boss, Central News Office, London City', and postmarked 'LONDON E.C. 3 – SP 27 88 – P'. This letter, written in red ink, ran as follows:

25 Sept. 1888

Dear Boss,

  I keep on hearing the police have caught me. but they wont fix me just yet. I have laughed when they look so clever and talk about being on the right track. That joke about Leather Apron gave me real fits. I am down on whores and I shant quit ripping them till I do get buckled. Grand work the last job was, I gave the lady no time to squeal How can they catch me now, I love my work and want to start again. You will soon hear of me with my funny little games. I saved some of the proper red stuff in a ginger beer bottle over the last job to write with but it went thick like glue and I cant use it. Red ink is fit enough I hope ha ha. The next job I do I shall clip the ladys ears off and send to the police officers just for jolly wouldnt you. Keep this letter back till I do a bit more work then give it out straight. My knife's so nice and sharp I want to get to work right away if I get a chance good luck.

   Yours truly

   Jack the Ripper

Dont mind me giving the trade name

wasnt good enough to post this before I got all the red ink off my hands curse it.

No luck yet. They say I'm a doctor now ha ha.

The name was simple but so very appropriate and effective. It was contrived merely by adding to the common name Jack – often used by criminals in the past, such as Jack Sheppard and Spring-Heeled Jack – the description of the killer's method of mutilation, which had frequently been referred to in the newspapers as 'ripping'. The use of American slang words such as 'Boss' and 'quit' may have been suggested to the writer by Wynne Baxter's report at the Chapman inquest on 26 September that an American had been attempting to purchase specimens of the female uterus.

   Although the letter was dated 25 September, significantly, it was not posted until the 27th, thus allowing the writer to use anything useful that may have emerged at the inquest. This could well explain the apparent delay between writing and posting, a delay which the letter-writer attempts to explain by claiming that he had red ink on his hands.

   The editor of the Central News forwarded the letter to Chief Constable Williamson on 29 September, attributing his own delay to the fact that he had thought that it was a joke. The timing was impeccable. In the early hours of Sunday 30 September there followed the murders of Stride and Eddowes.

   The letter had, at last, provided a name for the unknown Whitechapel murderer, a boon for the press. If not the work of the actual murderer it was, at least, well informed, and was quickly followed, in the wake of the double murder, by a postcard couched in similar terminology. This was received, again by the Central News, on

Monday 1 October, bearing no date but postmarked 'LONDON E. Oc 1 88'. It was addressed, 'Central News Office, London City, E.C.', and ran as follows:

> I wasn't codding dear old Boss when I gave you the tip. Youll hear about saucy Jacky's work tomorrow double event this time number one squealed a bit couldnt finish straight off. had no time to get ears for police. thanks for keeping last letter back till I got to work again.
> Jack the Ripper

The card, again apparently written in red ink, was obviously from the same source as the preceding letter to which it referred, but the handwriting, although similar, was not identical. Even if the police did not believe that the letter and postcard were written by the killer, it was at least in their interest to identify the writer. With a press agency the recipient of the correspondence, there was little chance of keeping the story quiet. On 3 October, the police took the bull by the horns and issued a poster bearing facsimiles of the envelope, letter and card, in a vain effort to identify the writer. All this achieved was to instigate a flood of similarly signed correspondence, some in the same hand, and to provide good copy for the press.

On 5 October, T. J. Bulling of the Central News again communicated with the Chief Constable:

> Dear Mr Williamson,
>   At 5 minutes to 9 oclock tonight we received the following letter the envelope of which I enclose by which you will see it is in the same handwriting as the previous communications.
>
> 5 Oct. 1888
> Dear Friend,
>   In the name of God hear me I swear I did not kill the female whose body was found at Whitehall.* If she was an honest woman I will hunt down and destroy her murderer. If she was a whore God will bless the hand that slew her, for the women of Moab and Midian shall die and their blood shall mingle with the dust. I never harm any others or the Divine power that

---

*The body found at Whitehall refers to a female torso found in the cellars of New Scotland Yard, then under construction (see Chapter Nine).

protects and helps me in my grand work would quit for ever. Do as I do and the light of glory shall shine upon you. I must get to work tomorrow treble event this time yes yes three must be ripped. will send you a bit of face by post I promise this dear old Boss. The police now reckon my work a practical joke well well Jacky's a very practical joker ha ha ha Keep this back till three are wiped out and you can show the cold meat

    Yours truly
    Jack the Ripper

Yours truly
    T. J. Bulling

The pot was truly being kept on the boil. And what was the reason for the Central News keeping back the original of this latest letter and merely forwarding the envelope as confirmation of its authorship? Similar terms had been used in this communication, but it was not accurate with its prediction: no 'treble event' followed. In many ways it devalues the earlier letter and postcard and indicates that the author was not the murderer.

There is nothing in any of this correspondence to indicate that it was from the killer. The facts contained in it were known to the press anyway. In 1910 Sir Robert Anderson, in his memoirs *The Lighter Side of My Official Life*, stated:

... So I will only add that the 'Jack the Ripper' letter which is preserved in the Police Museum at New Scotland Yard is the creation of an enterprising London journalist. Having regard to the interest attaching to this case, I am almost tempted to disclose the identity of the murderer [a matter the authors will address later] and of the pressman who wrote the letter above referred to. But no public benefit would result from such a course, and the traditions of my old department would suffer.

Four years later, in 1914, Sir Melville Macnaghten's book *Days of My Years* appeared. He wrote,

On 27th September a letter was received at a well-known News Agency, addressed to the 'Boss'. It was written in red ink, and purported to give the details of the murders which had been committed. It was signed, 'Jack the Ripper'. This document was sent to Scotland Yard, and (in my opinion most unwisely) was reproduced, and copies of same affixed to various police stations, thus giving it an official imprimatur. In this ghastly production I have always thought I could discern the stained forefinger of the journalist, indeed, a year later, I had shrewd suspicions as to the actual author! But whoever did pen the gruesome stuff, it is certain to my mind that it was not the mad miscreant who had committed the murders. The name 'Jack the Ripper', however, had got abroad in the land and had 'caught on'; it riveted the attention of the classes as well as the masses.

A further point of interest with regard to Anderson's comments on the authorship of the correspondence appears in a footnote to his serialised memoirs in *Blackwood's Magazine* in 1910:

I should almost be tempted to disclose the identity of the murderer and of the pressman who wrote the letter . . . provided that the publishers would accept all responsibility in view of a possible libel action.

It is obvious that these two senior Yard officials thought they knew the identity of the journalist responsible for the correspondence, though Anderson's apparent fear of libel action clearly indicates that he lacked positive proof. Indeed, if they had been in possession of such proof a police action against the author would most certainly have followed, as in the case of a certain Maria Coroner of Bradford, who had sent similar letters. Thus we have a mystery within a mystery: who did the Yard officials believe to have originated the correspondence, and the name Jack the Ripper? And did anyone else ever know?

To answer the latter question we must turn to a book published in 1935 entitled *Life and Death at The Old Bailey*. Despite the title, this contains a chapter on the Ripper murders, entitled 'Shadowing the Shadow of a Murderer'. In it the author, R. Thurston Hopkins, writes about the origin of the name Jack the Ripper, making observations that ring true and appear to have been missed by other authors:

But, first of all, who christened the phantom killer with the terrible soubriquet of Jack the Ripper? That is a small mystery in itself. Possibly Scotland Yard gave the name to the press and public. At that time the police post-bag bulged with hundreds of anonymous letters from all kinds of cranks and half-witted persons, who sought to criticise or hoax the officers engaged in following up the murders ... it was in a letter, received by a well-known News Agency and forwarded to the Yard, that the name first appeared. The Criminal Investigation Department looked upon this letter as a 'clue' and possibly a message from the actual murderer ... It was perhaps a fortunate thing that the handwriting of this famous letter was perhaps not identified, for it would have led to the arrest of a harmless Fleet Street journalist. This poor fellow had a breakdown and became a whimsical figure in Fleet Street, only befriended by the staff of newspapers and printing works. He would creep about the dark courts waving his hands furiously in the air, would utter stentorian 'Ha, ha, ha's,' and then, meeting some pal, would button-hole him and pour into his ear all the 'inner-story' of the East End murders. Many old Fleet Streeters had very shrewd suspicions that this irresponsible fellow wrote the famous Jack the Ripper letter, and even Sir Melville L. Macnaghten, Chief of the Criminal Investigation Department, had his eye on him.

This is tantalising stuff. Hopkins indicates that not only the police, but some pressmen also, suspected this mysterious character of being the originator of the name Jack the Ripper. It is disappointing to note that all these sources signally fail to identify the journalist. It has become one of the many side issues that have perplexed Ripper researchers over the years. The name we want to know, as Phil Sugden has succinctly put it, is the one that Sir Robert Anderson would give 'if we could put a gun to his head and make him divulge it'. However, all is not lost. One very senior retired police officer did indeed break the Yard silence on what they knew of the press origins of 'Jack the Ripper'. He was Chief Inspector John George Littlechild, head of the Secret Department (Special Branch) at Scotland Yard in 1888, and he divulged the information in the 'Littlechild letter':

With regard to the term 'Jack the Ripper' it was generally believed at the Yard that Tom Bullen of the Central News was the originator but it is probable Moore, who was his chief, was the inventor. It was a smart piece of journalistic work. No journalist of my time got such privileges from Scotland Yard as Bullen. Mr James Munro when Assistant Commissioner, and afterwards Commissioner, relied on his integrity. Poor Bullen occasionally took too much to drink, and I fail to see how he could help it knocking about so many hours and seeking favours from so many people to procure copy. One night when Bullen had taken a 'few too many' he got early information of the death of Prince Bismarck and instead of going to the office to report it sent a laconic telegram 'Bloody Bismarck is dead'. On this I believe Mr Charles Moore fired him out.

At last we have the names that the Yard officials had in mind as the originators of the famous correspondence. 'Bullen' is obviously one and the same as the 'T. J. Bulling' who forwarded the Jack the Ripper letters from the Central News to Mr Williamson. Littlechild, obviously writing from memory, makes an understandable mistake with the name: the habit of Londoners is to pronounce 'ing' as 'in', dropping the 'g', and it is likely that he remembered the name being pronounced as 'Bullen'. Littlechild's description of Bulling's decline through drink links in nicely with Thurston Hopkins' description of the 'poor fellow' he knew.

Bulling's boss at the Central News was Charles Moore, a man who would have been known socially to the journalist George R. Sims, as was Sir Melville Macnaghten. In Sims' autobiography, *My Life*, he writes:

> My friend of many long years, Sir Melville Macnaghten, late Chief of the CID at Scotland Yard, had the charming idea of giving little Corinthian dinners on Monday nights at his house, 32 Warwick Square. The little party generally consisted of Sir Melville, Colonel Vivian Majendie, Mr B. J. Angle, Mr Tom Anderson, Mr Charles Moore, an old Indian friend of Sir Melville, and myself.

Research by Keith Skinner shows that Moore and Bulling later visited Scotland Yard's Black Museum together, presumably they saw the 'Jack the Ripper' letter which was then displayed there. Their names even appear in the visitors' book!

The question of authenticity has significance beyond the academic or historical, for these letters are a primary source for the continuance of the mythical side of the Ripper story. They also originate the image of 'irony and wit' still so frequently associated with

Jack the Ripper, the mystique that transforms him into a stylish and impudent rogue.

There are still many questions to be answered concerning the exact roles played by Bulling and Moore in this matter. However, a fertile new avenue of research has now been opened with the identification, at last, of the journalist believed by the police to have invented 'Jack the Ripper'.

Chapter 9
The Ripper Hunt Continues

'I can bear and forbear or at least bide my time.'

October 1888 was a month in which there was not one Ripper murder. It started with great police activity in the wake of the Stride/Eddowes murders and much speculation over the receipt of the 'Jack the Ripper' correspondence, and continued with scares, false arrests and spurious leads. But were the police closer to the killer than we have ever realised? Did he know that they were on to him? Was he relocating himself, seeking new accommodation?

The *Star* of 1 October carried a small report headed 'Worth Inquiry' which ran as follows:

> A reporter heard a strange story this morning that may be connected with the murders. A gentleman living not far from the British Museum says: – In the room above mine there is an American lodging. He professes to be a doctor, but does not look like one. In fact, if one judged by his looks, he might be – well a perfect ruffian. No one knows anything about him. He never does any work, and always seems rather hard up, although he pays his rent regularly. He must wear something over his boots that enables him to walk silently, for no one ever hears him come in. At intervals he disappears for a time. On Saturday he went out, and has not been back since.

Although there were no Ripper murders in October, these were fraught times. In the East End, where large, morbid crowds gathered in the streets to view the murder scenes and indulge in rabid speculation, a terrible atmosphere prevailed. The *Star of the East* reported:

> The district of Whitechapel and Aldgate is, this morning, in a state of ferment and panic. All night long there have been people in the streets, standing round coffee stalls and at other points in

the main thoroughfares, talking of the latest horrors, and even the men seemed to be in a state of terror. Extra police have patrolled the streets, nine hundred additional constables having become available by reason of one of the crimes being in the precincts of the City. There is now a change in the demeanour of the police authorities, who now seem to have come to the conclusion that publicity is the greatest aid to the detection of the perpetrator of the murder, and all information is cheerfully imparted to the Press.

Unfortunately for Scotland Yard, the Whitechapel killings were not the only series of murders demanding investigation. They were presented with a 'torso' murder on Tuesday 2 October which became known as 'The Whitehall Mystery'. At 3.20 p.m. that day, a carpenter, Frederick Wildborn, employed by Messrs J. Grover and Sons, builders, of Pimlico, who were contractors for the new Metropolitan Police headquarters being built on the Thames Embankment, found a parcel tied up in paper, 2ft.6in. long by 2ft. wide, in the corner of one of the cellars. The parcel was found to contain the decomposed body of a woman minus head, arms, and legs. This was just one of a series of 'torso' murders which were, like the Ripper killings, to remain unsolved.

The newspapers of Wednesday 3 October added further American interest by recalling a recent series of murders of females in Texas. Headed 'After Texas – Whitechapel', an article in the *East Anglian Daily Times* was nothing more than press speculation cashing in on what was becoming a best-selling story: 'The theory has been suggested that the perpetrator of the latter [Whitechapel murders] may be the Texas criminal who was never discovered.' A leading Southern newspaper in the USA, *The Atlanta Constitution*, weighed in with its opinion: 'In our recent annals of crime there has been no other man capable of committing such deeds. The mysterious crimes in Texas have ceased. They have just commenced in London. Is the man from Texas at the bottom of them all?' The Superintendent of the New York Police stated that the theory was possible but not probable. 'There is the same brutality and mutilation, the same suspicion that the criminal is a monster or lunatic who has declared war literally to the knife against all womankind, but I hardly believe it is the same individual.' The Texas murders (1885–7) were in fact very different in their nature, were not all committed by the same killer, were brutal axe murders and were committed for motives of rape and robbery.

Wednesday 3 October also saw Mr Matthews, the Home Secretary, engaged for several hours at the Home Office with reference to the murders. He had prolonged interviews with Sir Charles Warren and others. At 6 p.m. the same day, a seaman, John Lock, was rescued by police from an excited crowd in the vicinity of Ratcliffe Highway. They were following him shouting, 'Leather Apron!' and 'Jack the Ripper!' The reason for this was not immediately obvious but when the police examined him at the police station his light tweed suit was found to bear paint stains which the crowd had mistaken for blood. His explanation was perfectly satisfactory but the police were unable to release him for some considerable time, until the crowd dispersed and he was able to depart.

At 9.30 p.m., Mrs Sewell, a cleaner at the Great Assembly Hall, was on her way to a temperance meeting at the hall. As she was passing along Redman's Road, a very dark thoroughfare, a man sprang out in front of her. She was alarmed and saw something glittering in his hand, held up against his sleeve. He said, 'I did not hurt you, missus, did I?' At this point a young man came by and her accoster took to his heels. The young man stated that the stranger was holding 'a huge knife, a foot long'. The two followed the man but lost him, and each other. Mrs Sewell, who continued to the hall in a state of alarm, described the man as rather tall, with red bushy whiskers, wearing a brown overcoat and accompanied by a white dog.

Between 9 and 10 p.m. that night, a Sergeant Adams made an arrest in Ratcliffe Highway. He heard a woman screaming for help in an adjoining court, and on going to investigate was confronted by a man, evidently foreign, leaving the place. Adams was immediately struck by the likeness of the foreigner to the published police description of the man seen with Stride. The man submitted to arrest quietly, stating that he was sailing from England for America the following day. At the station he was found to be Maltese and gave his name and address. He was carrying no weapon, and was released when his story was confirmed the following morning. Although no explanation was given for the woman's screams, it is reasonable to assume that it was another prostitute–client dispute.

Some two hours later the same night, a story circulated that the unknown murderer had been surprised in the act of attempting another outrage on a woman in Union Street, Whitechapel. The story went that she had been lured into a side street by the 'monster' but saw his knife and screamed. A man and two women went to the spot and the would-be murderer was pursued by a man who knocked the knife out of his hand. The alleged attacker then jumped into a passing cab, bidding the cabman to drive wherever he liked. A howling mob swarmed after the fugitive and the police soon stopped the cab and took the occupant to Leman Street police station.

Investigation, however, soon proved that this story had little foundation in fact. It was found that at about 10 o'clock a well-dressed man rushed out of the Three Tuns public house in Aldgate, followed by a woman who accused him of molesting her. To escape the crowd the man jumped into a cab and was pursued and captured. When he was formally charged, the woman stated that he had accosted her first in Whitechapel High Street and when she refused his proposals he threatened her with violence. However, the woman declined to press charges and left the police station. The man was detained pending enquiries. He was described as 'an athletic, determined fellow' of about forty-three years of age. No weapons were found on him and despite giving his name he refused to state his address. When taken to the cells, his attitude became defiant and he kept up a conversation in a slightly American accent. He was stated to have been a little under the influence of drink.

A report referring to this arrest appeared in the *Star* of 4 October:

An American, who refuses to give his name or any account of himself, was arrested last night on suspicion of being the East End murderer. He is well dressed, rather tall, of slight build, and clean-shaven. He accosted a woman in Cable Street, asked her to go with him, and threatened that if she refused he would 'rip her up'. The woman screamed, and the man rushed to a cab. The police gave chase, got upon the cab, seized the man, and took him to Leman Street Police Station, where he asked the Inspector in charge, 'Are you the boss?' The man is detained at the police station, as well as two others who were conveyed there during the evening.

Also at this time the opinions of Chief Inspector Thomas Byrnes of the New York Police appeared in the papers, illustrating the attention the murders were attracting in the USA:

An American Detective's Opinion – The Whitechapel murders are attracting widespread attention throughout America. Inspector Byrnes of New York was asked how he would proceed to solve the London mystery. He said, 'I should have gone right to work in a commonsense way, and not believed in mere theories. With the great power of the London police I should have manufactured victims for the murderer. I would have taken 50 female habitues of Whitechapel and covered the ground with them. Even if one fell a victim, I should get the murderer. Men un-uniformed should be scattered over the district so nothing could escape them. The crimes are all of the same class, and I would have determined the class to which the murderer belonged. But – pshaw! What's the good of talking? The murderer would have been caught long ago.'

One can imagine the feelings of his English counterparts when they read Mr Byrnes' remarks in the *Star*.

On Saturday 6 October the funeral of Elizabeth Stride took place at the East London Cemetery, with very little fuss or ceremony. Catherine Eddowes' funeral was held on Monday the 8th. At 1.30 p.m. the body was taken from the Golden Lane mortuary, where many hundreds of people had congregated. The cost of the funeral was borne by the undertaker, Mr G. C. Hawkes of 41A Banner Street. The polished elm coffin bore a plate inscribed, 'Catherine Eddowes, died 30th September, 1888, aged 43 years'. It was conveyed in an open glass car to the City of London Cemetery at Ilford, where nearly five hundred people witnessed the interment. The service was conducted by the Reverend J. Dunscombe, the cemetery chaplain.

The atmosphere in the East End was still highly charged. A newspaper article reported:

The police were nervously apprehensive that the night would not pass without some startling occurrence. The most extraordinary precautions were taken in consequence, and so complete were the measures adopted, both by the City and Metropolitan Police authorities, that it seemed impossible for the murderer to make his appearance in the East End without detection. Large bodies of plain-clothes men were drafted by Sir Charles Warren to the Whitechapel district from other parts of London, and these, together with the detectives, were so numerous that in the more deserted thorough-fares almost every man met with was a police officer.

Patrols were more than doubled, so that almost every nook and corner of the various beats came under police supervision every five minutes. A suggestion was made that bloodhounds could be used in the tracking of the criminal. The night patrols in the streets and courts in the area were reinforced by various vigilance groups, and there were only a small number of women to be seen on the streets at night.

The atmosphere of mistrust and fear that permeated the White-chapel and Spitalfields district is illustrated by the misfortune of a Suffolk doctor visiting the city. This was recorded in the *East Anglian Daily Times* of 16 October under the heading 'Adventure of a Suffolk Surgeon':

A medical gentleman residing at a town near the borders of Suffolk and Essex has just met with a singular and rather unpleasant adventure in Whitechapel. It appears that, being in London on business, he made a pilgrimage to Whitechapel, in order to visit the scene of the Mitre Square murder. Whilst examining the spot a case of surgical instruments was noticed to be in his possession, and he was immediately mobbed. His protestations that he was a medical practitioner living in a quiet Suffolk town only served to infuriate the crowd, whose ringleaders exclaimed, 'We always said it was a doctor who did the murder.' A constable coming up informed the surgeon – rather to his relief – that he must take him into custody on suspicion, and the unfortunate gentleman was hurried off in a cab, amid the howls of the angry mob, to the nearest police station. Here he succeeded in giving an explanation satisfactory to the authorities, and he was at once released. The constable had probably merely effected the arrest in order to extricate the doctor from his tormentors.

On the evening of Tuesday 16 October George Lusk, of 1 Alderney Road, Mile End, chairman of the Whitechapel Vigilance Committee (formed the previous month in response to the murders), received through the post a small cardboard box containing half a kidney, together with the following letter:

> From hell
>
> MrLusk
> Sir
>   I send you half the Kidne I took from one women prasarved
> it for you tother piece I fried and ate it was very nise. I may
> send you the bloody knif that took it out if you only wate a
> whil longer.
>   Signed Catch me when you can
>   Mishter Lusk.

As we know, Catherine Eddowes' left kidney was missing from her
body: it had been cut out by the killer and the left renal artery
severed. Dr Frederick Gordon Brown, the City Police surgeon, who
had conducted the post-mortem examination on the body, had
described the remaining, right, kidney as 'pale, bloodless, with slight
congestion of the base of the pyramids'.

Initially Lusk, perhaps not surprisingly, did not attach any importance to the package and letter, believing it to be a hoax. However,
on mentioning it to other members of his committee two days later
he was advised to show the piece of kidney to a medical man. He
duly took it to Mr F. S. Reed, assistant to Dr Wiles, of 56 Mile End
Road, and then to Dr Openshaw, Pathological Curator of the
London Hospital Museum. Both of these medical gentlemen gave
the opinion that it was a portion of a human kidney divided longi-
tudinally. Lusk then took the letter and kidney to Leman Street
police station, where a statement was taken from him.

The portion of kidney was forwarded to the City of London police
office in Old Jewry, where the investigation into the Eddowes murder
was being conducted. The letter was forwarded to Scotland Yard.
The kidney was submitted by the City Police to Dr Gordon Brown
for examination, he too agreeing that it was human. Inspector James
McWilliam of the City Police was in liaison with Chief Inspector
Swanson at Scotland Yard, and it was agreed by them that the
doctors' opinion should not be publicised. Swanson loaned the
'From hell' letter to McWilliam, who had it photographed and
returned it to the Yard.

Needless to say, despite the agreed non-publicity, the full story
and text of the letter soon appeared in the newspapers, giving rise
to much press speculation and comment. A report in the *Daily
Telegraph* of 20 October stated, without giving a source: 'It is
asserted that only a small portion of the renal artery adheres to the

kidney, while in the case of the Mitre Square victim a large portion of this artery adhered to the body.'

One enterprising reporter found his way to the house of Dr Brown the same night and spoke to the medical man in person. The details of the interview were published in the *Star of the East* of 22 October. This interview with the City Police surgeon has never before appeared in a book on the subject.

> Calling on Dr Gordon Brown, of the City Police, on Saturday night, a reporter found that he had not quite completed his examination of the kidney which had been submitted to him. He said: 'So far as I can form an opinion, I do not see any substantial reason why this portion of kidney should not be the portion of the one taken from the murdered woman. I cannot say that it is the left kidney. It must have been cut previously to its being immersed in the spirit which exercised a hardening process. It certainly had not been in spirit for more than a week. As has been stated, there is no portion of the renal artery adhering to it, it having been trimmed up, so consequently, there could be no correspondence established between the portion of the body from which it was cut. As it exhibits no trace of decomposition, when we consider the length of time that has elapsed since the commission of the murder, we come to the conclusion that the probability is slight of its being a portion of the murdered woman of Mitre Square.'

This very clear statement should dispose, once and for all, of the 'renal artery' argument. It is unequivocal on the point: the artery had been completely trimmed away from the portion of kidney sent to Lusk.

The Home Office, concerned as to the progress of the police investigation at this crucial time, sent a letter dated 7 October to Warren which evinced their frustration at the apparent lack of results. This was replied to, rather pointedly, by Warren on the 17th. Listing the Home Office questions with Warren's answers, the report is an interesting insight into the views of both sides and is worth repeating verbatim:

> *Question No. 1.* 'Is it your opinion that the Police and the CID have now exhausted all the means within their power of

discovering the criminal and have not only failed, but have no reasonable prospect of succeeding in any moderate time?'

To this I have to reply,

No. I think we have hardly begun: it often takes many months to discover a criminal.

Question No. 2. 'Has any information reached you which makes you think that there are persons who could give information but who are holding back either from fear of consequences, or in hope of a reward; or that any persons are harbouring the criminal, and assisting his concealment?'

There have been anonymous letters to this effect, but though they may be hoaxes, it shews that the offer of a reward has an effect upon the mind, and one of the logical solutions as to the murders is that there may be several persons who are more or less assisting the murderer.

Question No. 3. 'Has any special circumstance been brought to your knowledge which makes it proper to offer a reward in the case of these murders, and distinguishes them from other atrocious crimes such as the dynamite explosions, the shooting of PC Chamberlain, the rape and murder of Mary Cooper, and many others in which rewards were refused?'

I look upon this series of murders as unique in the history of our country, and of a totally different character to those mentioned above, and so far the case is in a totally different category.

I am,

Sir,

Your Most Obedient Servant,

  C. Warren

[Ref. MEPO1/55 pp.336–8]

Thus Warren updated the Home Office on the Whitechapel murders while giving very little away. It is interesting to see, though, the status that he was according the series of murders, apparently feeling that they exceeded even the Fenian dynamite outrages in their atrocity and unique character.

As far as the investigation was concerned, it was clear to both the police and the media that it was running out of steam. A report by Superintendent Arnold dated 22 October highlighted the problems of H Division, which was suffering from a manpower shortage to the degree that it was impossible to keep a constable on each beat in the division. Men were absent due to sickness, leave, attending various courts, special duties, and traffic regulation. Arnold continued:

> . . . a considerable portion of the population of Whitechapel is composed of the low and dangerous classes, who frequently indulge in rowdyism and street offences. With the exception of the recent murders crime of a serious nature is not unusually heavy in the District.

He explained the desirability of keeping the beats manned and asked for an augmentation of twenty-five constables for the duty. He felt they could be deployed by ten going to Leman Street, ten to the Commercial Street subdivision, which would embrace the greater part of the Whitechapel district, and the remainder to Arbour Square, which adjoined Whitechapel. The 'special arrangements' made in consequence of the recent murders would have to continue 'for a time to prevent if possible any further outrages', for which duty he asked that men be provided from other divisions 'as at present'.

Arnold finished:

> As regards the recent murders having had a disastrous effect on trade at the East End, there is no doubt that since those in Berner Street and Mitre Square were committed females have to some little extent discontinued shopping in the evening but I am of opinion that this will not prevail for any lengthened period there being at present very little excitement. [Ref. MEPO3/141 ff.164–6]

A study of reports from officers on the beat indicated that there were 62 houses known to be brothels in H (Whitechapel) Division, and a great number more other houses 'which are more or less intermittently used for such purposes'. There were 233 common lodging houses accommodating 8,350 people, about 1,200 of whom were prostitutes, 'mostly of a very low condition'. The lower class of common lodging houses was naturally frequented by prostitutes, thieves and tramps, as there was nowhere else for them to go and no law to prevent them congregating there. The study continued, 'I do not think there is any reason whatever for supposing that the murderer of Whitechapel is one of the ordinary denizens of that place.' (Ref. MEPO3/141 ff.158–63)

In October 1888 a strange series of events was documented in many of the newspapers. The underlying fact revealed in these reports was that the Ripper hunters were on to a promising suspect, not at all in the category of some of those who had already been disposed of. Here, at last, was a most promising lead in the hunt for the unknown killer of Whitechapel.

Chapter 10

The Lodger

'A little episode in the dark pages of our late history.'

The majority of the police arrests made following the double murder were on the flimsiest of evidence or suspicion and were followed by the early release of the persons detained, or their being held because of their mental condition. Most were suspects brought to police notice by overimaginative members of the public, or by their own odd behaviour. But in fact it was during October that the police were secretly engaged in the search for a definite suspect. We can now examine a peculiar and singular chain of events that were actually reported in the press, but were not, at least by the press, linked at the time, and which have been ignored by previous writers on the subject.

The investigating officers were actually on to something from the very day of the Berner Street/Mitre Square killings, and spent the ensuing weeks carrying out enquiries to locate a strong suspect. All this activity was shrouded in great secrecy and denials were made to the press when they approached the police with their questions.

This mysterious suspect, we will show, was an American, which probably accounts for the fact that, initially, the police attached some importance to the 'Dear Boss' correspondence, containing, as it did, its obvious Americanisms.

As we have seen, coroner Wynne Baxter's summing-up at the Chapman inquest introduced the idea of an American suspect, and received wide publicity via the press. However, the police were soon to be presented with some rather more substantial evidence indicating that an American was indeed their man. This, we hope to show, they received on Sunday 30 September, directly after the murders. This is the first time that the evidence has been pieced together and a recognisable chain of events deduced from it.

The first indication in the newspapers of this extraordinary story appeared in *The Globe* of Wednesday 10 October:

DETECTIVES ON A NEW SCENT

A well-informed correspondent states that he has gleaned the following information from an undeniably authentic source, and from careful and persistent inquiries in various quarters he is able to relate the news as fact, though for obvious reasons names and addresses are for the present suppressed: A certain member of the Criminal Investigation Department has recently journeyed to Liverpool and there traced the movements of a man which have proved of a somewhat mysterious kind. The height of this person and his description generally are fully ascertained, and among other things he was in possession of a black leather bag. This man suddenly left Liverpool for London, and for some time occupied apartments in a well-known first-class hotel in the West End. It is stated that for some reason or another this person was in the habit of 'slumming'. He would visit the lowest parts of London, and scour the slums of the East-end. He suddenly disappeared from the hotel leaving behind the black leather bag and its contents, and has not returned. He left a small bill unpaid, and ultimately an advertisement appeared in The Times, setting forth the gentleman's name, and drawing attention to the fact that the bag would be sold under the Innkeepers' Act to defray expenses, unless claimed. This was done last month by a well-known auctioneer in London, and the contents, or some of them, are now in the possession of the police, who are thoroughly investigating the affair. Of these we, of course, cannot more than make mention, but certain documents, wearing apparel, cheque books, prints of an obscene description, letters, &c., are said to form the foundation of a most searching inquiry now on foot, which is being vigilantly pursued by those in authority. It has been suggested that the mysterious personage referred to landed in Liverpool from America, but this so far is no more than a suggestion.

This remarkable story, showing that the CID were seeking a man from America, must have been written on 9 October, for publication on the 10th, and it may be safely assumed that the 'certain member of the Criminal Investigation Department' travelled to Liverpool on his quest in the first week of the month. What was it that caused him to be despatched on this enquiry? The answer seems to be given in subsequent reports which appeared over the next few days, as a gradual leak of information took place.

On Thursday 11 October, the *East Anglian Daily Times* carried an interesting item from a Liverpool correspondent stating that the police there had no knowledge of a report which had been circulated that they were aware of the movements of a man suspected of being concerned in the Whitechapel murders. The Chief Constable, however, had given instructions for the railway stations and departing steamers to be closely watched. The report concluded with the fact that up until then there had been no trace of the murderer in Liverpool, and that notices of the rewards had been posted at the Liverpool police courts.

Clearly the police believed their man was on the run and was likely to travel to Liverpool by train and attempt to leave the country on a ship. They also seemed keen to deny knowledge of such a suspect, possibly to avoid alerting him. In this, unfortunately, they failed.

The *Suffolk Chronicle* of Saturday 13 October confirmed the story, stating, 'The steamers leaving Liverpool for America and other ports are now carefully being watched by the police and the passengers are closely scrutinised by detectives, there being an idea that the perpetrator of the Whitechapel murders may endeavour to make his escape via Liverpool.' Liverpool, of course, was the main port of embarkation for the States.

Reports published three days later now assume huge significance. The following appeared in the *Daily News* of Tuesday 16 October:

According to a Correspondent, the police are watching with great anxiety a house at the East-end which is strongly suspected to have been the actual lodging, or a house made use of by someone connected with the East-end murders. Statements made by the neighbours in the district point to the fact that the landlady had a lodger, who since the Sunday morning of the last Whitechapel murders has been missing. The lodger, it is stated, returned home early on the Sunday morning, and the landlady was disturbed by his moving about. She got up very early, and noticed that her lodger had changed some of his clothes. He told her he was going away for a little time, and he asked her to wash the shirt which he had taken off, and get it ready for him by the time he came back. As he had been in the habit of going away now and then, she did not think much at the time, and soon afterwards he went out. On looking at his shirt she was astonished to find the wristbands and part of the sleeves saturated with wet blood. The appearance struck her as very strange, and when she heard of the murders her suspicions were aroused. Acting on the advice of some of her neighbours, she gave information to the police and showed them the blood-stained shirt. They took possession of it, and obtained from her a full description of her missing lodger. During the last fortnight she has been under the impression that he would return, and was sanguine that he would probably come back on Saturday or Sunday night, or perhaps Monday evening. The general opinion, however, among the neighbours is that he will never return. On finding out the house and visiting it, a reporter found it tenanted by a stout, middle-aged German woman, who speaks very bad English, and who was not inclined to give much information further than the fact that her lodger had not returned yet, and she could not say where he had gone or when he would be back. The neighbours state that ever since the information has been given two detectives and two policemen have been in the house day and night. The house is approached by a court, and as there are alleys running through it into different streets, there are different ways of approach and exit. It is believed from the information obtained concerning the lodger's former move-ments and his general appearance, together with the fact that numbers of people have seen this same man about the neigh-bourhood, that the police have in their possession a series of most important clues, and that his ultimate capture is only a question of time.

Here is a clear indication that the police had found the suspected lair of the killer in the East End. Perhaps realising this, he had fled, leaving property at his lodgings, clues to his identity, and, not daring to take it with him, most damning of all the bloodstained shirt.

It was a story that the police would rather have not seen published: indeed, they later tried to play it down and made denials. The result of the press report was that the killer now knew that he would be tracked and was therefore on the run.

The final part of this *Daily News* report is significant. It seems to show that the police now had information about the suspect's pre-vious movements, presumably obtained at his lodgings. This must have been what set them on the track to Liverpool.

A brief report in the following day's *Manchester Evening News* also relates to the incident:

The man suspected of the Whitechapel murders is shadowed, incriminating evidence of a certain character has already been obtained, [this we believe the blood-stained shirt, and his property seized by the police,] and a confession to the crime may be looked for at any moment. The accused is himself aware, it is believed, of the suspicions entertained against him.

This last sentence appears to refer to the suspect's hasty flight and failure to return to his lodgings where, he would be only too aware, the police would be waiting for him.

The *East Anglian Daily Times* of Wednesday 17 October sheds more light on the mysterious fleeing lodger and also highlights the efforts of the police to play the story down.

The startling story published on Monday, with reference to the finding of a blood-stained shirt, and the disappearance of a man from a certain house in the East End, proves, from investigation carried out by a reporter, on Tuesday, to be not altogether devoid of foundation, though on Monday afternoon the truth of the statement was given an unqualified denial by the detective officers, presumably because they were anxious to avoid a premature disclosure of the facts of which they had been for some time cognisant. The police have taken exceptional precautions to prevent a disclosure, and while repeated arrests have taken place with no other result than that of discharging the prisoners for the time being in custody, they have devoted particular attention to one particular spot, in the hope that a few days would suffice to set at rest public anxiety as to further murders. Our reporter, on Tuesday, elicited the fact that from the morning of the Berner Street and Mitre Square murders, the police have had in their possession a shirt saturated with blood. Though they say nothing they are evidently convinced that it was left in a house in Batty Street by the assassin.

Having regard to the position of this house, its proximity to the yard in Berner Street, where the crime was committed, and to the many intricate passages and alleys adjacent, the police theory has in all probability a basis of fact. The statement has been made that the landlady of the house was, at an early hour, disturbed by movements of her lodger, who changed some of his apparel, and went away after instructing her to wash the cast-off shirt. Although, for reasons known to themselves,

Location of Dutfield's Yard and 22 Batty Street

the police, during Saturday, Sunday, and Monday, answered in the negative all questions as to whether any persons had been arrested, there is no doubt that a man was taken into custody on suspicion of being the missing lodger from 22 Batty Street, and that he was afterwards set at liberty. [He would have had no option but to leave the tell-tale shirt behind, he could not risk carrying it into the street where he may have been stopped by the police.]

The German lodging-house keeper could clear up the point as to the existence of any other lodger absent from her house under the suspicious circumstances referred to, but she is not accessible, and it is easy to understand that the police should endeavour to prevent her making any statement. From our own inquiries in various directions on Tuesday afternoon, a further development is very likely to take place.

This report underlines the insignificance of the arrests made earlier, and points out that a great deal of importance was being placed on the address in the neighbouring road to Berner Street whence the mysterious lodger had fled. If we are correct in attributing the Stride murder to a domestic dispute, imagine the killer's consternation when, fleeing homewards from Mitre Square, he found his neighbourhood alive with police investigating the Berner Street affair. No wonder he fled his lodgings! Not only was he disturbed by his landlady, he must also have thought that the police were rapidly moving in on his address after the Mitre Square murder.

Why has this very important incident been ignored up till now? Because a counter-report was issued via our old friends at the Central News Agency, who it would appear syndicated their story at the instigation of the police. It was published in several newspapers on Wednesday 17 October, appearing with the story of the lodger in that day's *Manchester Evening News*. The Central News release ran as follows:

> The story is founded on some matters which occurred more than a fortnight ago. It appears that a man, apparently a foreigner, visited the house of a German laundress at 22 Batty Street, and left four shirts tied in a bundle to be washed. The bundle was not opened at the time, but when the shirts were afterwards taken out, one was found to be considerably bloodstained. The woman communicated with the police, who placed the house under observation, the detectives at the same time being lodged there to arrest the man should he return. This he did last Saturday, and he was taken to the Leman Street Police Station, where he was questioned, and within an hour or two released, his statements being proved correct.

This cryptic report, if it were true, would completely dispose of the 'bloodstained shirt' incident and that particular suspect. The whole thing seems very odd when we remember that the detectives had already made an unqualified denial of the story, and that the landlady (who becomes a laundress in the Central News piece) had been made incommunicado to members of the press. Also, the police were still watching the address, according to press reports, and were taking 'exceptional precautions to prevent a disclosure'. As has been seen, the initial information, obtained by a Press Association reporter for the *Daily News*, came from the landlady and neighbours and clearly stated that the person was a lodger who had returned to the house in the early hours of the morning of the murders. Suddenly the landlady was 'unobtainable' for further comment and the police denials had been issued. Clearly something significant was going on.

The *Daily Telegraph* of Tuesday 9 October had carried another 'bloodstained clothing' story which makes very interesting reading:

The Central News says the Metropolitan Police last night made an arrest through the instrumentality of the manager of a London clothes cleaning establishment near Holborn. The same news agency adds the following: Last Wednesday afternoon a man called at the shop between twelve and two o'clock in the afternoon with two garments – an overcoat and a pair of trousers – to be cleaned. They were both bloodstained; the coat was especially smeared near one of the pockets, and there were large spots of blood on various parts of the trousers. The manager was away at the time, and his wife took charge of the clothes; the owner of the garments said he would call for them on Friday or Saturday. The woman called her husband's attention to the bloodstains, and he communicated with the Metropolitan Police, who, having examined the garments, took them to Scotland Yard. Since then two detectives were secreted on the premises, awaiting the stranger's return. Friday and Saturday passed by without his calling, but last evening he entered the shop a few minutes before closing time. A detective sergeant and a companion seized him without much ceremony, and he was taken straight to Leman Street Police Station. Meanwhile the prisoner accounted for the presence of the blood-marks by the assertion that he had cut his hand. It is stated, however, that his explanation was not altogether consistent, as he spoke of cutting himself last Saturday, and then, as if recollecting himself, said he had also cut his hand previously. He further stated that he had had the garments by him, at his lodgings, for two or three weeks, but he refused to give his address. The prisoner is of good physique. On enquiry at Leman Street Police Station at midnight it was stated that no person suspected of participation in the Whitechapel murders remained under arrest.

Details of the release of this suspect appeared in the *Daily News* of 9 October: 'A later communication from the Central News says: The man was liberated after the police had satisfied themselves of his innocence. The apparent inconsistency of his explanation was doubtless due to his embarrassment.'

This report referring to a customer leaving bloodstained overcoat and trousers at a cleaning establishment near Holborn, and subsequently being arrested on his return by waiting detectives, seems to be the basis of the police denial of the lodger story. The cleaning establishment customer was arrested and taken to Leman Street police station, and released when he provided a satisfactory explanation. The parallels are there, and it would have provided an easy, though not very convincing way for the police to dispose of the lodger story which they wished to keep so very secret in view of their hunt for the man.

The report does seem finally to have had the desired effect, and the story was, apparently, followed up no further by the press. It would appear to be the earliest evidence of the police efforts to silence the story of the American suspect, and signally heralds the commencement of the search for this man.

As we have seen, the finding of the piece of bloody apron in Goulston Street indicated that the killer fled eastward from the scene of the Eddowes murder towards Whitechapel, avoiding the arterial route of Aldgate High Street, which would not give the cover afforded by the back streets. A route via Wentworth Street, Osborn Street, across Whitechapel Road, Church Lane, and across Commercial Road; or via Old Montague Street, Black Lion Yard, across Whitechapel Road, Fieldgate Street, then Greenfield Street – or Plumber's Row, Charles Street, into Greenfield Street – would lead directly back to Batty Street, avoiding too much use, other than crossing, of the major roads. It should also be noted that the lodgings could have been carefully chosen as having more than one way of exit or entry.

The location of the lodger's address was ideal for all the murders. He would have been able to come and go as he pleased, and might even have had more than one lodging room paid for in the area, thus giving himself more than one haven to retreat to. Where *had* he fled to? Was there another room ready for him in the area to cater for such an eventuality? If he fled his lodgings, leaving many of his belongings and attendant clues at that location, it would be obvious to him that the police would now know who he was.

Another story which emerged at this time, and which uncannily fits our fleeing suspect, appeared in the *Daily News* of Friday 19 October, entitled 'Remarkable Story'. It is all the more remarkable since the description furnished fits the Littlechild Suspect exactly, and indicates habits of approaching prostitutes, acting furtively when observed, and changing his clothing to alter his appearance:

The City Police have under observation a man whose movements in Whitechapel, Mile End and Bermondsey are attended with suspicion. A man, who is said to be an American, was arrested in Bermondsey at one o'clock yesterday morning, and taken to the police station. His conduct, demeanour, and appearance gave rise to great suspicion, and his apprehension and general particulars were wired to the City Police. Following this a conference took place yesterday afternoon between a young man named John Lardy, of Redman's Row, Mile End, and the head of the detective department at the Old Jewry, at which he stated as follows: 'At 10.30 last night I was with a friend and a young woman outside the Grave Maurice Tavern, opposite the London Hospital, when I noticed a man whom I had never seen before come across the road, look into each compartment of the tavern, and enter the house. He came out again directly, and carefully looked up and down the road, and then walked over the road to the front of the hospital, where two women were standing talking. They were, I believe, loose women. The man said something to them, but I did not hear his words. The women shook their heads and said, "No." I said to my friend, "What a funny-looking man! I wonder if he is the murderer." My friend replied, "Let's follow him." We said goodnight to our friend and followed the man. When opposite the Pavilion Theatre he drew himself up in an instant, and looked carefully round. We believe that he saw us following him, and he disappeared into a doorway. We stopped for a moment or two, and he came out of his hiding-place and went into a newspaper shop next door. During the whole time we saw him his right hand was in his overcoat pocket, apparently clutching something. He bought a paper at the shop, and folded it up on his chest with his left hand, and then left the shop, looking up and down the road as he did so, and carefully reading the placards outside the shop window. He afterwards started off towards Aldgate, and we followed him. When he got to the corner of Duke Street (the street leading to Mitre Square) he turned, and, seeing that we were following him, recrossed the road and walked back to Leman Street and went down it. When he reached Royal Mint Street he went into King Street, which is very narrow, and my friend and I ran round to the other end of the street, hoping to see him come out there. Just as we got to the other end of King Street we heard a door close, and we waited to see if the man reopened it, for we felt sure that he was the man, although we had not seen him go into the house. We both waited for 25 minutes, when we saw the same man come out of the house. He came up the street, and we stepped back and allowed him to pass, and he went in the direction of the Whitechapel Road. He went away so quickly that we lost sight of him in the fog, which was then very thick. The time then was just after 12. When he reappeared from the house we noticed that he was very differently dressed to what he was when we first saw him, the most noticeable being his overcoat. At first he was wearing a sort of frock coat reaching his knees only, but when he came out of the house in King Street he had on a large overcoat which reached to within three inches of the ground. From what I could see he appeared to be between forty and forty-five years of age, and from 5ft.11in. to 6ft. high.' (A man 5ft.11in. was placed before Lardy, who said, 'My man was a little taller than you.') 'He wore a low hat with a square crown, but I cannot describe his trousers or boots. He had the appearance of an American. His cheek-bones were high and prominent, his face thin, cheeks sunken, and he had a moustache only, his cheeks and chin being clean-shaven. The moustache was, I believe, a false one, for it was all awry, one end pointing upward and the other towards the ground. His hair was dark, apparently black, and somewhat long.'

From what has since come to the knowledge of the police it is inferred that on leaving King Street, the stranger made his way over London Bridge into Bermondsey, where he was apprehended, and there is no doubt that the description of the Bermondsey and King Street men tally in nearly every particular.

There was a brief report of the arrest in the *Manchester Evening News* of 18 October:

From the Central News Agency. Another man has just been arrested in Whitechapel by police on information received on suspicion of being concerned in the East End murders. He is about 35 years of age and has recently been living in Whitechapel. He is somewhat confused lately and will be detained pending further inquiries.

The next significant articles regarding the same arrest appeared in various newspapers on Saturday 20 October, and it was reported in the *Eastern Post and City Chronicle* as follows:

> On Thursday, the City Police had under observation a man whose movements in Whitechapel, Mile End, and Bermondsey are attended with suspicion. A man said to be an American was arrested in Bermondsey at 1 o'clock Thursday morning and taken to the police station. His conduct, demeanour, and appearance gave rise to great suspicion and his apprehension and general particulars were wired to the City Police.

The City Police interest, of course, was that they were hunting the Mitre Square killer. A report in the *East Anglian Daily Times* of the same date refers to this arrest but also includes some strange police denials, obviously indicating that the wrong man had been arrested:

> The Press Association reporter was informed today by the City Police that there is no truth whatever in the report of the arrest of an American in Bermondsey, and that no such statement as reported had been made. At the City Detective Office on inquiry last night it was found that no person was under arrest at present. The house-to-house search is completed, and has led to no result of any value. The householders have offered the fullest assistance to the police throughout the work of inspection.

The last thing the police wanted to admit was that they were seeking an American suspect, and that they had taken in the wrong man.

The tenacious witness, John Lardy, was felt to be so important that he warranted being seen by the head of detectives at Old Jewry. The only reason for this can be that his description of the suspicious man fitted that of the one the police were seeking, the missing lodger – and it also fits perfectly the American Littlechild Suspect. The man the police did arrest on the strength of this information, in Bermondsey, was obviously of very similar appearance, but younger and not the man whom Lardy and his friend had lost in the fog. As a result the man was released, and the police denied the arrest. They must have paled when they saw that their star witness had told his story to a reporter and it had appeared in the *Daily News*.

Do we now also have the answer to another minor mystery in the story of the Whitechapel murders? It is very important to note that the City Police were most interested in this American suspect, but that they denied all knowledge to the press and refused to discuss it. In his report to the Home Office on the Eddowes' murder, dated 27 October, Inspector McWilliam, head of the City Police detectives, makes no mention whatsoever of the suspect.

The Home Office, undoubtedly aware of the rumours surrounding this hunted man, obviously felt it strange that McWilliam should make no mention of the witness Lardy, the suspect, or the Bermondsey arrest. All that he had mentioned were the circumstances of the murder, the victim, Eddowes, enquiries made in lunatic asylums and the Lusk kidney episode. Indeed, Home Office officials show their surprise at this in notes made on the covering report dated 30 October (Ref. HO144/221/A49301C), where they state:

Mr Murdoch [Home Office Principal clerk]
This report tells very little.

i. The City Police are wholly 'at fault' as regards the detection of the murderer.

ii. The word on the wall was 'Jewes', not 'Juwes'. This is important; unless it's a mere clerical error.
[In margin] Not so I believe, GL. [Godfrey Lushington, Permanent Under Secretary to the Home Secretary]

iii. The ½ kidney sent to Mr Lusk is *human*. The printed report of the Inquest contains much more information than this. They evidently want to tell us nothing.
[In margin] I don't think so, GL.
?Shall we ask them

A. Did the writing on the wall resemble 'Jack the Ripper's', or the enclosed? [Presumably the 'From hell' letter]

B. Could the ½ kidney possibly be part of the victim's kidney?

WTB [unknown civil servant] Mr Lushington, Have you any private information from 30.10.88 Met. Police on the above points, or a facsimile of Jack the Ripper's letters. CW [probably C. B. Stuart-Wortley, a civil servant] Oct.30.
It is I think undesirable to ask these questions officially, but when Mr Matthews [the Home Secretary] comes to town I would advise that he should ask Sir J. Fraser [Commissioner of

the City of London Police] to come to the HO. He will then have full particulars. GL 30 Oct. 1888.

Why all this secrecy surrounding a murder suspect? Was it something the police wanted to keep to themselves?

Our research has revealed that despite police denials Scotland Yard, at this very time, were in communication with the Chief of Police of San Francisco concerning their suspect and were asking for samples of his handwriting. Who was this man? The *New York Times* of 23 November revealed that on the last day of October, Police Chief Patrick Crowley of San Francisco informed Scotland Yard that he had located specimens of the handwriting they required.

What is even more extraordinary about this suspect is the fact that the police were probably aware of his presence in England even before the Ripper murders, and that he was the subject of a large dossier kept by Scotland Yard. Chief Inspector John Littlechild, head of the then Secret Department, had a particular interest in Americans visiting England because of American support for the Irish cause. This man had relatives in Liverpool, a town full of Irish immigrant workers and, of course, the major port linking with the United States.

Is this why the killer lay low for over five weeks before killing again? The hunt was under way, the suspect was on the run, and the police knew who they were looking for.

Chapter 11

Bloody Finale

'The horrors of the scalpel and the amputating-knife.'

The Ripper's final foray was the most spectacular of all. It took place forty days after the 'double event' and was different from the preceding cases in several ways. The victim, though a prostitute, was young and attractive; she was killed indoors; and she was more horribly and extensively mutilated than any of the other victims. The murder occurred in the early morning of Friday 9 November 1888, the day of the Lord Mayor's Show.

Twenty-five-year-old Mary Jane Kelly, also known as 'Ginger' because of her hair colour, was murdered in her poorly furnished and uncarpeted room, number 13 Miller's Court, 26 Dorset Street, Spitalfields. Of all the victims she is the most mysterious. It is not even certain that Mary Kelly was her real name. Genealogical researchers are still trying to positively identify her, and her family, and many believe that the true identity of the victim is still unknown.

Much of the controversy surrounding Kelly is a result of the wildly conflicting evidence concerning *when* she died, certain witnesses claiming to have seen and even spoken to her after she was known to have been dead.

The only way to piece together the story of the Kelly murder is to examine the surviving inquest evidence. The police and Home Office records in respect of the Kelly murder are sparse, and much appears to be missing. The inquest, too, was subject to controversy.

Before the inquest even began, a member of the jury said, 'I do not see why we should have the inquest thrown upon our shoulders, when the murder did not happen in our district, but in Whitechapel.' Mr Hammond, the coroner's officer, replied, 'It did not happen in Whitechapel.' The coroner, Mr MacDonald, then spoke severely to the juror, saying, 'Do you think that we do not know what we are doing here, and that we do not know our own district? The jury are summoned in the ordinary way, and they have no business to object. If they persist in their objection I shall know how to deal with them. Does any juror persist in objecting?' The juror replied, 'We are summoned for the Shoreditch district. This affair happened in Spitalfields.' The coroner retorted, 'It happened within my district.' Another jury member chipped in, 'This is not my district. I come from Whitechapel, and Mr Baxter is my coroner.' The exasperated MacDonald replied, 'I am not going to discuss the subject with jurymen at all. If any juryman says he distinctly objects, let him say so,' and he paused for a response. There being none he continued, 'I may tell the jurymen that jurisdiction lies where the body lies, not where it was found, if there was doubt as to the district where the body was found.'

No further objections followed and the jury was sworn. They were then conducted by Inspector Abberline to view the body, an unpleasant duty for coroners' juries in those days. The body was 'decently coffined' in the mortuary adjoining Shoreditch Church. After this they were taken to Miller's Court to view the scene of the crime.

When the inquest hearing began, the coroner addressed the members of the press present and told them that a great fuss had been made in some papers about the jurisdiction of the coroner, and who should hold the inquest. He had not had any communication with Mr Wynne Baxter on the subject and the body was in his jurisdiction, it had been taken to his mortuary, and there was an end of it. There was no foundation in the reports that had appeared. In a previous case of murder which had occurred in his district the body was carried to the nearest mortuary, which was in another district. The inquest was then held by Mr Baxter who made no objection. The jurisdiction was where the body lay.

The inquest papers are headed with the name Marie Jeanette Kelly, according to her man friend the name she used. However, all the witnesses who knew her state they called her Mary Jane. Much of the information concerning her derives from this man friend, her ex-live-in lover, Joseph Barnett, a labourer and latterly a fish porter at Billingsgate Market. At the time of the inquest he was living at 21 Portpool Lane, Gray's Inn Road, his sister's address, and had been out of work for three or four months.

He had seen the body and had identified it by the ear and the eyes, which were all that he could recognise. He was positive that it was the same woman he had lived with. He had lived with her for eighteen months, eight of them in Room 13 Miller's Court, where the body was found. He had separated from her on 30 October because he was not earning enough money and she was resorting to prostitution. She took in another prostitute which he objected to. He left her between 5 and 6 p.m. that day.

He had last seen her alive between 7.30 and 7.45 p.m. the night before she was found. He was with her about an hour and they were on friendly terms. He told her when he left that he had no work and was very sorry that he had nothing to give her. They had not drunk together and she was quite sober. He claimed that whilst with him she had been of sober habits, although she had got drunk several times in his presence. With them that evening was another female, who had also lived in the court, and was the first to leave. He had left shortly afterwards at about 8 p.m.

Kelly had often told Barnett of her parents and had said that she was born in Limerick, and was twenty-five years old. From Ireland she had gone to Wales when still very young. Her father's name was John Kelly and he was a ganger at some iron works in Carmarthenshire or Caernarvonshire. She was married in Wales, possibly when she was sixteen, to a man named Davis or Davies, who was killed in some sort of explosion. She moved to Cardiff to live with a cousin. Whilst there she spent eight or nine months in an infirmary. She had said that she had one sister who was a traveller with materials from marketplace to marketplace, and was respectable. This sister was very fond of her. She also had brothers living in London and one was in the army. Another brother was named Henry. She had come to London about four years ago and had been resorting to prostitution for some time.

After leading an immoral life in Cardiff she had gone to a 'gay house' in the West End of London. A gentleman had induced her to go to France. She had returned after only two weeks and gone to live for some time in Ratcliffe Highway. Then she lived with a man called Morganstone opposite the Commercial Gas Works, Stepney. She had also described a man named Joseph Fleming who came to a 'bad house' in Pennington Street where she stayed. He was a mason's plasterer lodging in Bethnal Green Road and she was very fond of him.

Barnett had first met her in Commercial Street, where they had a drink together one Friday. He had met her again the next day and had then arranged to live with her. He took lodgings in George Street, after which they moved to Miller's Court. He stated that at her request he had read to her the reports of the previous

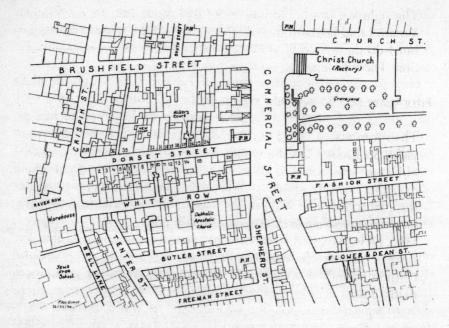

Location of Miller's Court

Whitechapel murders. He had never heard her express any fear of anyone.

Thomas Bowyer, of 37 Dorset Street, stated that at 10.45 a.m on Friday 9 November he went to Kelly's room to collect the rent for his employer, Mr McCarthy, whose shop was at the corner of Miller's Court. The room was rented at 4s. 6d. per week and she was 29s. in arrears. He knocked and received no answer. He found a broken window and pulled the curtain aside, then looked in and saw two lumps of flesh on the bedside table. Looking again he saw the bloody body on the bed and a pool of blood on the floor. He immediately returned to report his discovery to McCarthy.

John McCarthy, grocer and lodging-house keeper, of 27 Dorset Street, was informed by Bowyer that he had seen blood in the room and immediately went there with him. On seeing the body he was unable to say anything for a little time, but when he recovered he went with Bowyer to Commercial Street police station to inform the police. There he saw Inspector Walter Beck, who went to the scene shortly after 11 a.m. with beat constables.

Later McCarthy, still reeling from the shock of such a brutal sight, told a reporter from *The Times*:

The sight we saw . . . looked more like the work of a devil than a man. I had heard a great deal about the Whitechapel murders, but I do declare to God I never expected to see such a sight as this. The whole scene is more than I can describe.

Fifty years on, Walter Dew recalled:

The room was pointed out to me. I tried the door. It would not yield. So I moved to the window, over which, on the inside, an old coat was hanging to act as a curtain and to block the draught from the hole in the glass. Inspector Beck pushed the coat to one side and peered through the aperture. A moment later he staggered back, his face as white as a sheet. 'For God's sake, Dew,' he cried, 'don't look.' I ignored the order, and took my place at the window. When my eyes had become accustomed to the dim light I saw a sight which I shall never forget to my dying day.

Inspector Beck immediately sent for the doctor, ordered a search, and closed Miller's Court to all persons. McCarthy further stated that he knew Mary Jane Kelly and had seen the body and had no doubt as to the identity. He had often seen her the worse for drink, when she was noisy, but when sober she was a very quiet woman.

Mary Ann Cox was a widow living at Room 5 Miller's Court, which was the last room at the top of the court, opposite Kelly's. Mrs Cox explained that she got her living on the streets as best she could. She had known Kelly for eight or nine months. At about midnight on the Thursday she saw Kelly, very much the worse for drink, in Dorset Street. Kelly went up the court in front of Mrs Cox. She was in company with a man aged about thirty-six, around 5ft.5in. tall, stout, fresh-complexioned with blotches on his face, clean-shaven on his chin but with small sandy side whiskers and a thick carroty moustache. He was shabbily dressed, wearing a longish black coat and a hard black billycock hat. He was carrying a quart pot of ale. Kelly was dressed, as far as Mrs Cox could remember, in a dark, shabby linsey frock and a red knitted crossover around her shoulders, but with no hat or bonnet. As Mrs Cox passed she said, 'Good night, Mary,' and Kelly replied, 'I am going to have a song.' The man banged the door shut. A lamp facing Kelly's door cast enough light for Mrs Cox to see. Mrs Cox went into her room and could hear Kelly singing 'A violet I plucked from Mother's grave when a boy'. Mrs Cox stayed in her room for fifteen minutes and then went out again. At this time she could still hear Kelly singing in her room and the light was on.

At about 1 a.m. Mrs Cox returned to Miller's Court to find that Kelly was still singing in her room with the light on. After warming her hands in her room 'as it was raining', Mrs Cox again went out, to find that Kelly's singing had not abated. Her light was still on but nothing could be seen as the blinds were drawn. At 3 a.m. Mrs Cox finally returned to her room and found that by then the light in Kelly's room was out and all was silent. She couldn't sleep as she was upset, and she heard no sound other than the rain. Later, she heard men go out to work in the market, although, in response to a question, she stated that only one man living in the court worked in the market. At about 5.45 a.m., too late for the market, she heard someone go out, but from which room she could not tell as she heard no door close and no footsteps pass her room. She conceded it may have been a policeman. She further stated that she would know the man again and that she had heard no cry of 'murder' during the night but would have if there had been one.

Elizabeth Prater, wife of William Prater, a boot machinist who had deserted her five years previously, lived in Room 20 Miller's Court, which was situated upstairs, above Kelly's room. She went out at about 9 p.m. on the Thursday evening and returned at about 1 a.m. and stood on the corner by McCarthy's shop for about twenty minutes. She was waiting for a man she lived with but he did not arrive. The shop was open and she went in and spoke for a short while with Mr McCarthy, then ascended to her room, up the stairs adjacent to the partition at the rear of Kelly's room. By this time it was about 1.30 a.m. She saw no glimmer through the partition but admitted that she might not have noticed if there was a light as she took no particular notice. She heard no movement in the room.

On entering her room she placed two tables against the door as a barricade, possibly because of fears over the recent murders. She had been drinking and immediately went to sleep. At about 3.30 or 4 a.m. she was disturbed by a kitten walking across her neck and heard a suppressed cry of 'Oh, murder!' in a female voice nearby. She was used to hearing such cries and took no notice. She heard nothing else and fell asleep again, not waking until 5 a.m. She went down into the court at about 5.30 a.m. and saw no one, apart from two or three carmen harnessing their horses in Dorset Street. She then went across to the Ten Bells public house at the corner of

Church Street at about 5.45 a.m. and had some rum. After her early drink she returned to her room and slept until 11 a.m. She stated that whilst she was waiting outside the court during the night, Mrs Cox could have passed without her noticing her. She had not heard Kelly singing.

Caroline Maxwell, the wife of a Dorset Street lodging-house keeper, Henry Maxwell, claimed to have known Kelly for four months as 'Mary Jane', and also to have known Joseph Barnett. She also knew that Barnett had left Kelly because she was living as an 'unfortunate'. She was warned by the coroner to be careful when giving her evidence as it did not agree with that of other witnesses.

Mrs Maxwell was on speaking terms with Kelly, but had not seen her for three weeks until the morning of Friday the 9th. Between 8 and 8.30 a.m. she was positive she had seen Kelly standing at the corner of Miller's Court. Mrs Maxwell was carrying plates that her husband had to take care of to the house opposite. She spoke with Kelly across the street and asked her what brought her up so early. Kelly replied, 'Oh, Carrie, I feel so bad, I have the horrors of drink upon me.' Kelly stated that she had been drinking for some days past and she had just had a drink and brought it all up, and Mrs Maxwell saw it in the road. Kelly indicated that she had been to 'Ringer's', the Britannia public house, at the corner of Dorset Street and Commercial Street. Mrs Maxwell took her leave, saying that she pitied her feelings.

Mrs Maxwell went on to Bishopsgate to get her husband's breakfast, returning about thirty minutes later at around 8.45 a.m. She then saw Kelly speaking with a man outside the Britannia public house. The man was short and stout, aged about thirty, and was dressed as a market porter in dark clothes and a sort of plaid coat. She was doubtful if she could identify him. Kelly was wearing a dark dress, a black velvet bodice and a maroon shawl round her neck, but no hat. Mrs Maxwell had seen them at a distance of about twenty-five yards.

Sarah Lewis, a laundress, of 24 Great Pearl Street, went to Miller's Court to stay with Mrs Keyler, who lived at number 2, on the left on the first floor, as she had 'had a few words with her husband'. It was 2.30 a.m. when she arrived at the court and she saw a man standing alone in Dorset Street, opposite the court, outside the lodging house. She had noted the time from the Spitalfields Church clock. The man appeared to be looking up the court as if waiting for someone. She described him as short and stout and wearing a black wideawake hat. Another young man with a woman passed along the street. Mrs Lewis then went into the Keylers' and fitfully dozed in a chair. She woke at about 3.30 a.m. and heard the church clock strike the half-hour. A little before 4 a.m. she heard a female voice shout loudly, once, 'Murder!' The voice sounded like that of a young woman and was from the direction of Kelly's room. There was only one scream and she took no notice of it, as such cries were often heard. She did not leave the Keylers' until 5.30 p.m. as the police would let no one out.

Asked if she had seen any suspicious persons in the district Mrs Lewis recalled that on the Wednesday night, at about 8 p.m., she was in company with another female in Bethnal Green Road when they were accosted by a suspicious man carrying a black bag about nine inches long. He invited one of the women to accompany him but they refused. He went away but came back again saying he would treat them. He put his bag down and picked it up again, saying, 'What are you frightened about? Do you think I've got anything in the bag?' They disliked his appearance and ran away. He was short with a pale face and dark moustache, and was aged about forty. He was wearing dark clothes: a brownish overcoat with black short coat underneath, and a high round felt hat. She claimed that when she had gone to Dorset Street at 2.30 on the morning of the murder, she had seen the same man, talking with a woman, in Commercial Street, with the bag in his hand but no overcoat. As she entered Miller's Court they were standing at the corner of Dorset Street.

Julia Venturney, a widow and charwoman, living at number 1 Miller's Court with a man named Harry Owen, stated that she knew both Kelly and Barnett. She said that she had last seen Kelly at 10 a.m. on Thursday and had slept in the court that night and heard nothing. She had known Kelly and Barnett about four months and confirmed the circumstances of Barnett leaving her. She said that Barnett was very fond of Kelly and frequently gave her money but would not stay with her whilst she led that sort of life. She stated that Kelly had broken the window at number 13 a few weeks previously whilst drunk.

Another interesting remark by Venturney was that there was another Joe in Kelly's life, believed to be a costermonger, whom she was very fond of and who had ill-used her since she had been living with Barnett.

Maria Harvey, a laundress, of 3 New Court, Dorset Street, said that she had slept the Monday and Tuesday nights prior to the murder with Kelly, before taking a room at the above address. She had last seen her at about 6.55 p.m. on the Thursday night in her room, when Barnett called. Harvey said, 'Well, Mary Jane, I shall not see you this evening again,' and left. Kelly and Barnett seemed to be on the best of terms, she said. Harvey left in Kelly's room a black overcoat, two dirty cotton shirts, a boy's shirt, a little girl's white petticoat, a black crêpe bonnet, and a pawn ticket for a grey shawl upon which 2s. had been lent. She had subsequently been shown an overcoat, by the police, which was the one she had left there. She had been with Kelly all Thursday afternoon.

Shortly after 11 a.m. Dr George Bagster Phillips, H Division police surgeon, was called, and arrived at the scene at 11.15. He looked through the broken window and saw that the body on the bed was undoubtedly dead. He described the entrance door to Kelly's room, and produced photographs of the location. The door was locked and there were two broken panes of glass in the smaller of two rear windows facing out into the court. He looked through the lower of the two broken panes and satisfied himself that the dead woman was beyond human aid. He remained there, believing that it was advisable that entry should not be effected at that time.

At 1.30 p.m. the door was forced open by McCarthy under the direction of Superintendent Arnold. The door knocked against the bedside table when it was forced, the bedstead being between the table and the wooden partition in the room. The doctor was the first to enter the room and saw the mutilated remains lying two-thirds over towards the nearest edge of the bed. She was wearing only a linen undergarment. He examined the body and felt sure that it had been moved, after the fatal wound had been inflicted, from the side of the bed against the partition. A large quantity of blood under the bedstead and the saturated condition of the palliasse, pillow and sheet at the top corner of the bedstead nearest to the wooden partition led him to the conclusion that the severance of the right carotid artery, the immediate cause of death, had been inflicted whilst she was lying at that side of the bedstead with her head and neck in the top corner.

At this stage the jury had no questions and that was the sum total of the doctor's evidence that was heard. It was understood that further medical evidence would be given at a future hearing, though this was not to be the case. There was then a break of a few minutes and when the jury resumed their seats the coroner said, 'It has come to my ears that somebody has been making a statement to some of the jury as to their right to and duty of being here. Has anyone during the interval spoken to the jury, saying that they should not be here today?' Some of the jury replied in the negative and the inquest resumed.

Inspector Beck gave his evidence, also stating that he had not been aware that Kelly was known to the police.

Inspector Abberline stated that he was in charge of the case and that he had arrived at Miller's Court at about 11.30 on the Friday morning. He explained the delay in entering the room owing to an intimation from Inspector Beck that the hounds had been sent for, and a reply had been received that they were on the way. It was not until the arrival of Superintendent Arnold, who stated that the order to wait for the dogs in the event of a murder being discovered had been countermanded, that the door was forced.

Abberline had taken an inventory of the contents of the room and found traces of a large fire having been kept up in the grate. The ashes in the fireplace were later sifted through and remnants of clothing were found, including a portion of the brim of a hat, and a skirt. It appeared as if a large quantity of women's clothing had been burnt. When asked why the fire had been lit, Abberline replied:

> I can only imagine that it was to make a light for the man to see what he was doing. There was only one small candle in the room, on the top of a broken wine glass. An impression has gone abroad that the murderer took away the key of the room. Barnett informs me that it has been missing some time, and since it has been lost they have put their hand through the broken window, and moved back the catch. It is quite easy. There was a man's clay pipe in the room, and Barnett informed me that he smoked it.

With this Abberline's evidence was concluded and the coroner again addressed the jury, telling them that he felt that it was unnecessary for a second hearing to go through the same evidence again, causing expense and trouble, and that they merely had to find the cause of death. It would then be up to the police authorities to deal with the case and satisfy themselves as to any persons they may suspect.

> I do not want to take it out of your hands. It is for you to say whether at an adjournment you will hear minutiae of the

evidence, or whether you will think it is a matter to be dealt with in the police courts later on, and that, this woman having met with her death by the carotid artery having been cut, you will be satisfied to return a verdict to that effect. From what I learn the police are content to take the future conduct of the case. It is for you to say whether you will close the enquiry today; if not, we shall adjourn for a week or fortnight, to hear the evidence that you may desire.

This said, and leaving the jury in no doubt as to what he himself thought, the coroner firmly passed the ball into their court. After consultation with his colleagues the foreman stated that they felt they had heard sufficient evidence to be able to return a verdict. 'What is your verdict?' said the coroner. The foreman replied, 'Wilful murder against some person or persons unknown.'

And that was that as far as the inquest into Mary Kelly's death was concerned. There were definite signs that the coroner was on the side of the police, who had clearly indicated their interest in having a quick inquest at which they would have to reveal little of their investigation. Unlike the probing, lengthy inquests held by Wynne Baxter, this was an amazingly short one, involving no further sitting. And this at the climax of a baffling series of killings involving the employment of hundreds of police officers.

The paucity of accurate medical evidence on the grisly find at Miller's Court was remedied a hundred years later when, in 1988, a set of medical notes made by Dr Thomas Bond came to light among a bundle of documents posted anonymously to New Scotland Yard. Bond had worked with Dr Phillips at Miller's Court, and during the subsequent post-mortem, and his notes constitute the most detailed account of Mary Kelly's appalling injuries:

The body was lying naked [in fact the remains of her chemise were over her shoulders] in the middle of the bed, the shoulders flat, but the axis of the body inclined to the left side of the bed. The head was turned on the left cheek. The left arm was close to the body with the forearm flexed at a right angle and lying across the abdomen, the right arm was slightly abducted from the body and rested on the mattress, the elbow bent and the forearm supine with the fingers clenched. The legs were wide apart, the left thigh at right angles to the trunk and the right forming an obtuse angle with the pubes.

The whole of the surfaces of the abdomen and thighs was removed and the abdominal cavity emptied of its viscera. The breasts were cut off, the arms mutilated by several jagged wounds and the face hacked beyond recognition of the features and the tissues of the neck were severed all round down to the bone. The viscera were found in various parts, viz. the uterus and kidneys with one breast under the head, the other breast by the right foot, the liver between the feet, the intestines by the right side and the spleen by the left side of the body.

The flaps removed from the abdomen and thighs were on a [bedside] table.

The bed clothing at the right corner was saturated with blood, and on the floor beneath was a pool of blood covering about two feet square. The wall by the right side of the bed and in a line with the neck was marked by blood which had struck it in a number of separate splashes.

That same morning Doctors Phillips, Bond and Gordon Brown carried out a post-mortem at the mortuary. Dr Bond's newly discovered notes on the examination also reveal that Mary's throat had been cut with such ferocity that the tissues had been severed right down to the spinal column and the fifth and sixth vertebrae had been deeply notched by the knife. The air passage had been cut at the lower part of the larynx through the cartilage. There were also terrible mutilations to the face: it was gashed in all directions, the nose, cheeks, eyebrows and ears being partly removed. The lips were blanched and cut by several incisions running obliquely down to the chin. There were also numerous cuts extending irregularly across all the features.

The injuries inflicted on Mary's torso and limbs exceeded anything the Ripper had done before.

Both breasts were removed by more or less circular incisions, the muscles down to the ribs being attached to the breasts. The intercostals between the 4th, 5th and 6th ribs were cut and the contents of the thorax visible through the openings.

The skin and tissues of the abdomen from the costal arch to the pubes were removed in three large flaps. The right thigh was denuded in front to the bone, the flap of skin including the external organs of generation and part of the right buttock. The left thigh was stripped of skin, fascia and muscles as far as the knee.

The left calf showed a long gash through skin and tissues to the deep muscles and reaching from the knee to 5in. above the ankle.

Both arms and forearms had extensive and jagged wounds. The right thumb showed a small superficial incision about 1in. long, with extravasation [outflow] of blood in the skin and there were several abrasions on the back of the hand and forearm showing the same condition.

On opening the thorax it was found that the right lung was minimally adherent by old firm adhesions. The lower part of lung was broken and torn away. The left lung was intact; it was adherent at the apex and there were a few adhesions over the side. In the substances of the lung were several nodules of consolidation. The pericardium was open below and the heart absent.

The *Suffolk Chronicle* of 17 November reported:

As early as half past seven on Saturday morning Dr Phillips, assisted by Dr Bond (Westminster), Dr Gordon Brown (City), Dr Duke (Spitalfields), and Dr Phillips' assistant, made an exhaustive post-mortem examination of the body at the mortuary adjoining the Whitechapel Church. It is known that after Dr Phillips had 'fitted' the cut portions of the body into their proper places no portion was missing. At the first examination, which was only of a cursory character, it was thought that a portion of the body had gone, but this is not the case. The examination was most minutely made, and lasted upwards of 2½ hours, after which the mutilated portions were sewn to the body, and therefore the coroner's jury will be spared the unpleasant duty of witnessing the horrible spectacle presented to those who discovered the murder.

In the earlier cases the murderer must have attacked from the right side of the victim. In the case of Mary Kelly this would have been impossible because there would not have been room for him between the wooden partition and the bed. There is also the evidence of defensive wounds on her hands and arms indicating that she may have been aware of the initial attack on her; this is also indicated by the cry of 'Murder!' that was heard – if it was made by Kelly and not as the result of some other incident.

If the cry does not indicate the time of Kelly's death, then it is virtually impossible, from the evidence given, to say what time she did die. What medical evidence there is on this point is vague and, as we have seen, doctors of the era were notoriously inaccurate in their estimations. Factors that would have had a great effect in the case of Kelly were the extremely cold November day, the nakedness and evisceration of the body, and the delay, at least two hours and forty-five minutes, between the finding of the body and the doctor's first examination of it.

The other great difficulty about determining a time for the murder is the evidence of Mrs Maxwell, who claimed to have seen Kelly alive at around 8.30 a.m. and later around 9.30 a.m. This, in view of the foregoing evidence, cannot be correct unless we accept the fanciful theorising of those who assert that it was not Kelly who was murdered in Miller's Court. The authors feel that in the final reckoning we must accept that Mrs Maxwell was mistaken and had, in fact, seen Kelly on the Thursday morning. Her time of death, although by no means certain, we must place just before 4 a.m., in accordance with the cry heard by the witnesses.

Chapter 12

Aftermath

'But the night is past, the reign of terror that cast its shadow across the blue ether, and reflected an ominous cloud upon the fair land, is no more.'

In an effort to find a clue where no real clue existed, Dr Robert Anderson wrote to Dr Bond asking him to clarify 'the amount of surgical skill and anatomical knowledge probably possessed by the murderer or murderers.' To this end he asked Dr Bond to 'take up the medical evidence given at the several inquests and favour him [Sir Charles Warren] with your opinion on the matter'. Bond responded with a report dated 10 November 1888 (Ref. MEPO3/141 ff.151–7). This report has been published before but the authors feel it is too important to omit from this work.

I beg to report that I have read the notes of the 4 Whitechapel Murder [sic], viz.:

1. Buck's Row
2. Hanbury Street
3. Berners [sic] Street
4. Mitre Square

I have also made a post-mortem examination of the mutilated remains of a woman found yesterday in a small room in Dorset Street.

1. All five murders were no doubt committed by the same hand. In the first four the throats appear to have been cut from left to right. In the last case owing to the extensive mutilation it is impossible to say in what direction the fatal cut was made, but arterial blood was found on the wall in splashes close to where the woman's head must have been lying.

2. All the circumstances surrounding the murders lead me to

form the opinion that the women must have been lying down when murdered and in every case the throat was first cut.

3. In the four murders of which I have seen the notes only, I cannot form a very definite opinion as to the time that had elapsed between the murder and the discovery of the body.

In one case, that of Berners [sic] Street, the discovery appears to have been immediately after the deed. In Buck's Row, Hanbury St., & Mitre Square three or four hours only could have elapsed. In the Dorset Street case the body was lying on the bed at the time of my visit at 2 o'clock quite naked & mutilated as in the annexed report.

Rigor mortis had set in, but increased during the progress of the examination. From this it is difficult to say with any degree of certainty the exact time that had elapsed since death as the period varies from 6 to 12 hours before rigidity sets in. The body was comparatively cold at 2 o'clock & the remains of a recently taken meal were found in the stomach and scattered about over the intestines. It is, therefore, pretty certain that the woman must have been dead about 12 hours & the partly digested food would indicate that death took place about 3 or 4 hours after the food was taken, so one or 2 o'clock in the morning would be the probable time of the murder.

4. In all the cases there appears to be no evidence of struggling & the attacks were probably so sudden & made in such a position that the women could neither resist nor cry out – in the Dorset Street case the corner of the sheet to the right of the woman's head was much cut & saturated with blood, indicating that the face may have been covered with the sheet at the time of the attack.

5. In the four first cases the murderer must have attacked from the right side of the victim. In the Dorset Street case, he must have attacked from in front or from the left, as there would be no room for him between the wall and the part of the bed on which the woman was lying. Again the blood had flowed down on the right side of the woman and spurted on to the wall.

6. The murderer would not necessarily be splashed or deluged with blood, but his hands and arms must have been covered & parts of his clothing must certainly have been smeared with blood.

7. The mutilations in each case excepting the Berners [*sic*] Street one were all of the same character & showed clearly that in all the murders the object was mutilation.

8. In each case the mutilation was inflicted by a person who had no scientific nor anatomical knowledge – in my opinion he does not even possess the technical knowledge of a butcher or horse slaughterer or any person accustomed to cut up dead animals.

9. The instrument must have been a strong knife at least six inches long, very sharp, pointed at the top & about an inch in width. It may have been a clasp knife, a butcher's knife or a surgeon's knife. I think it was no doubt a straight knife.

10. The murderer must have been a man of physical strength & of great coolness & daring – there is no evidence that he had an accomplice. He must in my opinion be a man subject to periodical attacks of Homicidal & erotic mania. The character of the mutilations indicate that the man may be in a condition, sexually, that may be called satyriasis [a condition of being exceedingly oversexed]. It is of course possible that the Homicidal impulse may have developed from a revengeful or brooding condition of the mind, or that religious mania may have been the original disease but I do not think either hypothesis is likely. The murderer in external appearance is quite likely to be a quiet inoffensive-looking man probably middle aged & neatly & respectably dressed. I think he must be in the habit of wearing a cloak or overcoat or he could hardly have escaped notice in the streets if the blood on his hands or clothes were visible.

11. Assuming the murderer to be such a person as I have just described, he would probably be solitary & eccentric in his habits, also he is most likely to be a man without regular occupation, but with some small income or pension. He is possibly living among respectable persons who have some knowledge of his character and habits and who may have grounds for suspicion that he is not quite right in his mind at times. Such persons would probably be unwilling to communicate suspicions to the Police for fear of trouble or notorioty [*sic*], whereas if there were prospect of reward it might overcome their scruples. [Ref. MEPO3/141 ff.151–157]

This report of Bond's is most interesting, not least because it contains an early example of a professional medical man attempting to profile an unknown series killer. Points to note relevant to our own assessment of the case are as follows:

1. Bond clearly states that he feels all five murders were 'no doubt committed by the same hand'. This is obviously the origin of the 'canonical five' victims accepted by some police officers. Apart from the fact that her throat was cut, Bond offers no other reason for including Stride in this list.
2. He makes a misleading statement regarding the time that had elapsed between death and the finding of the bodies of Nichols, Chapman and Eddowes, stating that 'three or four hours only could have elapsed', which is totally erroneous.
3. He states that 'in all the cases there appears to be no evidence of struggling', which is inconsistent with the evidence in the cases of Chapman and Kelly, who both had defensive wounds as described.
4. He states that the mutilation 'was inflicted by a person who had no scientific nor anatomical knowledge', which does not agree with comments by other doctors who had seen the bodies.

On 10 November the Home Office sent a letter to the Commissioner of the Metropolitan Police, informing him of the Home Secretary's decision of, in connection with the Dorset Street murder, 'the grant of Her Majesty's gracious pardon to any accomplice, not being the person who contrived or actually committed the murder, who shall give such information and evidence as shall lead to the discovery and conviction of the murderer or murderers', and that the notice should be issued forthwith. At last Matthews was being seen to be making a positive, albeit futile, move in assisting in the detection of the murderer.

Throughout the Saturday and Sunday after the murder the police, under Inspectors Abberline and Reid, were busy making enquiries at lodging houses and anywhere else where information could be gleaned. Their efforts were without material result. The police made a complete census of Dorset Street, with special reference to anyone there on the night of the murder. Although a short thoroughfare, it was stated that there were no fewer than 1,200 men sleeping every night in the abundant common lodging houses in the street.

On the Sunday, at 3 a.m., an arrest was made as a result of the initiative of two young men, living in the neighbourhood of Dorset

Street, who had decided to act as amateur detectives and had been walking the streets on the lookout for suspicious persons. They noticed two men loitering in Dorset Street. The suspects separated and one of them was followed by the two youths into Houndsditch. They looked closely at him and noted that his appearance was that of a foreigner: about 5ft.8in. in height and wearing a long, pointed moustache. He was dressed in a long black overcoat and a deer-stalker hat. When near Bishopsgate Street, the young men spoke to a policeman, who stopped the stranger and took him into the nearby police station in order to confirm his identity. However, the man gave a satisfactory explanation and was released.

The same day, some men drinking at a beer house in Fish Street Hill began conversing about the Whitechapel murderer. A man named Brown, who lived at 9 Dorset Street, thought he detected blood marks on the coat of a stranger. On the latter's attention being called to it he said it was merely paint, but Brown insisted it was blood. Similar stains could be seen on the man's shirt, and he then admitted that they were bloodstains. Brown followed him from the house and when opposite Bishopsgate police station gave him into custody.

The prisoner claimed his name was George Compton. When brought before the inspector on duty he excitedly protested against being apprehended in the street, saying that in the present state of public feeling he might have been lynched. The same man had been arrested at Shadwell on Saturday by a police constable who considered his behaviour suspicious, but had been discharged. It was revealed that before he left the Fish Street Hill beer house he had, according to Brown, made contradictory statements about his place of residence and the locality in which he worked.

Compton did not bear any physical resemblance to the published description of the murderer, and he was later freed after the police had telegraphed the authorities at King David Lane station, Shadwell, and found his statements to be true.

At 10 p.m. that night, a man with a blackened face publicly proclaimed himself to be Jack the Ripper at the corner of Wentworth Street and Commercial Street, not far from the scene of the Dorset Street crime. This rash act resulted in two young men, one a discharged soldier, immediately seizing him. The 'great crowd' which always on a Sunday night paraded that neighbourhood raised a cry of 'Lynch him!' Sticks were brandished and the man was furiously attacked, and but for the timely intervention of the police, he would have been seriously injured. It took four constables, assisted by four civilians, to protect him from the infuriated crowd. The police took him to Leman Street police station where he refused to give any name, but asserted that he was a doctor at St George's Hospital.

He was aged about thirty-five, 5ft.7in. tall, with a dark complexion and dark moustache and wearing spectacles. He wore no waistcoat but had an ordinary jersey vest beneath his coat. In his pocket he had a double-peaked light check cap, and at the time of his arrest was bare-headed. He was detained in custody and it seemed at the time that the police considered his arrest of importance as his appearance corresponded with the description of the man wanted. He was eventually found to be Dr William Holt, aged twenty-four from Willesden, and attached to St George's Hospital. He stated that he had been walking round Whitechapel in various disguises hoping to discover the murderer. He was released the next day.

It was not until 6 p.m. on Monday 12 November that another witness appeared: George Hutchinson, an unemployed labourer who had known Kelly for three years, walked into Commercial Street police station and made a statement which was taken by Sergeant E. Bradshaw. He was then 'interrogated' by Inspector Abberline, who formed the opinion that his statement was true. Hutchinson's story was that at about 2 a.m. on the night of the murder he had met Kelly in Thrawl Street, near Flower and Dean Street. She said, 'Hutchinson, will you lend me sixpence?' He replied, 'I can't, I've spent all my money going down to Romford.' She said, 'Good morning, I must go and find some money.'

She walked away towards Thrawl Street, and a man coming in the opposite direction tapped her on the shoulder and said something to her at which they both laughed. Hutchinson watched. He heard Kelly say, 'All right.' The man said, 'You'll be all right for what I've told you.' He then put his right hand around her shoulders. He was carrying a 'kind of small parcel in his left hand with a kind of strap around it'.

Hutchinson told Abberline that he had occasionally given Kelly 'a few shillings'. He was surprised to see her with a man so well dressed, so he stood against the lamp outside the Queen's Head public house and watched them. When they walked past him, the stranger held his head down with his hat shading his eyes. Not to be foiled, Hutchinson stooped down and looked him in the face. At this the man looked at him in a stern manner. The couple then entered Dorset Street with Hutchinson following. They stood by the corner of Miller's Court for about three minutes.

The stranger then said something to Kelly, to which she replied, 'All right, my dear, come along, you will be comfortable.' At this he placed his arm on her shoulder and gave her a kiss. She said she had lost her handkerchief and he pulled out his own red handkerchief and gave it to her. They both then entered the court together and out of Hutchinson's sight.

Hutchinson went to the court to see if he could see them but he could not. He stood outside Miller's Court for about forty-five minutes to see if they would come out again. He then gave up his vigil and walked away.

Hutchinson was able to give a remarkably detailed description of the man: he was aged about thirty-four or thirty-five, height 5ft.6in., complexion pale, hair, eyes and eyelashes dark. He had a slight moustache curled up at each end and was surly-looking. He was wearing a long dark coat with collar and cuffs trimmed with astrakhan, a dark jacket underneath, light waistcoat, dark trousers, dark felt hat turned down in the middle, button boots and gaiters with white buttons. He wore a very thick gold chain, a white linen collar and a black tie with a horseshoe pin. His appearance was respectable. He walked 'very sharp' and was of Jewish appearance. Hutchinson stated that he would recognise him again. The police felt that this was a very important description, and it was circulated to all stations.

Abberline immediately arranged for two officers to accompany Hutchinson around the district for a few hours that night with a view to finding the man. It was also arranged that he would go with an officer at 11.30 the following morning to the Shoreditch mortuary to identify Kelly's body.

Hutchinson as a witness is very difficult to assess. There seems every possibility that he was the person seen by Sarah Lewis waiting outside Miller's Court. Nothing is known about him by which to judge his credibility, although Abberline seems to have been impressed by him. Even if the information he gave was accurate, the man he saw need not have been the murderer, although the time, if the murder occurred at about 4 a.m. is close.

The newspapers of 13 November were full of the resignation of Sir Charles Warren as Commissioner of the Metropolitan Police. Warren had handed in his resignation on Thursday 8 November, the day before the Kelly murder, although he would remain in his office until replaced. The resignation was the result of the building tensions between the Commissioner and his Home Office masters, with the strain reaching breaking point when Warren had the temerity to publish his feelings – without Home Office approval – in an article in *Murray's Magazine* on 'The Police of the Metropolis'.

On Monday 19 November the funeral of the last Ripper victim took place. As early as 10.30 a.m. a crowd had gathered outside Shoreditch Church, and despite the presence of a large body of police the road became blocked to traffic. Shortly after 12.30 p.m. the coffin was carried from the mortuary to an open car provided by Mr H. Wilton. There were three large wreaths on the coffin, which bore a plate with the simple legend: 'Marie Jeanette Kelly, died November 9, 1888, aged 25 years'. Two mourning coaches, the first containing Barnett, travelled via Hackney Road to the Roman Catholic cemetery at Leytonstone, where Kelly was buried.

On the morning of Wednesday 21 November rumours were broadcast of another murder, this time at 19 George Street, which ran between Flower and Dean Street and Thrawl Street, another rough area not far from Dorset Street. Most of the houses in the street were rented out as common lodging houses and were the resort of prostitutes and clients alike. As the story developed it was devalued first to attempted murder and finally to a prostitute-client dispute between one Annie Farmer, or 'Dark Sarah', who had a superficial wound to her throat, possibly self-inflicted, and an unknown man described as thirty-six years of age, 5ft.6in. tall, dark-complexioned, no whiskers and a black moustache. He was wearing a black jacket, vest and trousers, a round black felt hat and was of respectable appearance, and had made good his escape in the direction of Brick Lane when she had alleged an attack on her.

Farmer claimed to be thirty-four years of age but was probably older, and was 'a married woman of good appearance'. She was, however, of drunken habits and had been in custody in Commercial Street police station on many occasions.

On Friday 7 December, the new Commissioner, James Monro, reported to the Home Office that in connection with the recent murders in Whitechapel one inspector, nine sergeants, and 126 constables of the uniform branch of the force had been employed specially in plain clothes to patrol the neighbourhood of the murders with a view to preventing a repetition of the crimes.

The so-called 'Poplar Murder' took place in the early hours of the morning of Thursday 20 December 1888, when the body of a

woman was found in Clarke's Yard, Poplar, at 4.15 a.m. by PC
Robert Goulding, who was patrolling his beat. The woman was
identified as Rose Mylett and was thought by some to have been
murdered; she appeared to have been strangled. However, it was
possibly an accidental choking and was never satisfactorily resolved.
Although she was a prostitute it was not a Ripper killing.

On the last day of that eventful year the *East Anglian Daily
Times* printed a story in its ongoing coverage of 'The Whitechapel
Tragedies', subheaded 'Supposed Clue':

A gentleman who has for some time been engaged in philan-
thropic work in the East End recently received a letter, the
handwriting of which had previously attracted the attention of
the Post Office authorities on account of its similarity to that
of the writer of some of the letters signed 'Jack the Ripper'.
The police made enquiries, and ascertained that the writer was
known to his correspondent as a person intimately acquainted
with East End life, and that he was then a patient in a metropolitan hospital. It is stated that on inquiry at the hospital it was
discovered that the person sought had left without the consent
or knowledge of the hospital authorities, but that he has subsequently been seen, and is now under observation. The police
are of opinion that the last five murders were a series, and that
the first two were independently perpetrated. They believe the
murderer to live in the neighbourhood of Drury Lane – a locality
favourable for retirement after the deeds were done.

This interesting report contains an early indication that the police
had already discounted the murders of Emma Smith and Martha
Tabram as Ripper victims, and were concentrating on the 'canonical
five'.

Nevertheless, the grim shadow of Jack the Ripper was to continue
to fall over the slums of the East End. His name was certain to be
mentioned upon the finding of any fresh outrage, and frightened
women would continue to speak of him. The foul alleys and dark
courts of Whitechapel and its environs still harboured his evil spirit.

Chapter 13
The Ripper Still at Large?

'... so mystified and befogged ...'

At 12.50 a.m. on Wednesday 17 July 1889, the body of Alice McKenzie, a prostitute aged about forty, was found in Castle Alley, Whitechapel, by the patrolling beat PC, Walter Andrews. Her throat had been cut about two inches on the left side and the body was still warm. The constable saw no person nearby. PC Andrews blew his whistle and then saw Isaac Lewis Jacob of 12 Newcastle Place, Whitechapel, going towards Wentworth Street with a plate in his hand, on which he was going to fetch his supper. He stayed with the PC and they were immediately joined by Sergeant Bradshaw.

Bradshaw described the woman as aged forty to forty-five, 5ft.4 or 5in. tall, pale-complexioned, hair and eyes brown, top of left thumb missing and one tooth missing from the upper jaw. She was dressed in a red stuff bodice patched under the arms, and sleeves of maroon-coloured material, one black and one maroon-coloured stocking, brown stuff shirt, kilted brown linsey petticoat, white chemise and apron, paisley shawl, and button boots, all old and dirty.

She was lying on her right side with her clothing turned up to her waist, exposing her abdomen which had a deep zigzag cut extending across it. There was blood on the footpath.

Other constables from adjoining beats were summoned to assist, and Dr Phillips and the inspector on duty at Commercial Street police station were sent for, as was the local CID inspector, Edmund Reid. Dr Phillips examined the body and pronounced life extinct.

The Ripper murders were still fresh in the minds of the police and it was felt sufficiently important for the Commissioner, James Monro, to attend the scene. The body was afterwards taken to the Whitechapel mortuary. The area was thoroughly searched, but all that was found was an old clay pipe smeared with blood, and a farthing, both of which were lying under the body when it was removed. The usual enquiries were made at common lodging houses and coffee houses, but met with no success. After examining the body Dr Phillips' opinion was that 'the wounds had not been inflicted by the same hand as in the previous cases, inasmuch as the injuries in this case are not so severe and the cut on the stomach is not so direct.'

One person, a John Larkin Mills, was detained at 2.35 a.m., but was released at 4.30 a.m. when his story was checked out and was found to be satisfactory.

Monro, reporting to the Home Office later that day, stated:

I need not say that every effort will be made to discover the murderer, who, I am inclined to believe, is identical with the notorious Jack the Ripper of last year. It will be seen that in spite of ample Police precautions and vigilance the assassin has again succeeded in committing a murder and getting off without leaving the slightest clue to his identity. [Ref. HO144/ 221/A49301I ff.5–6].

Dr Bond was again asked to examine the body, and he called on Dr Phillips, who accompanied him to the mortuary. The post-mortem examination had taken place the day before and Dr Phillips assisted by pointing out the original wounds. Bond's opinion was that the wounds had been inflicted with a sharp, strong, pointed knife. Despite the superficial nature of the abdominal wounds Bond concluded:

I see in this murder evidence of similar design to the former Whitechapel murders, viz. sudden onslaught on the prostrate woman, the throat skilfully & resolutely cut with subsequent mutilation. Each mutilation indicating sexual thoughts & desire to mutilate the abdomen & sexual regions. I am of opinion that the murder was performed by the same person who commit-ted the former series of Whitechapel Murders. [Ref. MEPO3/ 140 ff.259–62]

Bond here shows some inconsistency in his findings: previously he had stated that the murderer had evinced no skill whatsoever, whereas here he judges that the throat wound was 'skilfully and resolutely cut'. There is little reason to think that Jack the Ripper had struck again, despite Bond's statement.

Dr Phillips made a very detailed report on his post-mortem findings (Ref. MEPO3/140 ff.263–71) and stated, *inter alia*: 'The abdominal injuries were caused subsequent to the throat being cut. The instrument used was smaller than the one used in most of the cases that have come under my observations in these "Whitechapel Murders".' The City Police surgeon, Dr Gordon Brown, was also consulted and concurred with Dr Phillips' conclusions. Phillips stated:

> After careful & long deliberation I cannot satisfy myself on purely anatomical & professional grounds that the perpetrator of all the 'Whi'chl murders' is our man. I am on the contrary impelled to a contrary conclusion, this noting the mode of procedure & the character of the mutilations & judging of motive in connection with the latter.

On the 17th William Wallace Brodie, of 2 Harveys Buildings, Strand, went into Leman Street police station and gave himself up for the McKenzie murder. He was seen by Inspector Moore, who examined his clothing for blood. There was none, but whilst making his examination Brodie confessed that he had now 'committed 9 murders in Whitechapel'. His story was investigated by Moore, and Sergeants Godley and Bradshaw. He was found to be a drunkard 'of unsound mind' and his story was groundless. The killer of Alice McKenzie was never discovered.

Two months later, at 5.20 a.m. on Tuesday 10 September 1889, the headless and legless torso of a woman was found under a railway arch in Pinchin Street, south of Commercial Road, by a patrolling constable on his beat. The Ripper killings were still in people's minds but it was concluded by Monro and Chief Inspector Swanson that this crime was not linked with the Whitechapel series. Indeed, it bore no signs of a Ripper killing and had been committed elsewhere and the remains dumped where they were found.

There was a cut on the trunk extending from the sternum leading to the left side of the labia major, but this appeared to have been inflicted in the course of dismemberment.

Swanson reported to Superintendent Arnold on the same day:

> What becomes most apparent is the absence of the attack upon the genitals as in the series of Whitechapel murders beginning

at Buck's Row and ending in Miller's Court. [Ref. MEPO3/140 ff.136–40]

Monro reported on the murder on 11 September:

> If this is a fresh outrage by the Whitechapel murderer known by the horribly familiar nickname of Jack the Ripper the answer would not be difficult although this murder committed in the murderer's house would be a new departure from the system hitherto pursued by this ruffian. I am however inclined to believe that this case is not the work of the Ripper. [Ref. MEPO3/140 ff.125–33]

Monro added that there was no evidence to show that death was caused by cutting the throat, there was no mutilation, although there was dismemberment, no evisceration, or removal of any organs, neither was there any sign of frenzied mutilation of the body, just deliberate and skilful dismemberment with a view to removal. He pointed out:

> These are all striking departures from the practice of the Whitechapel murderer, and if the body had been found elsewhere than in Whitechapel the supposition that death had been caused by the Ripper would probably not have been entertained.

Monro ended by saying:

> This is not the work of the Whitechapel murderer but of the hand which was concerned in the murders which are known as the Rainham mystery, the new Police buildings case, and the recent case in which portions of a female body [afterwards identified] were found in the Thames.

Over a year later, on 13 February 1891, the last real Ripper scare occurred. The victim this time was another prostitute, Frances Coles, an attractive twenty-six-year-old. Her body was discovered at 2.15 a.m. by PC Ernest Thompson, a new recruit to the Metropolitan Police, pounding the beat for the first time. He passed from Chamber Street into a narrow, dark alley named Swallow Gardens. There he found the body, and on turning his lantern on to it saw blood flowing from a severe cut to the throat. At the same moment he heard the sound of footsteps going off into Royal Mint Street at the opposite end of the thoroughfare. He blew his whistle to summon assistance. Thompson later claimed that he thought he saw the woman's eye move, and remained with her instead of pursuing the unknown person.

Two cuts found in the throat were declared to be the cause of death. Dr Phillips made his usual examination and came to the conclusion that the murder had no connection with the previous killings. This time the police had a prime suspect, in the shape of James Thomas Sadler, a ship's fireman, who had recently been on a lengthy pub crawl with Coles and had quarrelled with her. Sadler, who was feared by his wife, was the subject of prolonged police attention, but despite strong suspicion the crime remained unsolved.

The murder of Coles marked the end of any real fear that the Ripper had returned to his old haunts. No further killings were attributed to him, and the file was closed the following year and never reopened.

Chapter 14

Suspects

' "What, sir," said I, with a perceptible flush of indignation, "do you mean to say that you have been impersonating me?" '

When the killings ended in November 1888, a perplexing mystery was spawned. Many questions are still unanswered. Who was the Whitechapel serial killer? What manner of man could have mutilated with such taunting, callous indifference? How did he evade capture? Why did he stop? Was there a police cover-up?

To analyse and dispose of even a fraction of the Ripper suspects – more than 130 according to *The Jack the Ripper A-Z* – would be pointless and would defeat even the most enthusiastic student of the murders. Over a century of false trails leading nowhere, ludicrous scenarios and outrageous suspects have fogged the path and obstructed any serious attempt to discover the Ripper's identity.

There is one document which suggests that the police had a short list of probable suspects. Most Ripper experts have treated the Macnaghten report as one of the most important documents about the Whitechapel murders, but we suggest that it should be viewed with a great deal of caution.

In his 1910 autobiography, Sir Robert Anderson, head of the CID, stated that Jack the Ripper's identity was a 'definitely ascertained fact'. In 1894, Sir Melville Macnaghten, the Chief Constable of CID, who had joined the Metropolitan Police in June 1889, wrote the report which aimed to refute claims being made by the *Sun* newspaper that a man named Thomas Cutbush was Jack the Ripper.

These two important senior officers of the CID, both of whom have contributed so much to the suspects controversy, were known to Major Arthur Griffiths, who in 1898 painted excellent pen-pictures of them in his three-volume work:

Sir Robert Anderson, chief of the Criminal Investigation Department until 1901, when he resigned, was an ideal detective officer, with a natural bias for the work, and endowed with gifts peculiarly useful in it. He is a man of the quickest apprehension, with the power of close, rapid reasoning from facts, suggestions, or even impressions. He could seize on the essential point almost by intuition, and was marvellously ready in finding the real clue or indicating the right trail. With all this he was the most discreet, the most silent and reserved of public functionaries. Someone said he was a mystery even to himself. This, to him, inestimable quality of reticence is not unaided by a slight, but perhaps convenient, deafness. If he is asked an embarrassing question, he quickly puts up his hand and says the enquiry has been addressed to his deaf ear. But I shrewdly suspect that he hears all that he wishes to hear; little goes on around him that is not noted and understood; without seeming to pay much attention, he is always listening and drawing his own conclusions.

Mr Macnaghten, the Chief Constable, or second in command of the Investigation Department, is essentially a man of action. A man of presence is Mr Macnaghten – tall, well-built, with a military air, although his antecedents are rather those of the public school, of Indian planter life, than of the army. His room, like his chief's, is hung with speaking tubes, his table is deep with reports and papers, but the walls are bright with photos of officials, personal friends, and of notorious criminals which Mr Macnaghten keeps by him as a matter of business. Some other and more gruesome pictures are always under lock and key, photographs, for instance, of the victims of Jack the Ripper, and of other brutal murders, taken immediately after discovery, and reproducing with dreadful fidelity the remains of bodies that have been mutilated almost out of human semblance, but it is Mr Macnaghten's duty, no less than his earnest desire, to be first on the scene of any such sinister catastrophe. He is therefore more intimately acquainted, perhaps, with the details of the more recent celebrated crimes than anyone else at New Scotland Yard.

Thomas Cutbush had been arrested in March 1891 and arraigned in April of that year on a charge of maliciously wounding Florence Grace Johnson and attempting to wound Isabella Fraser Anderson. He had stabbed both women in the backside with a knife. Despite strenuous efforts by some writers to brand Cutbush the Ripper, it is clear from the evidence that he was nothing more than a violent, mentally unbalanced minor offender.

The Macnaghten report, dated '23 Feb. 1894', is headed 'Confidential'. There are two versions, one which is now in the Scotland Yard files, and the other which is with Macnaghten's descendants. The latter, which appears to have been Macnaghten's original draft, passed, after Lady Macnaghten's death in 1929, to Julia Donner, their eldest daughter. In the early 1950s a friend of the family, Philip Loftus, apparently saw it in the possession of Gerald Melville Donner, Julia's son. The text was preserved by Christabel Aberconway, Julia Donner's younger sister, who made a copy of her father's notes, evidently in the early 1930s.

The seven-page official report was written in Macnaghten's own hand whilst he was Assistant Chief Constable. He joined the Force too late to participate in the true Ripper inquiry. The relevant section reads:

A much more rational theory is that the murderer's brain gave way altogether after his awful glut in Miller's Court, and that he immediately committed suicide, or, as a possible alternative, was found to be so hopelessly mad by his relations that he was by them confined in some asylum.

I may mention the cases of three men, any one of whom would have been more likely than Cutbush to have committed this series of murders:

1. A Mr M. J. Druitt, said to be a doctor and of good family, who disappeared at the time of the Miller's Court murder, whose body (which was said to have been upwards of a month in the water) was found in the Thames on 31st – or about 7 weeks after that murder. He was sexually insane and from private info I have little doubt but his own family believed him to have been the murderer.

2. Kosminski, a Polish Jew, and resident in Whitechapel. This man became insane owing to many years' indulgence in solitary vices. He had a great hatred of women, specially of the prostitute class, and had strong homicidal tendencies; he was removed to a lunatic asylum about March 1889. There were many circs connected with this man which made him a strong 'suspect'.

3. Michael Ostrog, a Russian doctor, and a convict, who was

subsequently detained in a lunatic asylum as a homicidal maniac. This man's antecedents were of the worst possible type, and his whereabouts at the time of the murders could never be ascertained. [Ref. MEPO3/141 ff.177–83]

Of the three suspects presented in Macnaghten's report, it seems that Anderson and Macnaghten preferred different ones. Anderson, as stated in his later writings, favoured a Polish Jew as the miscreant. This must, in the light of all evidence, refer to the suspect listed by Macnaghten as Kosminski. For his part, as evidenced in his report and later memoirs, *Days of My Years*, Macnaghten seems to have been more convinced by Montague John Druitt. This is a strange anomaly considering that we are looking at the views of the head of the CID and his immediate subordinate. Macnaghten obviously did not share his chief's opinion that the identity of the murderer was known, and we will also see, elsewhere, that he apparently held an alternative view as to the identity of the murderer, one that he did not air publicly.

The details of Macnaghten's three named suspects were first committed to print by Major Arthur Griffiths, in his 1898 book *Mysteries of Police and Crime*. Griffiths knew both Anderson and Macnaghten, and there is little doubt that he consulted the two men before writing the following:

The police, after the last murder, had brought their investigations to the point of strongly suspecting several persons, all of them known to be homicidal lunatics, and against three of these they held very plausible and reasonable grounds of suspicion. Concerning two of them the case was weak, although it was based on certain suggestive facts.

One was a Polish Jew, a known lunatic, who was at large in the district of Whitehchapel at the time of the murder, and who, having developed homicidal tendencies, was afterwards confined in an asylum. This man was said to resemble the murderer by the one person who got a glimpse of him – the police constable in Mitre Court [*sic*].

The second possible criminal was a Russian doctor, also insane, who had been a convict in both England and Siberia. This man was in the habit of carrying about surgical knives and instruments in his pockets; his antecedents were of the very worst, and at the time of the Whitechapel murders he was in hiding, or at least, his whereabouts was never exactly known.

The third person was of the same type, but the suspicion in his case was stronger, and there was every reason to believe that his own friends entertained grave doubts about him. He also was a doctor in the prime of life, was believed to be insane or on the borderline of insanity, and he disappeared immediately after the last murder, that in Miller's Court, on the 9th of November, 1888. On the last day of that year, seven weeks later, his body was found floating in the Thames, and was said to have been in the water a month. The theory in this case was that after his last exploit, which was the most fiendish of all, his brain entirely gave way, and he became furiously insane and committed suicide.

Griffiths' descriptions contained some strange additional information, of mysterious origin. In the case of Kosminski, he states that the suspect was identified by a police constable who had seen him in 'Mitre Court'. But from what source did this originate? Possibly Anderson, who in his 1910 book stated: ' . . . the only person who had ever had a good view of the murderer unhesitatingly identified the suspect the instant he was confronted with him; but he refused to give evidence against him.' Macnaghten refers to the individual seen by the City PC near Mitre Square in the draft of his report that was retained by his family, information revealed by Lady Aberconway, his daughter, to both Tom Cullen and Dan Farson, and used in their books *Autumn of Terror* and *Jack the Ripper*.

Anderson's statements with regard to his Polish Jew have been argued over at length, but his conviction is misplaced, as is shown by the fact that no known witness ever had 'a good view of the murderer'. However, Anderson would seem to be Griffiths' source for stating that a witness had identified the Polish Jew.

It is also important to remember that Kosminski has never been positively identified, and arguments still continue as to whether he was a person named Aaron Kosminski, the only Kosminski historically identified by researchers who more or less fits the known facts.

With regard to Ostrog, Griffiths adds the facts that he had been a convict in 'both England and Siberia', and that he was 'in the habit of carrying about surgical knives and instruments in his pockets'. Again, the source for this additional information must be the police. We now know that Ostrog had been arrested in April

1891, and sent to Surrey County Asylum for about two years. He was released and again arrested in 1894, the year of Macnaghten's report, for stealing the Fives Challenge Cup at Eton. This subsequent information on Ostrog was revealed by the diligent research of D. Stuart Goffee, who disposes of Ostrog as a viable suspect.

Griffiths' third and undoubtedly preferred suspect is Druitt. In this, it is clear that Macnaghten was the influence, added confirmation that Griffiths must have spoken to both him and Anderson about the murders.

The *Referee* of 22 January 1899 saw G. R. Sims making his first reference to the newly proposed suspects. George Robert Sims was a prominent figure in British journalism, and was also a renowned poet, playwright and author. He wrote a regular column in the *Sunday Referee* under the pseudonym 'Dagonet', covering the murders in some detail. He stated:

> There are bound to be various revelations concerning Jack the Ripper as the years go on. This time it is a vicar who heard his dying confession. I have no doubt a great many lunatics have said they were Jack the Ripper on their death beds. It is a good exit, and when the dramatic instinct is strong in a man he always wants an exit line, especially when he isn't coming on in the little play of 'life' any more. I don't want to interfere with this mild little Jack the Ripper boom which the newspapers are playing up [as] in the absence of strawberries and butterflies are good, exciting murders, but I don't quite see how the real Jack could have confessed, seeing that he committed suicide after the horrible mutilation of the woman in the house in Dorset Street, Spitalfields. The full details of that crime have never been published – they never could be. Jack, when he committed that crime, was in the last stage of the peculiar mania from which he suffered. He had become grotesque in his ideas as well as bloodthirsty. Almost immediately after this murder he drowned himself in the Thames. His name is perfectly well known to the police. If he hadn't committed suicide he would have been arrested.

Here we see that Sims has taken on board entirely the views of Griffiths with regard to Druitt, and, consequently, the information fed out by the police. Sims almost certainly knew Griffiths, a fellow criminologist, and he definitely knew Macnaghten, referring to him, in *My Life*, as 'my friend of many long years'.

In the *Referee* of 16 February 1902, Sims returned to the White-chapel murders, and the suspect. He was writing on the subject of homicidal lunatics and their release from asylums: 'The homicidal maniac who shocked the world as Jack the Ripper had been once – I am not sure that it was not twice – in a lunatic asylum. At the time that his dead body was found in the Thames, his friends, who were terrified at his disappearance from their midst, were endeavour-ing to have him found and placed under restraint again.' This is another clear reference to Druitt, which also indicates that Sims may have obtained additional information from his 'friend' Macnaghten.

In the *Referee* of 13 July 1902, the vexed question of Ripper suspects again commands Sims' attention, prompted this time by a piece on the unidentified and mutilated remains of a woman that had recently been found in Salamanca Place. Sims mused:

> If the authorities thought it worth while to spend money and time, they might eventually get at the identity of the woman by the same process of exhaustion which enabled them at last to know the real name and address of Jack the Ripper. In that case they had reduced the only possible Jacks to seven, then by a further exhaustive inquiry to three, and were about to fit these three people's movements in with the dates of the various mur-ders when the one and only genuine Jack saved further trouble by being found drowned in the Thames, into which he had flung himself, a raving lunatic, after the last and most appalling mutilation of the whole series. But prior to this discovery the name of the man found drowned was bracketed with two others as a possible Jack, and the police were in search of him alive when they found him dead.

Sims had totally accepted the 'drowned man in the Thames' theory, and seemed to be adding to the story. As we will see, however, there was no evidence at all to show that Druitt was a contemporary suspect.

If, as has been supposed, the Macnaghten report was a sop to the Home Office, and later to the public via Griffiths and Sims, then much makes sense. Macnaghten, signally, never did state that he knew the identity of the killer: in *Days of My Years* he merely said, 'I incline to the belief that the individual who held London in terror resided with his own people; that he absented himself from home at certain times, and that he committed suicide on or about the 10th of November 1888, after he had knocked out a Commissioner of Police and very nearly settled the hash of one of Her Majesty's principal Secretaries of State.'

In the 1950s the author Douglas Browne, whilst writing his history of Scotland Yard, apparently saw official information that Macnaghten actually identified the Ripper 'with the leader of a plot to assassinate Mr Balfour at the Irish Office'. Unfortunately the official source for Browne's statement cannot now be found and it remains a tantalising mystery.

In his book *The True Face of Jack the Ripper*, Melvin Harris wrote:

> I contend that the efforts put into looking for Jack the Ripper among the main police suspects have been sadly misdirected. The police were never looking for a sexual serial murderer, they were hunting for their imaginary homicidal lunatic. Druitt alone, of the selected three, had never been an asylum inmate; but his suicide brought him into the same category and this matched police expectations. And all other candidates had to measure up to these same archaic standards.

Let us now assess the key suspects in more detail. We do not intend to dwell long on the more outrageous and hysterical suggestions, and will give short shrift to those we believe are falsified or complete non-starters.

Druitt

Montague John Druitt was born on 15 August 1857 at Wimborne in Dorset. He was educated at Winchester College, where he was a prefect, played cricket for the First XI, was an outstanding fives player, and won a scholarship to New College, Oxford. There he studied Classics and in 1880 obtained a third-class honours degree. He may then have studied medicine for a year (he had a cousin who was a doctor) before switching to law, enrolling at the Inner Temple in May 1882. While he studied law, he taught at a crammer school in Blackheath. He was called to the Bar in April 1885. His father died in September, after which Druitt rented chambers at 9 King's Bench Walk in the Temple.

He had a self-confident, competitive spirit, and his passion for sport, especially cricket, was evident at an early age. In 1876, he became a member of Kingston Park and Dorset County Cricket Club, the principal club side in his native county. He would have possessed the strength and confidence to commit the murders, though there is nothing to back up Macnaghten's claim that he was sexually insane or that he was in any way violent or a woman-hater. It has long been contended that the Whitechapel murderer must either have lived in or had knowledge of the East End. Druitt had no connection with the area.

Druitt's last years were marred by tragedy. He continued to teach at the Blackheath school until he was sacked in December 1888. The reason for the dismissal is not known: he may have shown homosexual tendencies or behaved unreasonably or oddly – the latter being not unlikely, as his mother had been certified as insane in July that year.

By that time Druitt himself seems to have been financially secure, but apparently he feared for his own sanity. He was last seen alive on Monday 3 December 1888, after which he penned a note – 'Since Friday I felt I was going to be like Mother and the best thing was for me to die' – weighted the pockets of his overcoat with stones and jumped or waded into the River Thames. His body was found floating in the river near Chiswick on Monday 31 December, four weeks after his disappearance. He was thirty-one.

Druitt's suicide must have shocked his friends and acquaintances. On 5 January 1889, the *Southern Guardian* reported that he was 'well known and much respected in the neighbourhood. He was a barrister of bright talent, he had a promising future before him, and his untimely end is deeply deplored.'

A member of the MCC, for several years he played cricket for Blackheath and also for teams in Dorset. The day after Mary Ann Nichols was murdered, Druitt played for Canford against Wimborne, in Dorset. Some five hours after the murder of Annie Chapman he was playing for Blackheath, in south London. Could it be possible that Montague Druitt was Jack the Ripper?

Of all the suspects, Druitt seems to be the one most favoured by writers and experts. But as in every other case there is in reality no connection with the murders. The main, if not the only, reason why Druitt stands high on the list of suspects is simply because of what Macnaghten wrote in 1894. The key phrase is: ' . . . after much careful & deliberate consideration I am inclined to exonerate the last

2 [Kosminski and Ostrog], but I have always held strong opinions regarding no.1, and the more I think the matter over, the stronger do these opinions become.'

However, Macnaghten himself never claimed actually to know for certain that Druitt was the Whitechapel murderer. It seems possible that he only suspected him because he committed suicide within a matter of weeks of the murder of Mary Jane Kelly, which neatly explained the sudden cessation of the murders.

Crucially, one of the key detectives involved with the Whitechapel investigation of 1888 put paid to any sort of speculation in an interview he gave to the *Pall Mall Gazette* in 1903. Inspector Abberline answered the suggestion that the Whitechapel murderer was 'a young medical student who was found drowned in the Thames' by saying:

> I know all about that story. But what does it amount to? Simply this. Soon after the last murder in Whitechapel the body of a young doctor was found in the Thames, but there is absolutely nothing beyond the fact that he was found at that time to incriminate him.

Abberline also refuted any claim that the CID knew for certain that the murderer was dead.

> You can state most emphatically that Scotland Yard is really no wiser on the subject than it was fifteen years ago. It is simple nonsense to talk of the police having proof that the man is dead. I am, and always have been, in the closest touch with Scotland Yard, and it would have been next to impossible for me not to have known all about it. Besides, the authorities would have been only too glad to make an end of such a mystery, if only for their own credit.

It is a fact that Macnaghten knew almost nothing about his suspects. He is mistaken on a number of points: Druitt, for example, was a barrister and schoolmaster, never a doctor; Ostrog was a confidence trickster and thief, not a killer. Macnaghten believed that Druitt lived with his family and stayed away from home at certain times; other records show that he lived at the school in Blackheath. Macnaghten said that Druitt committed suicide 'on or about the 10th of November' – he was three weeks too early! Despite these

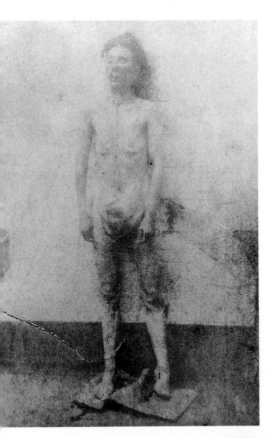

The body of Catherine Eddowes,
murdered 30 September 1888.
Her wounds have been stitched
up.

Church Passage, Aldgate, leading
into Mitre Square, site of the murder
of Catherine Eddowes.

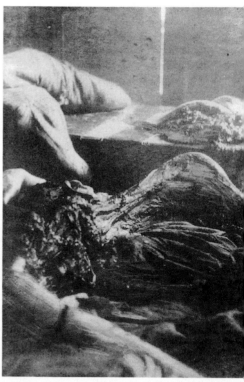

Miller's Court, 26 Dorset Street, where Mary Jane Kelly was murdered on 9 November 1888.

The newly-found photo of Mary Kelly: the table piled with flesh can be seen behind the bed.

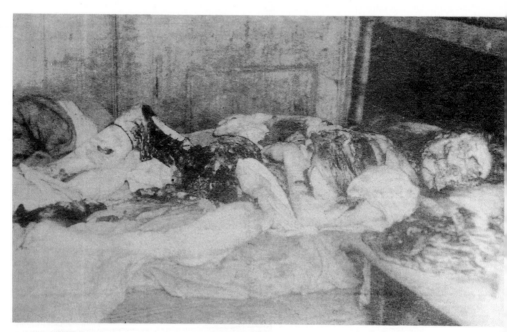

The fearfully mutilated body of Mary Kelly, found on her bed at Room 13, Miller's Court.

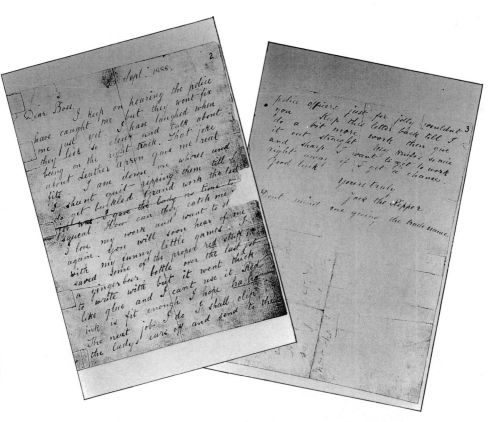

The original 'Dear Boss' letter sent to the Central News Agency on 27 September 1888.

The second Jack the Ripper communication – the 'Saucy Jacky' postcard of 1 October 1888.

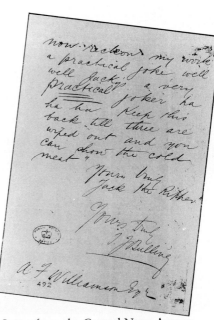

Letter from the Central News Agency to Scotland Yard, reporting receipt of a third 'Dear Boss' letter, 5 October 1888.

HANG THE WANTON! MURDER HER!

Contemporary cartoon (1889) showing how the press visualised Jack the Ripper.

St Louis in 1895 – Tumblety was based there until his death in 1903.

The type of ship on which Tumblety, using the alias 'Frank Townsend', escaped from France to sail to America on 4 December 1888.

A contemporary American sketch of Tumblety, prior to his arrival in Britain.

St John's Hospital, 307 South Euclid, St Louis, where Tumblety died of a heart condition in May 1903.

(*Below*) The shaky signature of Dr Francis Tumblety, taken from his will.

The portrait of Tumblety which appeared on the front cover of his second booklet, 1889.

fairly fundamental mistakes, Macnaghten's observations have served as the basis for most of the serious research undertaken by modern Ripper theorists.

Kosminski

Writer Martin Fido searched through the records of public asylums and workhouse infirmaries and in the admissions book of the Colney Hatch Asylum found a reference to one Aaron Kosminski. Unfortunately, it did not tally with the facts that were known about Kosminski the suspect. Aaron was a poor wretch who searched for bread in the gutters of the street. This could not possibly be the man who murdered prostitutes and disappeared without a trace.

Fido came up with his own revised theory that suggested that there had been a confusion of names and the man described in the asylum record was, in fact, a certain Nathan Kaminsky, a Polish Jew who on 24 March 1888 began a six-week course of treatment for syphilis at the Whitechapel Workhouse Infirmary. There are no other references to this man. Fido then theorised that Kaminsky had been incarcerated under a different name and concluded that he and a patient called David Cohen were one and the same. Cohen had been brought in to Colney Hatch on 21 December 1888 and had died there on 20 October 1889. He was an extremely violent man more often found in a straitjacket than without. He was also, in Fido's view, unmistakably Anderson's Polish Jew, and therefore Jack the Ripper. A bold claim with no evidence to support it.

Phil Sugden's research has revealed that those senior officers writing about Kosminski; if Aaron Kosminski made mistakes about the most basic of facts. Kosminski was not committed to Colney Hatch in 1889 but in 1891, and far from dying shortly afterwards, he lived for a further twenty-eight years. What is also clear from the records is that he was not considered violent. His official record reveals that he was not dangerous to others and doctors did not diagnose him as a homicidal patient. According to his case notes, only one of nine reports on him while at Colney Hatch mention violence: 'Incoherent; at times excited and violent – a few days ago he took up a chair, and attempted to strike the charge attendant; apathetic as a rule, and refuses to occupy himself in any way; habits cleanly; health fair.'

Kosminski was discharged to Leavesden Asylum on 18 April 1894, where he resided for the remainder of his life.

Anderson's comments about his 'Polish Jew' would lead most

right-thinking people to expect hard and clear evidence that Kosminski was in some way implicated in the murders. There is none. There are also important objections to attempts to identify him with the killings. Whereas Druitt's death might explain the cessation of the crimes, Kosminski's incarceration took place more than two years after the Miller's Court murder. If he was the killer, we would have to accept that after committing the murders he quietly went to ground and remained inactive for another two years and three months.

The question that must be asked is: does Kosminski, a sad and shambling twenty-three-year-old foraging for bread in the gutter, unemployed, dirty, with voices in his head, sound like the sort of man who could persuade prostitutes to come with him and then show the necessary cunning and discipline to kill them so expertly? Macnaghten's claim that he had strong homicidal tendencies is not substantiated anywhere. There is no evidence to connect him with any of the killings. Our conclusion must be that Kosminski, a harmless imbecile, was not involved in any way in the Whitechapel murders.

Ostrog

Michael Ostrog, the third man named by Macnaghten, was a thief and confidence trickster accustomed to living under numerous aliases. The elusive Russian first came to the notice of the police in 1863, following a series of break-ins at Oxford University. Ostrog was then calling himself Max Kaife Gosslar.

On 11 February, he stole an opera glass and case at Oriel College, and six days later was arrested in Cambridge. He pleaded guilty and was sentenced to ten months' hard labour in the House of Correction. Shortly after his release, he went to Bishop's Stortford, where he posed as Count Sobieski, the son of a fallen Polish nobleman, who had escaped from Warsaw after being sentenced, like his father, to end his days in Siberia. For several months he kept up his front, and managed to con money and favours out of several people. His luck then ran out. He was arrested as a rogue and vagabond and sentenced to three months' imprisonment. His life in Britain seems to have consisted of petty thieving and conning gullible people out of money. And he was not very accomplished at that: he was nearly always caught and found himself back in gaol.

In July 1866, Ostrog was once again brought to trial, this time at the Kent Summer Assize in Maidstone. He was convicted of stealing books and robbing one Esther Carpenter and sentenced to seven years' penal servitude for each offence. On his release in May 1873, he again returned to his life of petty crime.

One incident is unique in Ostrog's record because it is the only time when he is known to have attempted violence. He was arrested in Burton-on-Trent by Superintendent Thomas Oswald, and while on his way to the police station pulled a gun out of his pocket. Oswald seized the weapon and disarmed Ostrog. In January 1874, he was sentenced to ten years, and spent the following decade in various government prisons. The next evidence of him is in August 1887, when he was caught stealing a tankard at the Royal Military Academy, Woolwich. Before getting six months' imprisonment he tried to drag a gaoler under a train in an attempt at suicide. In September 1887 he was certified insane and was taken to the Surrey County Lunatic Asylum in Tooting. Having served his sentence, he was discharged on 10 March 1888.

On 26 October 1888, during the Ripper inquiry, his details were published in the *Police Gazette* for failing to report at a police station. He was described as a Polish Jew, aged fifty-five and a 'dangerous man'.

Why was Ostrog named by Macnaghten as a possible suspect? There appears to be no evidence to link him with the crimes. It must be that the general consensus at the time was that the murderer was a lunatic, and so the police were focusing on people who possessed anatomical knowledge and were known to be insane. Ostrog fitted this simple equation perfectly. He had pretensions to medical knowledge and had been discharged from an asylum less than six months before the murders began. His long criminal record also marked him out as someone the police should be looking at. However, following his release from the Surrey asylum, Ostrog could not be traced and eliminated from inquiries. Was this the sole reason why his name remained on police files? Macnaghten admitted that Ostrog's whereabouts at the time of the murders 'could never be ascertained'.

The police believed that Ostrog was back to his old tricks in 1889, posing in Kidderminster as a French captain, and they suspected he was back in Whitechapel when Alice McKenzie was murdered. 'Special attention is drawn to this dangerous man, and enquiry requested at hospitals, infirmaries, work houses etc.', said the *Police Gazette* in another call for Ostrog in July. Yet he was not arrested at that time.

In April 1891 he was detained again and sent to Surrey County Asylum for two years. In 1894 he was arrested for stealing the Fives Challenge Cup at Eton but was instead convicted of another Eton offence dating back to 1889. His tendency to repeat crimes occurred again when he went back to Woolwich Royal Military Academy and stole some books. He was lucky to escape with six weeks' imprisonment as a rogue and a vagabond.

What is crucial to any consideration of Ostrog as a possible suspect is the police lack of concern about him when he was arrested in 1894. They made no effort to keep him incarcerated, which suggests they did not consider him a Ripper suspect. D. Stuart Goffee researched Ostrog's last known offence, ironically committed in Whitechapel itself, the stealing of a microscope from the London Hospital. He received five years' penal servitude for his trouble, and the judge in sentencing said that because of his partial paralysis he would not be given any work to do in prison. After his release in August, 1904, he disappeared without trace.

Macnaghten stated that Ostrog was 'unquestionably a homicidal maniac' and was 'said to have been habitually cruel to women'. But his criminal record does not show this. A liar, a trickster, a petty thief, but no murderer. If his name had not appeared in the Macnaghten report there would be no reason at all to consider him a suspect.

Ostrog is the least plausible of Macnaghten's totally improbable selection of three; not a shred of evidence can be found or any strong case made against any of them. After careful consideration, the Macnaghten report seems much more like a deliberate smoke-screen than a serious attempt to identify the Whitechapel murderer. And this from a senior officer who had ready access to all the files on the murders, files which should have contained full information on the leading suspect, who had escaped to America.

Stephenson/D'Onston

Dr Robert Donston Stephenson, or Roslyn D'Onston, was the son of a Yorkshire seed-oil mill owner, who studied chemistry in Munich and medicine in Paris. An alleged doctor, army officer, Garibaldian freedom-fighter and black magician, he went to elaborate lengths to suggest to two women that he was the Whitechapel murderer. A truly colourful contender for the Ripper's cloak!

In 1863, under family pressure, he took a post with Customs in

Hull, but was often in trouble, largely because of his belief in his own superiority, and was eventually fired. He moved to London and worked as a freelance journalist, contributing most notably to the *Pall Mall Gazette*, which accepted from him an article on the Whitechapel murders. During the 1890s his interest in black magic appears to have waned, and in 1904 he published *The Patristic Gospels*, a serious exercise in comparative Biblical studies.

In November 1888 Stephenson was a patient in the London Hospital, sharing a private ward with a Dr Evans, who was nightly visited by Dr Morgan Davies. On one of these visits he witnessed a graphic and overexcited re-enactment of the Ripper's supposed modus operandi that persuaded him that Davies was the Ripper.

Stephenson told his story to an unemployed ironmongery assistant named George Marsh, and the pair decided to turn private detective and investigate Dr Davies. On Christmas Eve 1888, however, Marsh went to Scotland Yard and told Inspector Roots his suspicions that the killer might in fact be Stephenson himself, whom he described as a habitual drinker. Roots, who had known Stephenson for years, dismissed him as a plausible suspect.

In 1890, Stephenson was living in Southsea with Mabel Collins, novelist and editor of *Lucifer*, the journal of the Theosophical Society. The two met Baroness Vittoria Cremers and went into business with her as the Pompadour Cosmetics Company. On one occasion, Cremers went into Stephenson's room and found several blood-encrusted ties in a black-enamelled deed box. Stephenson, unaware of this discovery, subsequently told her a variant of the story about Dr Davies being the Ripper that he had been peddling in 1888, with the additional claim that the Ripper concealed the organs he stole under his neckties.

In 1987 author Melvin Harris, having come to the conclusion that Stephenson/D'Onston was the Ripper, published the first of his three excellent contributions to the Ripper genre. He believed that Stephenson uniquely satisfied all requirements, and claimed that the murders stopped because he underwent a 'religious conversion'. Harris maintained that Stephenson and Marsh's visits to Scotland Yard were deliberate and successful efforts to throw the police off the scent, making them believe that Stephenson was one of those familiar cranks who turn up with demonstrably false accusations or confessions in all notorious criminal cases.

Stephenson was first written about in 1975 in Elwyn Jones and John Lloyd's *The Ripper File*, and his status as a suspect was discussed in Richard Whittington-Egan's *Casebook on Jack the Ripper* and further explored in Stephen Knight's 1976 book, *Jack the Ripper: The Final Solution*.

His credibility as a suspect was elevated by Melvin Harris's three books, and he was well and truly put under the microscope in the third of these, *The True Face of Jack the Ripper*. Harris has also comprehensively disposed of many of the earlier ridiculous suspects, and some later ones.

The strongest indications that Stephenson was not the Whitechapel murderer can be found in his own writings. In the article, he made several wrong deductions about the murders – something the real killer would not have done.

Klosowski/Chapman

Severin Klosowski, the son of a carpenter, was born in the village of Nagornak, Poland, in 1865. He was hanged in 1903, aged thirty-eight, for the murder of a barmaid.

Phil Sugden, in his recent invaluable study of the Whitechapel murders, proposed that Klosowski is a plausible Ripper suspect. Sugden does not seriously advance him as the murderer, but the mere fact that he rates him higher than Druitt, Ostrog and Kosminski – 'the least unlikely of an unlikely bunch' – does warrant further investigation.

Klosowski arrived in England from his native Poland some time during 1887 or 1888. He resided in the East End, where he was employed as a barber's assistant. He had some basic medical knowledge gained in apprenticeship to a surgeon between 1880 and 1885. By 1889, aged twenty-four, he was running his own hairdressing business at 126 Cable Street, St George's in the East. In October 1889 he married a Polish woman, Lucy Baderski, who, by September 1890, had borne him a son. This son died in March 1891, at which time the couple were living at 2 Tewkesbury Buildings, Whitechapel. In April 1891, they emigrated to the USA and lived in the New York area. Klosowski was a womaniser and violent towards his wife, resulting in her returning to England alone and pregnant in February 1892. He followed some two weeks later.

Reunited with Lucy, Klosowski again worked as a hairdresser's assistant. By 1893 he had found himself another woman, by coincidence called Annie Chapman, whose surname he assumed. In late 1894, as a result of his womanising, Annie left him.

In 1895, Chapman became a barber's assistant at a shop at 7 Church Lane, Leytonstone, and lodged in Forest Road, where he conducted a relationship with a woman also lodging at that address. Her name was Mrs Mary Spink. Chapman falsely stated that he married her in October 1895. They moved to George Street, Hastings, in 1896, where Chapman conducted his own barber shop business using money supplied by Mrs Spink.

Chapman soon reverted to his violence and began to beat this adopted 'wife'. He then began seeing another woman, a servant called Alice Penfold. In April 1897 he purchased an ounce of tartar-emetic, a powder containing antimony, a metallic poison, and used it to gradually poison Mary Spink because she had become an unnecessary hindrance. They moved back to London in 1897 and took over the lease of the Prince of Wales public house in Bartholomew Square. By the end of the year Mary was dead. In 1898 Chapman took on a barmaid, Bessie Taylor. A relationship developed between the two and a similar stormy lifestyle began. By 1901 Bessie was suffering similar symptoms to her predecessor and she died in the February. Both deaths had been put down to natural causes.

In August 1901, Chapman hired a new barmaid, Maud Marsh, and she too became his common-law wife. They moved into the Crown at 213 Borough High Street. By the summer of the following year the usual pattern had emerged and he was making advances to a new barmaid, Florence Rayner. On 22 October 1902, Maud died in a similar fashion to her two predecessors. Unfortunately for the scheming Chapman, doctors realised that a poison was at work and he was duly arrested on suspicion of murder. His two previous 'wives' were exhumed and the telltale poison discovered. He stood trial for Maud's murder, and was convicted and duly hanged on 7 April 1903.

Only now did the Chapman/Ripper theories begin to emerge. There had previously been absolutely no contemporary evidence, nor even suspicion, that he was the Ripper. The *Daily Chronicle* of 23 March 1903, however, made the astonishing claim that officers who had previously worked on the Ripper investigation were now forming theories based on a study of Chapman's antecedent history. What is staggering is that almost every detail supposedly used to illustrate some sort of link between Chapman and the Ripper is incorrect.

Although he had a powerful sex-drive, Klosowski was a different sort of killer from the Ripper, slowly and patiently poisoning his three partners rather than resorting to the crazed frenzy of the Whitechapel murderer. Klosowski needs no further consideration. He most definitely was not Jack the Ripper.

Bogus suspects and hoaxes

The misinformation found in books about the Ripper is not always simply a product of reliance upon untrustworthy sources. Unfortunately, many writers have their own theories and suspects and deliberately shape the facts to fit their pet theory. Fiction is dressed up as fact, which in turn becomes hardened fact in the retelling. However, once errors creep in, they are often repeated in book after book and are believed by most who read them.

Then there are those who insist on the involvement of the Crown. The Queen knew the identity of the killer; the killer's wife held a position at Court; the 'royal medium' was responsible for the capture of the Ripper; and the Queen herself asked the medium to leave town in order to make the cover-up foolproof. The theory that the Duke of Clarence was the Ripper, which also includes the claim that the royal physician Sir William Gull was involved, is fully disposed of in Melvin Harris' *Jack the Ripper – The Bloody Truth*.

Joseph Gorman/Sickert, who claims to be the son of the artist Walter Sickert, sold his own version of the Court cover-up to the BBC and then to Stephen Knight, who used it as the basis for his best-selling *Jack the Ripper: The Final Solution*. Other authors have also drawn on his stories, notably Melvyn Fairclough in his *The Ripper and the Royals*.

In Knight's ludicrous scenario, Mary Jane Kelly witnesses the secret marriage of Prince Albert Victor, Queen Victoria's grandson and heir presumptive, to a Catholic shop assistant called Annie Elizabeth Crook, and then bands together with a group of fellow East End prostitutes to blackmail the Government.

Lord Salisbury, the Prime Minister, is alarmed. If it comes out that the Prince has taken a Catholic bride the very future of the monarchy itself might be under threat. Salisbury hands the problem to Sir William Gull, the Queen's physician, who, together with Walter Sickert and sinister coachman John Netley, tracks down and murders the blackmailers.

Author Michael Harrison rejected the idea of Clarence as the Ripper, but proposed Clarence's friend J. K. Stephen as an alternative. Frank Spiering then combined Clarence and Stephen into a deadly alliance. After that, one would have thought that the fantasies had run themselves to earth. No shred of proof was ever offered for any of these outlandish claims.

If the royal conspiracy theory is rubbish, then we must view the alleged Jack the Ripper 'diary' in the same light. The owner of the diary, Mike Barrett, a one-time scrap-metal dealer who lives in Liverpool, claimed it was given to him by retired newspaper type-setter Tony Devereux, who died several months later. Barrett put it up for auction to publishers via a literary agency, it was snapped up by Smith Gryphon and on 7 October 1993 was launched on an unsuspecting world in a blaze of hype. It purports to be the diary of James Maybrick, a wealthy cotton merchant, and identifies him as the Ripper.

Maybrick died at Battlecrease House in Aigburth, a suburb of Liverpool, in May 1889, and his American wife Florence was accused of poisoning him with arsenic extracted from flypapers. Florence was convicted and sentenced to death but her sentence was commuted to one of penal servitude for life. She was released in 1904 and died in the United States in 1941. One of the early theories concerning the provenance of the diary was that it was found by electricians under the floorboards of Battlecrease House in 1990 or 1991. However, neither the present owner nor the workmen employed in the house at that time have any knowledge of such a find.

In July 1994, the *Liverpool Daily Post* ran a story about a con-fession by Barrett that he had forged the diary. This was later retracted by solicitors. In an attempt to prove that the diary was a fake, it was subjected to forensic, handwriting and language tests. Not only did the handwriting not match that of Maybrick, but also the conclusive proof that the whole thing was a forgery came when tests demonstrated that the ink used was of modern origin. In his confession, Barrett revealed the name of the shop where the ink used in the 'diary' came from. This shop (Bluecoats Art Shop) confirmed that they had indeed sold a special manuscript ink, made by Diamine, a Liverpool company. It contained iron salts and nigrosine as colour-ing matter, with chloroacetamide as its preservative. Chloroacet-amide is a modern commercial product, first used in ink manufacture in 1974. Its presence in the diary would prove beyond doubt it was a fake. Melvin Harris obtained six ink samples from the original twelve taken from the diary during the Warner Books investigation into its authenticity. The test was made by Analysis For Industry, a body headed by Dr Diana Simpson. Dr Simpson was asked to test for one substance only. Did the diary ink-spots contain chloroacetamide? Her report was written on 19th October 1994; it confirmed that her thorough tests showed that the diary ink samples contained chloroacetamide. It did not exist until 1974. This means that the diary is a recent forgery. Since then, Mike Barrett has made a full confession of his hoax in a sworn affidavit.

Chapter 15

Discovery of the Littlechild Letter

'I will here introduce some documentary evidence, which must speak for itself.'

The dream of any researcher seeking the identity of Jack the Ripper is to find some dusty, long-lost document revealing information on the case known to no one else. That such a find should ever be his had never seriously entered Stewart Evans' mind.

In 1965, Stewart, then a sixteen-year-old schoolboy, purchased two books that appeared simultaneously on the shelves at his local branch of W. H. Smith's. These were *Autumn of Terror* by Tom Cullen and *Jack the Ripper in Fact and Fiction* by Robin Odell. The two books contained a wealth of information on the case and were the first of the modern studies. Two years later Stewart travelled to the East End of London, aiming to walk around the surviving Ripper murder sites and take photographs.

Armed with sketch maps made from the books and a primitive Kodak Brownie 127 camera, he headed for the nearest murder location to Liverpool Street Station – Mitre Square, Aldgate. He passed from Duke Street through the narrow Church Passage into Mitre Square, as had the Ripper and his victim some seventy-nine years previously. He found 'Ripper's corner', where Catherine Eddowes' body had been discovered, and took photographs of the cobbled square surrounded by high office and warehouse buildings.

Stewart then visited and photographed the other surviving sites. The forbidding George Yard Buildings was regrettably locked. Derelict 29 Hanbury Street, with its faded and peeling pale green paint, was also inaccessible. Through towering grey edifices he went into narrow Durward Street, formerly Buck's Row, where still stood the row of terraced houses which had witnessed the crime. Henriques Street, formerly Berner Street, site of Dutfield's Yard, but in 1967 a school, had altered beyond recognition. Today these sites no longer exist as they did at the time of Stewart's visit.

Over the years, Stewart collected many of the books that were published on the subject, but refrained from serious research on his own part as he felt that this was already being more than adequately conducted by several authors. Open-minded on the subject of suspects, if forced to give an opinion Stewart would probably have plumped for Druitt as the most likely.

In February 1993, however, Stewart's whole thinking on the case was turned upside down. One night, the phone rang and the voice of an elderly gentleman said, 'You won't have heard of me, but I have some Jack the Ripper letters for sale and wondered whether you were interested.' Stewart *had* heard of the gentleman, and was most certainly interested. Within a week, an envelope arrived at his home containing four letters written at the beginning of the century to the noted journalist and author George R. Sims. Undoubtedly these letters had been penned as a result of Sims' prolific crime-writing, especially on the subject of Jack the Ripper. Also in the envelope were two yellowing press cuttings, one a review of the Ripper entry in Major Griffiths' 'new' book, the other relating the theory of Dr Forbes Winslow, an alienist, who believed that the Ripper was known to him. Winslow had related his theory to Scotland Yard who dismissed it as worthless.

Two of the letters were handwritten and dated from 1907. One had been written on 24 September by a certain Ernest Crawford of 2 Rosehill Terrace, Larkhall, Bath, and had been prompted by Sims' recent article on the Ripper case in *Lloyds Weekly News*. Mr Crawford wrote of the 'curious theory of the crimes' held by an acquaintance of his whom he called 'Mr S.' The theory had been brought to his mind by a map of the murders that Sims had reproduced. Mr S. believed that the outrages were 'instigated by the Jesuits who had reasons for getting foreign detectives into the London service' and that 'the miscreant never passed through the cordon of police because in the centre of the district was a Jesuit college in which he took refuge after his deeds.' According to Mr S. the Jesuits left the sign of the cross on all their work, and lines drawn on the map of the murders formed a 'fairly regular cross'.

Conceding that this theory was 'wild speculation', Crawford went on to give Mr S.'s alternative theory that the cut in the throat indicated that the murderer was left-handed. Mr S. believed that the

Ripper 'had induced the woman to allow connection from behind; a very convenient position for concealing his purpose and using the knife effectively.'

The second letter had been written on 25 September by one John Kimber of 8 Cavendish Drive, Leytonstone, again as a result of Sims' recent article. Mr Kimber, obviously feeling that the Ripper's career extended to 1891, pointed out to Sims that he had omitted to mention 'the murder committed in a court off Royal Mint St., Whitechapel, which was attributed to that fiend'. This of course refers to the Frances Coles murder, and the writer's interest in this lay in the fact that he knew the unfortunate policeman who had found the body.

The third letter had been written by a lady in Gorleston, Norfolk, and referred to another unsolved murder, unrelated to the Ripper case.

The fourth letter had been signed 'J. G. Littlechild', whom Stewart immediately recognised to be Chief Inspector John Littlechild, head of the Secret Department at the time of the Whitechapel murders. Indeed, a copy of Littlechild's reminiscences was already in Stewart's vast crime-book collection. The Littlechild letter was apparently sent in response to a previous enquiry of Sims' about the Ripper case. Incredibly, on the very first page Littlechild identified a suspect whose name Stewart had never seen in any of his books on the subject.

It is clear from this that the document's provenance is excellent: it was purchased by Stewart in a batch of Sims' correspondence in the normal course of a transaction between a collector of crime and police ephemera and an antiquarian dealer who had no specialist interest in the Ripper case.

The dealer in question, Eric Barton, of the Baldur Bookshop, Richmond, was himself a collector of memorabilia connected with many classic murder cases and had handled items connected with Jack the Ripper, Dr Crippen, Constance Kent, Dr Pritchard the Glasgow poisoner, Dougal the Moat Farm murderer, Bennett the Yarmouth beach murderer, Edgar Edwards the Camberwell murderer, William Gardiner the alleged Peasenhall murderer, James Berry the hangman, and many others. In the musty, dusty, esoteric world of the antiquarian book dealer, Eric's name was legendary, his knowledge in the field unsurpassed.

The collection of Ripper items of which Stewart's letters formed a part had first surfaced at Sotheby's in the early 1960s. Experts believed the items, including horrific photographs of Ripper victims, to be too gruesome to offer for general sale to the public. Knowing of his interest in crime, Sotheby's asked Eric if he wanted to buy the collection. He decided he would, and in turn sold some of the more obviously commercial items to Madame Tussaud's.

For thirty years, the remainder of the collection lay undisturbed among Mr Barton's rich collection of books, manuscripts, and ephemera. In 1993 he retired and, sadly, his bookshop closed forever. It was then that he learnt of Stewart's interest in all things criminological and made contact.

The Littlechild letter contains four points of huge importance to Ripper studies. The first, and most obvious, is that it introduces a completely new and, more importantly, very likely suspect. Second, it indicates that there was no contemporary police interest in Druitt as a suspect. Littlechild simply says that he had never heard of a 'Dr D.' in connection with the Whitechapel murders.

Third, the letter casts huge doubt over the credibility of Robert Anderson, who stated several times in writing that the identity of the Ripper was known. A great deal of Ripper research has been based on his thoughts and memoirs, given that everyone believed it was a solid foundation from which to begin. This revelation throws a serious question mark over Anderson.

Lastly, as we have seen, Littlechild names the probable inventors of the nickname that has so memorably forced its way into public awareness: Jack the Ripper.

The letter's key passage, naming Littlechild's suspect reads:

> I never heard of a 'Dr D.' in connection with the Whitechapel murders but amongst the suspects, and to my mind a very likely one, was a Dr T. (which sounds much like D.) He was an American quack named Tumblety.

A contemporary police suspect fitting the most crucial criteria was thus revealed. And he had escaped English justice. Littlechild continued:

> [He] was at one time a frequent visitor to London and on these occasions constantly brought under the notice of police, there being a large dossier concerning him at Scotland Yard. Although a 'Sycopathia [sic] Sexualis' subject he was not known as a 'Sadist' (which the murderer unquestionably was) but his feel-

ings towards women were remarkable and bitter in the extreme, a fact on record.

He concluded:

> Tumblety was arrested at the time of the murders in connection with unnatural offences and charged at Marlborough Street, remanded on bail, jumped his bail, and got away to Boulogne. He shortly left Boulogne and was never heard of afterwards. It was believed he committed suicide but certain it is that from this time the 'Ripper' murders came to an end.

Here is confirmation of one of the most important requirements for any suspect: a complete explanation for the sudden cessation of the murders. But Littlechild leaves some crucial questions unanswered. What was the reason for Tumblety's arrest? Why was he bailed if suspected of the murders? And what became of him? We are going to reveal the answers to these questions.

At this stage of the story the talented and indefatigable researcher Keith Skinner arrived on the scene. An old friend of Stewart's from the time they had researched the mysterious Peasenhall murder together, Keith was the obvious person to enlist. When he heard the details of Stewart's discovery, he realised that Tumblety's name, in an odd sort of way, rang a bell. He would begin research immediately.

Then Stewart remembered a story that had appeared in the *Pall Mall Gazette* of 31 December 1888, and which, he knew, must refer to his man:

> Inspector Andrews, of Scotland Yard, has arrived in New York from Montreal. It is generally believed that he has received orders from England to commence his search in this city for the Whitechapel murderer. Mr Andrews is reported to have said that there are half a dozen English detectives, two clerks, and one inspector employed in America in the same chase. Ten days ago Andrews brought hither from England Roland Gideon [and] Israel Barnet, charged with helping wreck the Central Bank, Toronto, and since his arrival he has received orders which will keep him in America for some time. The supposed inaction of the Whitechapel murderer for a considerable period and the fact that a man suspected of knowing a good deal about this series of crimes left England for this side of the Atlantic three

weeks ago, has, says the Telegraph correspondent, produced the impression that Jack the Ripper is in that country.

A short while later, Keith Skinner telephoned Stewart with the news, 'I've found him!'

Chapter 16

John George Littlechild

'. . . a man of much literary culture, and whose reputation as a high-toned, honourable gentleman is recognised throughout.'

John George Littlechild was born in Royston, Hertfordshire, on 21 December 1848, and was not a Scot as claimed in some books. He joined the Metropolitan Police on 18 February 1867. On 11 January 1871 this promising young officer was transferred to Central Office at Scotland Yard, under Superintendent Williamson, and on 23 March was promoted to sergeant. According to the *Police Review*:

It was the tracking of a would-be wife murderer upon no clue at all, but following up an ingenious theory, which led to Mr Littlechild's promotion to the rank of Sergeant. It was his indefatigable and successful efforts to weave the net around loan office swindlers and a bogus assurance office which gained the Detective's great distinction. During this period, he was involved in detecting the 'Great Turf frauds' and arrested the principal offenders.

Littlechild himself told a reporter from *Cassell's Saturday Journal*:

I have followed up the whole story of Fenian outrage, and I spent five months in Dublin after the Phoenix Park murders [6 May 1882], which gave me a wonderful insight into it. I assisted the Dublin Police by posing as a certain character, and staying in low hotels in the city, in which it was thought that information might be gained of the perpetrators of the deed.

As we have seen, author Douglas Browne wrote of Macnaghten's identification of the Ripper with the leader of a plot to assassinate Balfour at the Irish Office. The source of Browne's information is not known but appears to have been found in the official files. Could it be possible that he is describing Tumblety? With all the Irish connections, and the interest of Littlechild, head of the Secret Department, it seems that there is a possibility that Tumblety was the man.

Ripper expert Nick Warren also makes an interesting connection, pointing out that a certain Dr Hamilton Williams, who was a Fenian and had a practice in Demerara, British Guyana, bought the amputating knives used to assassinate the Irish Secretary in Phoenix Park in 1882 in Bond Street, London. Nick regards Williams as an important and curious historical figure. He came to London in 1882 from the West Indies, was obsessed with knives and tried, albeit unsuccessfully, to attach himself to the Irish cause. This mysterious figure hung around the capital for several weeks attempting to gain employment with the Irish revolutionaries, only to be refused by them because of his 'violent language'. As a 'dodgy doctor', who may have been of interest to the Special Branch, Williams and Tumblety had much in common, leading Nick to believe that they could be one and the same person. He points out Tumblety's known use of an alias, his Irish sympathies, and his visits to England prior to 1888.

In the same year as Littlechild was promoted to sergeant. Littlechild was a seasoned and brave officer. A leader of a gang of horse-racing fraudsters, William Kurr, who had four Scotland Yard inspectors bribed to report police activities, tried to escape while being arrested. Littlechild gave chase, and realising he could not escape Kurr turned on his pursuer and levelled a revolver at the Scotland Yard man.

Littlechild warned, 'For Heaven's sake, don't make a fool of yourself, it means murder.' 'I won't,' responded Kurr, who tamely submitted to arrest, and was disarmed by Littlechild. He was promoted to inspector on 8 April 1878 and chief inspector on 3 February 1882. He was later involved with the Irish troubles and had to arrest several Irish MPs, in the course of which he met Charles Parnell. Littlechild later told a reporter from the *Daily Graphic*:

Mr O'Kelly subsequently introduced me to Mr Parnell on the night of the arrest of William O'Brien and John Dillon, in my room at Scotland Yard, and Mr Parnell cordially shook hands with me, saying he had heard very good accounts of me from his lieutenants, which, of course, I thought very gratifying...

Everything relating to Irish disaffection came into my scope, but the 'special' branch of which I was made chief was not formed until the explosions at Salford, Chester Barracks, and Liverpool in 1883. Then there was the attempt to blow up the Mansion House, frustrated, fortunately, by the arrival of a policeman who saw the machine and bravely extinguished the fuse.

Then came the period of Fenian problems which may have led to Littlechild's first contact with Dr Francis Tumblety. Describing the pulse of dissatisfaction throughout the whole country, Littlechild commented: 'All kinds of suspects were coming into London, and people thought they saw a dynamiter in every Irish-American who took private lodgings.'

In 1883 he was made head of the newly formed Special Irish Branch. It was then that he started to investigate the dynamite explosions and the Anglo-American Fenian conspiracies. When asked whether he was actually in Scotland Yard when it was blown up by the dynamitards, he replied:

Fortunately, I was not. It was my room which was destroyed. I was in the habit of working late, but I owed my life to the happy chance that a friend of mine had sent me a couple of orders for the opera, and as a musical man I couldn't resist the temptation to use them. I remained at the office until 8 o'clock and then rushed off. The explosion took place at 8.40, and when next I saw my office I found it in ruins, with a large perforated brick upon my chair.

Littlechild's activities as head of the Special Branch are shrouded in mystery. With activities that included keeping a watch on possible terrorists in London, Fenians from America, Russian anarchists and the like, Littlechild and his men would have been very active in the East End.

In 1886 he was living at 2 Turret Grove, Clapham and the Whitechapel murders were only two years in the future. We do not know when he first became aware of Tumblety, but the elusive and mysterious doctor had spent much time in England and Littlechild states that he 'was at one time a frequent visitor to London and on these occasions constantly brought under the notice of police'.

In 1888 the Scotland Yard departments were under the direction of Superintendent John Shore. There were five chief inspectors: namely Greenham, Neame, Butcher, Littlechild and Swanson. Littlechild would undoubtedly have liaised closely with Swanson, who was conducting the investigation into the Ripper murders, and would certainly have been totally *au fait* with the inquiry.

It has been suggested by Paul Begg in his *Jack the Ripper: The Uncensored Facts* that the Secret Department would have been especially closely involved, as its administrative chief, James Monro, was specifically recommended by the Home Office to liaise with the full-time Whitechapel murders enquiry team. The Special Branch men would also, as a matter of course, have maintained surveillance on potential subversive centres in the East End, such as the International Working Men's Institute adjacent to the Stride murder site. Many of these clubs were merely fronts for anarchist organisations.

Littlechild's views are therefore of considerable interest and importance. In addition, the suspect would have been the subject of his personal interest due to the Irish-American terrorism connection.

One curious aspect of Littlechild's career was his sudden and unforeseen resignation in 1893, when he was only forty-five years old. It is not clear why he made this decision at the height of a hugely successful career, but the indications are that it was for reasons of health and, possibly, business opportunity.

The *Daily Graphic* paid its own tribute to Littlechild in April 1893:

His bearing, no less than his record, stamps him as a straight-forward but keenly intelligent and alert officer, whose zeal in the public service has forced him to retire from Scotland Yard at the early age of forty-six [*sic*].

When asked by the *Daily Graphic* to what extent a detective had to report failure Littlechild replied:

If you refer to the number of crimes the authors of which are never punished, I should say that the percentage is not great. Much has been said with regard to undetected murders, but without a proper understanding of the law and the powers of the police. Murders have been committed in my time in which it has been morally certain who the perpetrator was, but owing to the lack of positive and direct evidence it has been impossible to bring him before a magistrate.

This is a particularly relevant quote when we relate it to Tumblety, who was bailed, without doubt because the police were unable to prove him the murderer, and subsequently escaped.

After his retirement, Littlechild worked as a private investigator. Although little is known about this phase of his life, it is common knowledge that he was involved in the case of Oscar Wilde. At the time of the great playwright's arrest in 1895, the prosecution needed more evidence against him, and Littlechild was hired. He was assigned to follow up a lead that led him to a lodging house, where, after pushing past the woman on the door, he found a roomful of young boys with whom Wilde had been involved. The Littlechild letter also contains an interesting reference to Wilde: 'It is very strange how those given to "contrary sexual instinct" and degenerates are given to cruelty, even Wilde used to like to be punched about.'

In 1906 Littlechild was involved in investigating a thirty-four-year-old American, Harry Kendall Thaw, who was in London at that time. Thaw, something of a playboy, was the millionaire son of a railway magnate, and was married to a beautiful model named Evelyn Nesbit, an ex-chorus girl. He was responsible for the shooting of Stanford White, a noted architect, in the roof garden at New York's Madison Square Garden.

The fatal shooting took place on 25 June 1906, and the alleged motive was revenge: White had seduced the teenage Evelyn before she married Thaw. During Thaw's trial for murder in January 1907, some unsavoury stories emerged concerning his ill-treatment of women; it was even alleged that he meted out brutal whippings to his wife. The jury was unable to reach a verdict and he was tried a second time and found not guilty by reason of insanity, the Thaw millions having no small part to play in his escape from the ultimate penalty of the law.

Chapter 17

The Littlechild Suspect

'The good physician is known by his works.'

Francis J. Tumblety was born, as near as can be at present ascertained, in 1833 in Canada. The family moved, whilst he was still at an early age, to Rochester, New York. His father, Frank, was Irish, and his mother's name was Margaret. He was the youngest of eleven children, with two brothers, Patrick and Lawrence, and eight sisters, Jane and Bridget (twins), Alice, Margaret, Ann, Julia, Elizabeth and Mary.

Some details of this early life were provided by Captain W. C. Streeter, an old resident of Rochester who in 1888 was the owner of a canal boat plying between Rochester and Buffalo.

The first recollection I have of him is along about 1848. I should judge he was something like fifteen years old and his name was Frank Tumblety. I don't know when he changed it to Twomblety [referring to the name that was appearing in the 1888 newspaper accounts]. He was selling books and papers on the packets, and was in the habit of boarding my boat a short distance from town. The books he sold were largely of the kind Anthony Comstock suppresses now [Comstock was a reformer who gained some fame as superintendent of the Society for the Prevention of Vice in New York]. His father was an Irishman and lived on the common south of the city on what was then known as Sophia Street but is now Plymouth Avenue and is about a mile from the centre of the city. There were but few houses there then and the Tumbletys had no near neighbours, I don't remember what the father did. There were two boys older than Frank and one of them worked as a steward for Dr Fitzhugh, then a prominent physician. Frank continued to sell papers until 1850, I think, and then disappeared, and I did not see him again for ten years.

So Tumblety disappeared from his childhood stamping ground at the age of about seventeen. He returned in great style around 1860, as Streeter recalled:

... when he returned to Rochester as a great physician and soon became the wonder of the city. He wore a light fur overcoat that reached to his feet and had a dark collar and cuffs, and he was always followed by a big greyhound. When a boy he had no associates, and when he returned he was more exclusive and solitary than ever. I don't remember ever having seen him in company with another person in his walks. When I met him on his return, having known him quite well as a boy, I said, 'Hello, Frank, how d'ye do?' and he merely replied, 'Hello, Streeter,' and passed on. He had become very aristocratic during his absence. The papers had a great deal to say about him and he created quite a sensation by giving barrels of flour and other provisions to poor people. Afterwards he went to Buffalo and did likewise, and I understand visited other cities.

Streeter was unsure of the doctor's origins but said:

I think Frank was born in Rochester. He had no foreign accent when I met him, and I understood at the time that he was a Rochester boy. I remember after he became famous his two brothers quarrelled because each imagined the other was thought more of by the 'doctor'. I have not heard anything about him for fifteen years as I moored away from Rochester.

A valuable physical description of Tumblety was then provided by Captain Streeter:

He was about five feet ten inches high, of rather slight build, and fine-looking, but evidently avoided society. I thought that his mind had been affected by those books he sold, and am not at all surprised to hear his name mentioned in connection with the Whitechapel murders.

Another boyhood acquaintance of Tumblety, Edward Haywood, was tracked down by reporters in December 1888 at the Bureau of Accounts in the State Department. He said that he had known Tumblety since boyhood, and when it was first mentioned in the newspapers that there were suspicions connecting him with the Whitechapel murders he believed the theory was quite tenable. He said:

> I am in my fifty-second year and I fancy Frank Tumblety must be two or three years older. I remember him very well when he used to run about the canal in Rochester, a dirty, awkward, ignorant, uncared-for, good-for-nothing boy. He was utterly devoid of education. He lived with his brother, who was my uncle's gardener. About this time I went West. Tumblety turned up in Detroit as a 'doctor'. The only training he ever had for the medical profession was a little drug store at the back of the Arcade, which was kept by a 'Doctor' Lispenard, who carried on a medical business of a disreputable kind.

Mr Haywood further recalled, of Tumblety's later Washington days:

> A few years later I saw him here in Washington and he was putting on great style. He wore a military fatigue costume, and told me he was on General McClellan's staff. Lieutenant Larry Sullivan, who belonged to a Rochester regiment, came up to him one day. He tried to palm the same tale off upon Sullivan, but the latter, being perfectly familiar with McClellan's staff, told the imposter plainly just how great a liar he was. During the war and for some time after, Tumblety remained in Washington and played the 'doctor' as he had done in Detroit. He got up some sort of patent medicine, and at one time the walls were covered with large posters advertising the virtues of the Tumblety Pimple Destroyer. He must have made money, for he was able to spend plenty and live in the most extravagant elegance.

Mr Haywood then added another telling indictment of his erstwhile acquaintance: 'Knowing him as I do I should not be the least surprised if he turned out to be Jack the Ripper.'

For a young man of high intelligence and political ambition, there were many routes to success, but all of them depended on a system of personal preferment and patronage. It was all a matter of who you knew.

Tumblety claimed that at the age of twenty-four he was distinguished enough to be asked by some of the key political figures in

Montreal to stand for the Colonial Parliament in opposition to
Thomas Darcy McGee. Others urged him to enter the political arena
in Ottawa City. It was an offer which he declined. On 7 December
1857 he put forward a public disclaimer in the *Montreal Commercial
Advertiser*:

> As a candidate to represent the suffrages of the people of Mon-
> treal in opposition to Darcy McGee and that I am about to
> receive a most numerously signed address and I may add have
> resolved to come forward for the representation of the Irish
> interest. In allusion to the above statements, I may say it is not
> my intention at the present time to contest an election, but I
> have every hope, were I to do so, of ultimate success.

The press also lavished praise on the doctor and his herbal rem-
edies. The *St Johns Albion* printed a poem about him which
Tumblety, may well have written himself:

DR TUMBLETY

Dr Tumblety rode a white steed
Into St Johns in its time of need
Determined to cure with herbal pills
All the ailing of all their ills
Dr Tumblety had a grey hound
A beautiful animal I'll be bound
The dog looked up in the doctor's face
As he rode along at a slapping pace

Tumblety had a killing air
Though curing was his professional trade
Rosy of cheek and glossy of hair
Dangerous man to widow or maid

Eschewing beef, and mutton and pork
Like Daniel of old, he fatted on pulse
His thumb the knife his finger the fork
He lived on herbs and moss and dulse

Of simples all he knew the use
He also knew the use of the weed
But, ah! He played the dickens and deuce
With doctors who physic and purge and bleed

Cures he had wrought of each disease
With healing herbs and barks of trees
Simples culled from mountain and glen
Plucked from the moor or dragged from the fen
The mandrake, elm, and bitter bog bean
Sarsparilla and horehound, I ween
Butternut, colt's foot and Irish moss
The bark of the widow and garlic sauce
With these the doctor's wondrous skill
Each killing disease was sure to kill
Gouts, consumption, and shivering ague
Deathly diseases – complaints that plague you
All things nasty, for which physic's given
Out of you soon by these herbs will be driven
See certificates, given galore –
Citizens all, at least three-score
Blind and lame, who walk and see
Given up by the doctors, twenty-three
All grown sound and healthy by taking
Medical potions of Tumblety's making

So all the cramped rheumatic and stuffed
Seeing how the Doctor was puffed
Besieged his door at morn and noon
Blessing their stars to have met such a boon
Of a doctor who knew their disease without telling
Whether by seeing or only by smelling
Thousands came, who went assured
Satisfied all, for all were cured

In July 1858, Tumblety was practising medicine in Toronto. However, it was in St John, New Brunswick, that the first dark cloud of suspicion descended on the doctor. He had arrived there in 1860 and established himself in his usual manner, proclaiming himself to be an 'electric physician of international reputation'. He lived at the leading hotel in the city and 'by his pretentious airs convinced the people that he was all he represented himself to be'. He adopted the system of personal advertisement that he was to continue to use with great success in other locations. He was 'given to extremes in dress' and would ride through the streets 'arrayed in the most gorgeous style', mounted on a superb white horse, and followed by 'a troop' of thoroughbred hounds.

Soon however, rumours were whispered about that the doctor was a 'pretentious humbug and vulgar charlatan'. The more respectable members of the community dropped him. Eventually one of his patients died under 'very peculiar circumstances'. The patient, a locomotive engineer named Portmore, was well known in St John's and had many friends, and his death caused a local sensation. Portmore's family, their suspicions aroused, requested an autopsy, which revealed that the man's death was entirely due to the doctor's 'atrocious treatment'. So gross was this malpractice that the case was immediately put into the hands of the coroner.

A jury was empanelled and an inquest convened to more fully investigate the circumstances. Hampered by local red tape, the procedure was unduly prolonged, but eventually sifted the evidence and Tumblety was proved guilty of manslaughter. The shrewd 'doctor' was aware of the peril he was in and by this time had fled to Boston.

He was soon as conspicuous in Boston as he had been in St Johns. There was the same white horse, the same dogs and the same extravagant mode of attire. However, a subtle change had taken place. His narrow escape from justice had made him more careful about the general practice of medicine; he presented himself in Boston primarily as the inventor of a sure cure for pimples, and soon accumulated a healthy business, 'devoting his time entirely to ladies'. His trade increased to such an extent that he opened a branch office in New York and afterwards worked Jersey City, Pittsburgh, and many Western cities, extending as far south as San Francisco, and as far north as Canada. [New York World 27 November 1888]

He wrote his own personal motto:

> We use such balms as have no strife
> With Nature or the laws of Life;
> With blood our hands we never stain,
> Nor poison men to ease their pain.
>
> Our Father – whom all goodness fills,
> Provides the means to cure all ills;
> The simple herbs beneath our feet
> Well used, relieve our pains complete.
>
> A simple herb, a simple flower,
> Culled from dewy lea –

These, these shall speak with touching power
Of change and health to thee.

His travels also took him to the famous watering places such as 'exclusive and aristocratic' White Sulphur Springs, where he paraded himself with all 'his offensive vulgarity of attire', to the great horror of the staid old Virginia aristocracy.

On 18 March 1861, Tumblety received from the Board of the Commissioners of Health, Mayor's Office, New York, a copy of the health laws and ordinances published under their auspices, showing that they recognised him as a member of the medical fraternity.

A close friend, A. McDonnell, a lawyer from Buffalo, wrote to Tumblety, after reading about him in the newspapers. In his letter he said: 'I perceive by the papers that you continue to astonish the natives. God and your own indomitable will have furnished you with a marvellous healing art, perhaps unequalled by any other man of your age now walking this earth.'

Colonel C. A. Dunham, a well-known lawyer in Fairview, New Jersey, was tracked down by a reporter in 1888 and gave much valuable information on Tumblety, whom he had known in his Washington days. He furnishes perhaps the most important insight of all:

When, to my knowledge of the man's history, his idiosyncrasies, his revolting practises, his antipathy to women, and especially to fallen women, his anatomical museum, containing many specimens like those carved from the Whitechapel victims – when, to my knowledge on these subjects, there is added the fact of his arrest on suspicion of being the murderer, there appears to me nothing improbable in the suggestion that Tumblety is the culprit.

He is not a doctor. A more arrant charlatan and quack never fattened on the hopes and fears of afflicted humanity. I first made the fellow's acquaintance a few days after the first battle of Bull Run. Although a very young man at the time I held a colonel's commission in the army, and was at the capitol on official business. The city was full of strangers, 90 per cent of them military men. All the first-class hotels resembled beehives. Among them were many peculiar-looking men, but of the thousands there was not one that attracted half as much attention as Tumblety. A titanian stature, with a very red face and long flowing mustache, he would have been a notable personage in any place and in any garb. But, decked in richly embroidered coat or jacket, with a medal held by a gay ribbon on each breast, a semi-military cap with a high peak, cavalry trousers with the brightest of yellow stripes, riding boots and spurs on for a show window, a dignified and rather stagey gait and manner, he was as unique a figure as could be found anywhere in real life. When followed, as he generally was, by a valet and two great dogs, he was no doubt the envy of many hearts. The fellow was everywhere. I never saw anything so nearly approaching ubiquity. Go where you would, to any of the hotels, to the War Department or the Navy Yard, you were sure to find the 'doctor'. He had no business in either place, but he went there to impress the officers whom he would meet. He professed to have had an extensive experience in European hospitals and armies, and claimed to have diplomas from the foremost medical colleges of the Old World and the New. He had, he declared, after much persuasion accepted the commission of brigade surgeon at a great sacrifice pecuniarily, but, with great complacency, he always added that, fortunately for his private patients, his official duties would not, for a considerable time, take him away from the city.

Colonel Dunham elaborates further on the most significant point – Tumblety's hatred of women:

At length it was whispered about that he was an adventurer. One day my Lieutenant-Colonel and myself accepted the 'doctor's' invitation to a late dinner symposium, he called it – at his rooms. He had very cosy and tastefully furnished quarters in, I believe, H Street. There were three rooms on a floor, the rear one being his office, with a bedroom or two a storey higher. On reaching the place we found covers laid for eight – that being the 'doctor's' lucky number, he said – several of the guests, all in the military service, were persons with whom we were already acquainted. It was soon apparent that whatever Tumblety's deficiencies as a surgeon, as an amphitryon he could not be easily excelled. His menu, with coloured waiters and the et ceteras, was furnished by one of the best caterers in the city. After dinner there were brought out two tables for play – for poker or whist. In the course of the evening some of the party, warmed by the wine, proposed to play for rather heavy stakes, but Tumblety frowned down the proposition at once and in such a way as to show he was no gambler. Someone asked why he had not invited some women to his dinner. His face instantly became as black as a thunder-cloud. He had a pack of cards in his hand, but he laid them down and said, almost savagely, 'No, Colonel, I don't know any such cattle, and if I did I would, as your friend, sooner give you a dose of quick poison than take you into such danger.' He then broke into a homily on the sin and folly of dissipation, fiercely denounced all women and especially fallen women.

He then invited us into his office where he illustrated his lecture so to speak. One side of this room was entirely occupied with cases, outwardly resembling wardrobes. When the doors were opened quite a museum was revealed – tiers of shelves with glass jars and cases, some round and others square, filled with all sorts of anatomical specimens. The 'doctor' placed on a table a dozen or more jars containing, as he said, the matrices [wombs] of every class of women. Nearly a half of one of these cases was occupied exclusively with these specimens.

Not long after this the 'doctor' was in my room when my Lieutenant-Colonel came in and commenced expatiating on the charms of a certain woman. In a moment, almost, the doctor was lecturing him and denouncing women. When he was asked why he hated women, he said that when quite a young man he fell desperately in love with a pretty girl, rather his senior, who promised to reciprocate his affection. After a brief courtship he married her. The honeymoon was not over when he noticed a disposition on the part of his wife to flirt with other men. He remonstrated, she kissed him, called him a dear jealous fool – and he believed her. Happening one day to pass in a cab through the worst part of the town he saw his wife and a man enter a gloomy-looking house. Then he learned that before her marriage his wife had been an inmate of that and many similar houses. Then he gave up all womankind.

If Tumblety's story is true, or even partly true, we have here an explanation for his loathing of women. Having fallen deeply in love with a woman older than himself, possibly even a mother-figure, to whom he devoted himself, he was devastated to learn that not only had she deceived him, she was also a prostitute.

Tumblety's time in Washington was not without its adversities, as the following extract from a Washington newspaper shows:

> On Saturday afternoon, a charge of libel was preferred before Justice Johnson, by Dr Francis Tumblety, against Mr George Perceval, the proprietor of Canterbury Music Hall. Dr Tumblety charges that George Perceval did on the 7th instant, and on divers other occasions, utter and publish a false and malicious libel, to the great injury and detriment of his reputation as an authorised physician.
>
> The complainant (Dr T.) exhibited to the Justice a programme of the amusements of Canterbury Hall, in which one of the farces proposed to be performed was entitled 'Doctor Tumblety's First Patient'. The publication of the same in this connection, the Doctor very positively stated, was intended to ridicule him and his profession, and to bring into disrepute his character as a physician. He said that he had previously requested the proprietor of the Canterbury Hall not to use his name on the stage in a burlesque performance. The Doctor also exhibited his diploma, to prove that he was a regularly authorised physician, and a gold-medal testimonial to his efficiency as a physician, which he had received in Canada.
>
> The Doctor, who, by the way, is a very handsome man, is rather eccentric and odd in his manner, appearing at times on the streets dressed as an English sportsman, with tremendous spurs fastened to his boots, and accompanied by a pair of greyhounds, lashed together. His skill as a physician, however, is undoubted, his practice in Washington being very extensive, and among the higher classes of society.

A different account of this incident is furnished by Colonel Dunham:

> Tumblety would do almost anything under heaven for notoriety, and although his notoriety in Washington was of a kind to turn people from him, it brought some to him. Let me tell you of one of his schemes. At that time there was a free – or it may have been a 10-cent – concert saloon known as the Canterbury Music Hall. The performance embraced music, dancing, farces, etc. One day Tumblety told me, apparently in great distress, that the management of the Canterbury Hall had been burlesquing him on the stage. An actor, he said, was made up in

minute imitation of himself, and strutted about the stage with two dogs something like his own, while another performer sang a topical song introducing his name in a ridiculous way. That night, or the next, I went with some friends to this concert hall, and, sure enough, about 10 o'clock out came a performer the very image of Tumblety. In a minute a dog, that did not resemble the 'doctor's', sprang from the auditorium upon the stage and followed the strutting figure. The longer I examined the figure the greater became my surprise at the perfection of the make-up.

Before I reached my hotel I began, in common with my companions, to suspect that the figure was no other than Tumblety himself. The next day the Lieutenant-Colonel told the 'doctor' our suspicions. The fellow appeared greatly hurt. He at once instituted an action against the proprietor of the hall for libel. The action was another sham, and three or four nights afterwards the 'doctor' was completely unmasked. When the song was under way a powerful man suddenly sprang from the auditorium to the stage, exclaiming at the figure, 'See here, you infernal scoundrel, Dr Tumblety is my friend, and I won't see him insulted by such an effigy as you are. Come, off with that false mustache and duds,' and quick as a flash he seized the doctor's hirsute appendage and pulled it for all it would stand, threw his cap among the audience and otherwise showed the fellow up. The 'doctor', though a powerful man, made no struggle except to get behind the scenes as soon as possible.

The Colonel makes interesting comment on Tumblety's book, *Kidnapping of Dr Tumblety. By Order of the Secretary of War of the US*, published in Cincinnati in 1866:

Tumblety's book contains, as subscribers to testimonials to his high social standing and medical skill in Canada, the names of some of the best-known people in the Dominion and elsewhere. Evidently the testimonials are bogus. The book was doubtless intended for distribution among persons who would never suspect or discover the fraud, and there was little or no danger of its reaching any of the parties whose names accompanied the lying commendations. Tumblety, I am sure, would rather have lost $1,000 than that a copy should have fallen into my hands. I obtained it in this way. Meeting him one day in Brooklyn, near his office, he urged me to go in for a chat. As I was standing by his desk, about to leave, I involuntarily picked up the book and, while I was yet talking, mechanically turned over the leaves. The name of a friend having suddenly caught my eye and aroused my curiosity, I asked the 'doctor' to let me take the book. This he good-naturedly objected to, making various excuses for refusing. I, however, insisted, and when he found me in dead earnest he reluctantly yielded.

When General George McClellan was appointed commander of the army of the Potomac Tumblety made up his mind to tender his professional services as a surgeon in one of the regiments. He stated in his book: 'My feeling and sympathy have ever been with the Union and the Constitution, under which Young America progressed in strength, power, and wealth, with almost miraculous growth.' McClellan gave him passes which enabled him to move freely. He mixed with the officers of the General's staff and was always cordially received and trusted. He later claimed on oath that he never betrayed any trust or proved false to any friendship that he had professed. He also claimed that through a distinguished officer with whom he became acquainted in Boston he was introduced to President Abraham Lincoln, for whom he professed 'feelings of the warmest respect and admiration'.

The provost-marshal, or military governor of Washington, General Wordsworth, who was acquainted with Tumblety's family in Rochester, repeatedly invited him to his headquarters to dine with him. It was during these evenings that Tumblety became acquainted with several high-ranking military officers. He often stayed late at these soirées, and at such times the General furnished him with some of his staff officers as escorts back to his rooms at Willard's Hotel. One of these escorts, Captain Bacus, believed to be a relative of the General and who had previously been well acquainted with Tumblety's brother in Rochester, became a personal friend of the doctor's.

Over a two-year period, Tumblety earned in excess of $30,000 through his herbal cures and was, he claimed, frequently present at receptions held by President Lincoln. He stated that an 'alarming decline in health' prevented him from joining the army as a full-time surgeon and caused him to contemplate a recuperative trip to Europe. But was this just an excuse to hide the fact that someone had realised that he was not what he claimed to be?

His relations with the President, he claimed, were of 'the most gratifying character, and as I informed him of my projected trip, he kindly furnished me with letters, one of which was an introduction to Mr Adams, the American Minister at the Court of St James.' Circumstances, however, apparently forced him to abandon the idea of the trip, and some time later his professional duties called him to St Louis, where he speedily established a reputation which he said excited a feeling of jealousy amongst the medical practitioners of that city, and subsequently 'lent itself to the persecution of an innocent and unoffending man'.

In St Louis Tumblety took rooms at the Lindell Hotel, which at the time was claimed to be the largest hotel in the world. Built in 1863, it was seven floors high, and had become the gathering place for the cream of the city's society. Within two weeks of his arrival the real or imagined persecution that he felt he suffered began. He wrote:

> I have been charged with eccentricity in dress, but I presumed, as this is a free country, that so long as a person does not outrage decency or propriety, he has a perfect right to suit his own taste in the colour and fashion of his garments. It seems, however, that I was mistaken, and even my partiality for a fine horse and a handsome dog – weaknesses which must be constitutional in my case, as I am happy to know they are in many of the most amiable individuals in this and every other country – has, in connection with the cut of my apparel, furnished sufficient foundation, in the estimation of the might-is-right party, to annoy and persecute me.

He went to Carondelet, Missouri, to look at some property with a view to purchase.

> While there, I was unceremoniously arrested and incarcerated for two days, for no other offense, that I could learn, than that I was 'putting on foreign airs', riding fine horses, dressing in a semi-military style, with a handsome robe, high patent-leather boots and spurs; that I kept a large greyhound, sported a black mustache; and, in short, as one of my gallant captors affirmed, 'You're thinking yourself another God Almighty, and we won't stand it.'

However, as there was neither treason, murder, arson, or any other hanging or penitentiary crime in all this, and as I fortunately had an influential friend at hand, I was, after, as I have said, an imprisonment of a couple of days, set free, once again to resume my professional labours, much to the chagrin of my medical rivals, to whom, as I was informed by the Chief of Police, I, in a great measure, was indebted for my arrest.

But I was destined soon to fall a victim to another and more serious annoyance, or, to call it by its proper name, tyrannical and monstrous persecution.

On returning to St Louis, he was arrested again. This event was a pivotal point in his life and one which seems to have left him full of hatred. To his bewilderment, the doctor was taken into custody suspected of being involved in the conspiracy to assassinate President Lincoln.

His own feelings on the assassination he sums up as follows:

I, who had known and esteemed him for his many amiable and social qualities, felt, I am sure, the great national loss as keenly as any; and from an innate respect to the man, and in sacred reverence to his memory, I attended his obsequies at Springfield, Illinois, although I could ill afford the time: for at no former period of my life was I so professionally pressed, my practice at that time netting me some $300 per day.

Almost the first person I met on my arrival at Springfield was the steward of the late President's household, who knew me at once, for he had frequently seen me at the White House, and bursting into tears, he caught my hand, exclaiming, 'O, Doctor, this is a sad time for us to meet!'

The last sad, solemn ceremony performed, I returned, Heaven knows in how melancholy a mood, to St Louis, and the day after I was once again arrested, thrown into prison, and this time my office and apartments were searched, ransacked, and plundered of every article of portable value, including a considerable amount of money.

He remained incarcerated in St Louis for two days, and was visited by several military officers, whom he questioned as to the reason for his arrest. They laughingly replied, 'Oh, they have such an immense amount of excitement in Washington that Colonel Baker [under whose order the arrest was made] thinks that we ought to have a little sensation here.'

The *Missouri Republican* reported, under the headline 'Arrest of the Indian Herb Doctor':

A sensation was produced in police circles yesterday, by the arrest of the famous Indian herb doctor, J. H. Blackburn, alias Tumblety. He was arrested at his office on Third Street, opposite the Post Office, by a United States policeman, and is charged, as it is stated, with some knowledge of complicity in the late assassination of President Lincoln.

We are not informed of the grounds of the suspicion under which he has fallen. He is said to have been a former partner of Herold's, in Brooklyn, New York. A few facts in relation to the Doctor's history may be interesting in this connection.

Several years ago, at the time the practice was fashionable of giving flour and bread to the poor, Dr Tumblety visited Buffalo, New York, and announcing to the public, through the columns of the Buffalo Express, that he would on the day following meet any merchant of that city on the steps of the Merchants Exchange, and there distribute fifty sacks of flour to the poor, the proprietors of the Express, desiring to know more about the Doctor, telegraphed to Toronto, Canada, from which city the Doctor hailed, inquiring who he was. The answer came from the Bank of Toronto: 'His check is good for $60,000 in this bank.'

At the appointed hour the Doctor was present with fifty bags of flour, which he distributed to the poor. The next day he published advertisements, and issued hand-bills, announcing that he would cure 'all the ills that flesh is heir to'.

Tumblety explained his actions in the following manner, 'I do not court fame, for with Colton [presumably an American celebrity], of present fame, I think little, and of the future less; for the praises we receive after we are buried, like the flowers that are strewed over our grave, may be gratifying to the living, but they are nothing to the dead; the dead are gone, either to the place where they hear them not, or where, if they do, they will despise them. No, I do not covet fame for my alms, but if I can leave behind me a name and reputation as an alleviator of the bodily ills that afflict poor humanity, my mission upon earth will be accomplished.'

Several months ago the Doctor came to this city, announcing himself as the Indian Herb Doctor, and that he was prepared to cure every known disease, and published certificates from those under his treatment. When he first came to the city, he affected a half-military dress, but upon being arrested by the provost guard for wearing military clothing, the Doctor concluded to change his style of dress.

Tumblety himself stated that no person was better personally known in and around Washington than himself:

thus the absurdity of confounding me with the notorious individual for whom I was arrested will be strongly apparent. Nay, not only in Washington but in every city throughout the United States, as well as the British provinces, I am recognised: for there are few places in which I cannot be identified by some of my former patients.

He asked:

How was it possible for Stanton's [Lincoln's Secretary of War] myrmidons to mistake me for the notorious Dr Blackburn whose person is the antipodes of the following description, which was embodied in a military pass I obtained during the memorable period of martial law in 1865. 'Age, thirty-two; height, six feet; eyes, blue; complexion, fair; hair, dark; occupation, physician.' I will venture to assert that the only point of resemblance between myself and the individual on whose account I was so fearfully victimised is in the last item, otherwise, I am rejoiced to state, we have no nearer likeness than 'I to Hercules'.

The 'notorious Dr Blackburn' was Dr Luke Pryor Blackburn, a Confederate agent, who had been praised for his excellent work in Mississippi and Louisiana fighting yellow fever outbreaks. In 1864 he went to Bermuda to assist in the fight against the disease there.

In April 1865 it was announced by Charles Allen, the US Consul in Bermuda, that Blackburn's real reason for being in the colony was to hatch what was to become known as 'the yellow fever plot' to infect the North with the disease. To accomplish this he would ship soiled, infected clothing to northern cities, though in reality this would not have worked, as the germs would not have survived. Blackburn's arrest was ordered. Unfortunately for Tumblety, 'Dr J. H. Blackburn' was one of his current aliases. The St Louis police mistook him for the wanted man and he was arrested.

Tumblety wrote bitterly: 'The fact is, my arrest was one of those open-handed acts of wantonness that could only spring from a reckless and irresponsible official, wielding absolute authority, and without the pale of the fear of God or of mankind.' He claimed to have suffered 'great pecuniary loss, bodily and mental suffering, and a broken constitution'.

He then made the following curious observation:

The chronicles of Ireland will furnish many instances of undue harshness exercised during troubled times, and the suspension of the writ of habeas corpus, but I challenge the record to produce such a flagrant use of power, and wanton outrage of the liberty of the citizen, as was exemplified in my case, and I may say hundreds, if not thousands of others . . .

According to Colonel John P. Baker, Provost Marshal General of Missouri, in a report forwarded to Assistant War Secretary Dana, Tumblety knew nothing at all about the assassination plot:

I have the honour to forward herewith, in compliance with your telegram of this date, Dr Tumblety, alias Blackburn. All his papers had been carefully examined previous to the arrival of your order, but nothing was found in them tending to implicate him with the assassination.

Tumblety's papers and his own admissions show that he has tramped the continent from Quebec to New Orleans, in the character of an 'Indian Herb Doctor'; has gained an extensive notoriety as an impostor and quack; has been compelled to leave several towns and cities in Canada for his rascality and trickery, and is being continually importuned and threatened by those he has deluded and swindled.

Tumblety's principal associates in Saint Louis have been one J. W Blackburn, his assistant in the 'medical profession', and one Oregon Wilson, an artist. There appears to be nothing against them, except they belong to a class of adventurers that encumber and prey upon society. [Ref. National Archives, War Dept. Records, File 'B', Doc. 261, JAO]

In light of the Missouri provost's initial report, what can be made of Assistant War Secretary Charles Dana's insistence on Tumblety's imprisonment and questioning? As reported in Chapter 1, Dana advised Judge Advocate General Joseph Holt that he felt the prisoner 'should be confined in the Penitentiary'. To this advice he added the suggestion: 'Let the Indian Doctor tell all he knows about Booth and Booth's associates.'

What did Dr Tumblety know? The files fail to cast any light on the question. His name is registered in the Old Capitol jail inventory, but particulars are not specified. Then he disappears from the prison records.

One extract from his own writings describes a tense episode while a prisoner in the Old Capitol. One of his fellow inmates was a Southern belle who on hearing a military band and the marching of hundreds of feet outside their cell window – Sherman's grand entry into the capital – was overcome by 'the natural curiosity of her sex', looked from the window and was seen by one of the prison guards.

At this, the guard raised his rifle and fired at her, as she was in breach of prison rules. The bullet struck the brickwork a few inches from her face, but the recalcitrant woman merely stamped her foot, shook her fist and cried: 'Fire again, I won't stir!' It would seem that Tumblety was impressed by this display of defiance by the 'Southern heroine'.

Both the *Washington Star* and the *New York Herald* carried accounts by Tumblety of his incarceration:

After three weeks' imprisonment in the Old Capitol prison in this city, I have been unconditionally and honourably released from confinement by the directions of the Secretary of War, there being no evidence whatever to connect me with the yellow fever or assassination plot, with which some of the Northern journals have charged me of having some knowledge. My arrest appears to have grown out of a statement made in a low, licentious sheet, published in New York, to the effect that Dr Blackburn, who has figured so unenviously in the hellish yellow fever plot, was no other person than myself. In reply to that statement, I would most respectfully say to an ever generous public that I do not know this fiend in human form named Dr Blackburn; nor have I ever seen him in my life. For the truth of this assertion I can bring hundreds of distinguished persons throughout the United States to vouch for my veracity, and, if necessary, can produce certificates from innumerable numbers of gentlemen in high official positions.

While in imprisonment, I noticed in some of the New York and other Northern papers a paragraph setting forth that the villain Herold, who now stands charged with being one of the conspirators in the atrocious assassination plot, was at one time in my employment. This, too, is false in every particular, and I am at a loss to see how it originated, or to trace it to its origin. For the past five years I have had but one man in my employment, and he is with me yet, his character being beyond reproach. I never saw Herold, to my knowledge, and I have no desire to see him.

Another paper has gone so far as to inform the public that I was an intimate acquaintance of Booth, but this too is news to me, as I never spoke to him in my life, or any of his family.

I do hope the persons which so industriously circulated these reports, connecting me with these damnable deeds, to the very great injury of my name and reputation, will do me the justice to publish my release, and the facts of my having been entirely exonerated by the authorities here, who, after a diligent investigation, could obtain no evidence that would in the least tarnish my fair reputation.

With these few remarks in justice to myself, I will close by submitting them to the public.

He also wrote bitterly of his experiences in his pamphlet, *Kidnapping of Dr Tumblety*. The following passage shows the rage that bubbled below the surface:

I cannot trust myself to reflect upon the cruel manner in which I have been treated and the indignity I have suffered: for at such times I feel the hot blood tingling to my finger ends, and it requires a strong effort to calm an indignation which, if allowed full scope, might lead the victim of a tyrannical despot to contemplate redress, by personal chastisement upon the author of his misfortunes. Thank heaven, there is considerable philosophy in my composition, and I can bear and forbear or at least bide my time.

> For time at last sets all things even –
> And if we do but watch the hour,

> There never yet was human power
> Which could evade, if unforgiven,
> The patient search and vigil long
> Of him who treasures up a wrong.

Tumblety summed up his confusion thus:

A few more remarks will not be inapplicable concerning my arrest, and the presumed cause, for it was all presumption, and the arrangement was so mystified and befogged, that at the time I was almost tempted to question my own identity. Indeed, I was somewhat in the same predicament of the rustic wagoner, who while asleep, some rogues unhitched the team and carried them off. Awakening soon after he rubbed his eyes in a state of bewilderment, and after a few minutes' intense cogitation, was delivered of the following soliloquy: 'Am I Hodge, or aint I Hodge? If I am Hodge, I've lost four spanking fine horses. If I aint Hodge, I have found a wagon.' In my case, however, if I lost my identity, I discovered something far less agreeable than a wagon, in the shape of the Old Capitol Prison.

He continued to harbour feelings of ill will about his false incarceration, and quoted Dickens to illustrate the 'old barbarous system of imprisonment', saying that the author 'never realised the horror of being a State prisoner, and, worse than all, the State prisoner of such a man as Stanton, under whose iron despotism the unfortunate victim could not even speculate upon the fate in store for him.'
He also wrote bitterly:

For three or four years, persons innocent, like myself, had been summarily arrested and made away with, Heaven knows where, and the resemblance of many cases I had from time to time read of, now that I was another added to the number, crowded thick and fast upon me. Under such circumstances, to look philosophically upon the situation is an impossibility. The chronicles of the past were conjured up, nor could I glean one ray of consolation, in comparing the tyranny of a past age with the despotism of the present. The legends of the Tower of London, the horrors of St Marc, the dark record of the Bastille, even the chronicles of the Spanish Inquisition, crowded upon my excited fancy, compared to which the Marshalsea, the King's

Bench, the Fleet, and the various receptacles for the unfortunate debtor, described by 'Boz', were agreeable retreats.

Tumblety maintained that he became ill after his wrongful imprisonment: 'I feel that I shall never again realise the hardy and robust physique for which I was distinguished previous to my arrest in St Louis.'

Fearing that some of his readers might find his views extreme or unbalanced, Tumblety continued:

To the inexperienced all this may appear the effect of a morbid and overstrained imagination; but place the strongest-minded person in the situation with an Edwin Stanton the controller of his destiny, and the incertitude of the future would unstring his nerves, were they originally of iron strength.

After his release, Tumblety left Washington for New York, where he resumed his medical career. As usual, his arrival and activities were documented by the local papers.

The *Sunday Mercury* included in an article the following reference to Dr Tumblety returning to his healing ways.

We were honoured with a visit from the celebrated Indian Doctor last evening, who has escaped the toils of the War Department, and is once more going about curing diseases with the most magical success, and threatening to send all the undertakers, sextons, and gravediggers to the alms house.

The article continued in such flattering terms about him that he could almost have written it himself. It also had a vitriolic reference to Stanton which tends to reinforce this supposition.

Tumblety then left the east to return to St Louis, where his arrival was once again announced in the local press. The hostility that he encountered there from most of the other medical practitioners he put down to jealousy. It is likely that they saw him as an eccentric fraud, with a flair for self-publicity. His own view of his medical philosophy he recorded on paper:

I am, in a great measure, the disciple of Abernethy, especially in his horror of cutting, unless as a last recourse. That great physician was a contemporary of Sir Astley Cooper, but there was no sympathy in their mode of practice, and he at all times expressed abhorrence at the sanguinary practice of Sir Astley.

He illustrated this with a story about Cooper, royal physician to George IV, being unable to cure the monarch. The royal family sent for Abernethy, who was treating the poor. Abernethy dismissed the royal summons: 'No, no, let him send for his butcher; I can't go, for I have my poor hospital patients to attend to, and I won't neglect them for all the kings in Christendom.' Tumblety concluded: 'There is no disputing the fact that the knife is the source of immense mischief to the human family. Every day brings us tidings of some unfortunate man or woman being ushered into eternity through the means of a surgical operation.' Tumblety recalls several unnecessary deaths caused on the operating table, and continues his crusade for greater use of the medical properties of plants as a substitute for 'the horrors of the scalpel and amputating knife'. Was the death of his patient in St Johns on his mind when he penned these lines?'

While residing in Boston, from around 1863, Dr Tumblety befriended Captain Anderson of the Royal Navy. Anderson also knew Tumblety's relatives in England, who, it seemed, believed that he had joined the United States Army and been killed in an engagement. The captain frequently pressed the doctor to take a trip with him to Europe to visit his friends there, 'among whom I had a near relative and namesake, Tumblety, who has been connected over 20 years with the Cunard line. On one of his trips the Captain took my daguerreotype to my uncle in England, who has since died, in order to satisfy him that I was still in the land of the living.'

Captain Moody, a distinguished Cunard commander, was also an intimate friend of the family and used to meet Dr Tumblety at the Old Tremont in Boston. Tumblety writes: 'I recall these reunions with pleasurable emotion, for they were magnetic links that connected me with dear friends far away across the stormy Atlantic.'

But what of his other traits, his outspoken hatred of women and his remarkable and extremely bitter feelings towards them? His 'psychopathia sexualis'?

In 1888 the *New York Daily Tribune* reflected upon aspects of Tumblety's murky past:

During the war he lived in the vicinity of Broome Street. At that time he had some money, and his chief aim seemed to be to have everybody imagine that he was a great man. His odd ways always won attention. He used to ride up and down Fifth Avenue in an elegant equipage attired in the uniform of a major-general. A coloured coachman in gaudy clothes drove him about. In 1865 Tumblety was known as 'the great quack doctor', and, despite that fact, was eagerly sought after by old people who suffered from rheumatism. Soon after the [1863] draft riots that doctor posed as an Irish patriot, and used to hold indignation meetings in East Broadway, which were largely attended. During these meetings the doctor would tell his auditors what a great man he was, and, among other things, the hairbreadth escapes he had had during the war of the rebellion.

Six years ago the doctor was arrested in St Louis for parading himself about the city as a retired army surgeon. He was soon afterward released on condition that he would leave the town. The next heard of him was in connection with the Whitechapel crimes, when he was arrested as a suspect.

In the latter half of the 1860s Tumblety visited England:

I visited London where I was induced to prolong my stay beyond the anticipated period, through the request of parties who were anxious for me to prescribe for them. It was at this time that I had the gratification of an introduction to Charles Dickens, the immortal 'Boz', and my brief acquaintance with this eminent writer constitutes one of the most pleasant episodes of my life. During my sojourn in London I was the recipient of marked courtesies from many of England's most illustrious men and women.

He went from England to Berlin, where he spent two weeks before returning to London, 'whence, after a brief sojourn, I posted for Liverpool, and embarked for New York.'

Another witness to Tumblety's past life was Colonel James L. Sothern of Chicago, a lawyer. When Tumblety's name was mentioned in conversation with friends, he said:

I have met that fellow all over America and Europe. The first time I saw him was in London. It was along about 1870, I believe, and he was dressed up in the most startling fashion. I never saw anything quite equal to it. He had an enormous

Epesian shako [a form of military hat with a peak and an upright plume] on his head, an overcoat, the front of which was covered with decorations; earrings in his ears and by his side a very black negro, fantastically got up in a parti-coloured dress that appeared to be a blending of the flags of all nations. A great crowd followed him but he didn't appear to notice them. I saw him afterwards in San Francisco, and have seen him a hundred times in Chicago. Once I met him in Cincinnati parading through the Burnet Homes, and I asked the clerk who he was. He told me the fellow's name was Twomblety, but said he knew nothing about him, except that he didn't live there, and appeared to know no one. He said that he was a kind of patent medicine man he believed, who sold some off-colour medicine.

Another lawyer who had known the errant doctor was William P. Burr who stated in the *New York World* of 2 December 1888:

I met him in July 1880. He brought a suit against a Mrs Lyons, charging her with the larceny of $1,000 worth of bonds, and I was retained to defend her. It seems that several years before he met the son of Mrs Lyons while walking on the Baftery. The lad had just come from college and was a fine-looking young man. He was out of employment. Tumblety greeted him and soon had him under complete control. He made him a sort of secretary in the management of his bonds, of which he had about $100,000 worth, mostly in governments, locked up in a downtown safe-deposit company. He employed the youth as an amanuensis, as he personally was most illiterate. On April 28th 1878, the 'Doctor', as he was called, started for Europe by the Guion line steamer, Montana. See, here is his name on the passenger list, 'Doctor. Tumbety.' He gave a power of attorney to the young man, and under that some South Carolina railroad bonds were disposed of, as it was claimed and shown, under an agreement that they were to be taken as compensation. When Tumblety got back the young man had disappeared and the mother was arrested, charged by the 'Doctor' with having taken the bonds. I remember the examination to which I subjected him at the Tombs police court.

James D. McClelland was his lawyer, and I went into a history of the doctor's life. I remember well how indignant he became when I asked him what institution had the honour of graduating so precious a pupil. He refused to answer, and was told that the only reason for which he could refuse was that the answer would tend to humiliate or criminate him. He still refused to answer, and I thought he would spring at me to strike. There was quite a commotion in court. The case fell through and the old lady was not held. The son returned and brought a suit against the doctor, charging atrocious assault, and the evidence collected in this case was of the most disgusting sort. The lawyer who had the matter in hand is now dead, but I remember that there was a page of the Police Gazette as one exhibit, in which the portrait of the doctor appeared, with several columns of biography about him. This suit was not pushed, and then came another suit brought this time by Tumblety against William P. O'Connor, a broker, for disposing of the bonds. Boardman & Boardman defended and gathered up a great mass of evidence against the doctor. Charles Frost and Charles Chambers, detectives of Brooklyn, had evidence against him. At this time he kept an herb store, or something of that sort at No. 77 East Tenth Street. The suit did not come to anything, and I do not know of any other law matters in which this notorious man was concerned.

This interesting story raises the question of Tumblety's dubious sexuality and preference for the company of young men. Burr goes on to add more valuable information:

I had seen him before that time hovering about the Old Post Office building, where there were many clerks. He had a seeming mania for the company of young men and grown-up youths. In the course of our investigations about the man we gathered up many stray bits of history about him, but nothing to make a connected life story. He had a superabundance of cheek and nothing could make him abashed. He was a coward physically, though he looked like a giant, and he struck me as one who would be vindictive to the last degree. He was a tremendous traveller, and while away in Europe his letters to young Lyons showed that he was in every city of Europe. I had a big batch of letters sent by him to the young man Lyons and they were the most amusing farrago of illiterate nonsense. Here is one written from the West. He never failed to warn his correspondent against lewd women, and in doing it used the most shocking language. I do not know how he made his money. He had it before he became acquainted with the Lyons family, and was a very liberal spender. My own idea of this case [the White chapel murders] is that it would be just such a thing that Tumblety would be concerned in, but he might get one of his victims to do the work, for once he had a young man under his control he seemed to be able to do anything with the victim.

Further information on Tumblety's partiality for the company of young men was given by ex-Assemblyman Jimmy Oliver, who was tracked down by a *Daily Tribune* reporter at a meeting of the Young Men's Democratic Club in New York, after the doctor's arrest in England:

The stories that the doctor used to tell of his wonderful exploits when I was a boy living in East Broadway would make a fellow's hair curl. I remember once that he told of riding a coal black charger across a ravine twenty feet wide in his endeavour to escape a party of rebels whom he had accidentally fallen in with during the Peninsular campaign. The gravity with which he told that creepy story was enough to bring tears to the most hardened wretch's eyes. The boys always pretended to believe everything the old fellow would say, and he thought they did too. After he had finished one of his war stories he would change off on the wrongs which Ireland has suffered for so long, and then tell about the time when he put a company of English dragoons to flight by an ambuscade trick only known and practised by himself. The doctor, however, always spent plenty of money with the boys and none were ever known to doubt a statement made by him – that is, while he was around.

James Pryor, the house detective of the Fifth Avenue Hotel in New York, also recalled the dandified doctor. He had first seen him around 1868 and gave a familiar description of him: 'He had a big black mustache, one of the blacking-brush kind, black eyes, a good complexion and a walk like he had just been elected Alderman.' His dress was described as an army officer's cap, a big cape, and light-coloured trousers. At that time he had a 'kind of fake medicine shop' on Grand Street where he sold his patent medicine. Pryor said that the doctor was 'chased away from there' and opened up a place in Jersey City. He added:

> Wherever he went he was followed by a thick-set young man, who kept about twenty paces behind him. They never spoke to each other; and when the 'doctor' would come into the hotel his shadow would lounge in after him. They got to telling tough stories about the 'doctor', and the guests complained about him – the gentleman, I mean – and they said they didn't care to have him so near them, so I determined to bounce him. I remember that day very well, because I fired another fellow just before I did the 'doctor' . . .
>
> I never had trouble with the 'doctor', he was very quiet, and soon as he tumbled to the fact that I knew him he went right out. I saw him a year afterwards passing the hotel. He never came in, though.

Pryor thought that in twenty years of encountering curious characters on Broadway Tumblety was the oddest he had seen. He expressed his puzzlement at the origins of the doctor's wealth, stating that he always appeared to have plenty of money and paid his bills promptly.

Pryor's opinion, when asked, was that he did not think that Tumblety was the Whitechapel murderer, a view echoed by a hotel clerk. Pryor said:

> If I were to search New York for a man less likely to be guilty than the 'doctor' I wouldn't find him. Why, he hasn't the nerve of a chicken. He just had enough nerve to put some molasses and water together and label it a medicine – the biggest nerve being the label – and sell it.

Of Tumblety's attitude to women, Pryor commented:

> He seemed indifferent to them. I never saw him, in all his walks up and down Broadway, look at a woman. He never appeared to care for them, and many a time I have seen women look after him, for he was a very handsome fellow. He had the smallest hand and foot I ever saw. During the later years of his residence here he wore fewer diamonds and appeared to be getting a little toned down in his dress. He used to go abroad

often and what he went for nobody ever knew. I never heard the sound of his voice in all the years I saw him.

It is interesting to note these remarks by someone who was not acquainted with Tumblety personally. Those who knew him, as we have seen, felt quite differently. The reporter who had interviewed Pryor concluded his article with an interesting observation:

However impressed with the belief in the 'doctor's' harmlessness those to whom he was a familiar figure may be, the London police evidently do not share it. Although nothing tangible was produced connecting the eccentric wanderer with the Whitechapel crimes, the English authorities have evidently not abandoned their suspicions. Only a few days ago the London Chief of Police telegraphed to San Francisco requesting that specimens of Twomblety's handwriting in possession of the Hibernia Bank there be forwarded to him. When these are compared with the chirography of 'Jack the Ripper' another chapter may be added to the life story of this man of mystery.

The history of Tumblety in the 1880s was further clarified by another young man who fell in with him and who declared undying gratitude to the doctor. A reporter from the *New York World* newspaper tracked down Martin H. McGarry, a young New York businessman, on 4 December 1888:

In the first place the Doctor's name is Thomas F. Tumblety, and he is not an herb doctor any more than I am a street contractor. It was July, 1882, that I applied for work at No. 7, University Place. I saw a big fine-looking man standing on the stoop. He had on a braided English smoking jacket, black striped trousers, Oxford ties and a peaked cap. He told me there was no work for me in the house, but if I wanted to work he would give me a trial. I asked him what he wished me to do, and he said he was in need of a young man to act as a travelling companion. We walked upstairs to his rooms, and he told me all about himself, and I afterwards found it was true.

Tumblety told McGarry that he had been born in Dublin in 1835 and was the son of a wealthy Irish gentleman. He claimed to have graduated from the University of Dublin, and displayed a diploma as proof of this. He also claimed to have studied medicine in Dublin and produced another diploma to this effect. He said that he left Ireland for America in 1853, landing at New York. Here, he continued, he studied surgery, and on the outbreak of the Civil War became an army surgeon. The doctor then produced his honourable discharge from the army, and a number of personal letters from General Grant speaking of his efficiency and good conduct. He also claimed that on the death of his father he had been left a large amount of money, which kept him from having to do anything for a living.

McGarry seems to have been suitably impressed by the doctor's bogus credentials and agreed to work for him. He provides an interesting insight into Tumblety's lifestyle in the years preceding the Whitechapel murders:

My duties were not hard. I was always to be near him. He got up at 11 o'clock, when he would usually send out his jug for a pint of old ale. He breakfasted in the house and then walked around town. Usually he went up about the Morton House, where he pointed out the actors to me and told me who they were and what they did. Sometimes in the afternoons we would drop into the matinées. In the evenings we would stay at home generally. After we had been in New York a while he said we were to go to Niagara Falls. We stopped at a French hotel, where everybody knew the doctor and seemed glad to see him. He showed me about, and after a short time grew tired of the place and we started off to Rochester.

After we saw everything about Rochester we went to Saratoga. The doctor took rooms at No. 151 Congress Street. It was the finest suite of rooms at the Springs, there was nothing at the Grand Union that could approach them. We stayed there two months and enjoyed life. He was very kind to me and sent my people presents. We came back to New York where we spent the Winter. He had nothing to do but amuse himself, and he used to walk about town, ride, and drive through the Park, and read to me, and have me read to him. He kept everything that was said about him in the newspapers. He had no associates or companions but me, and sometimes for days I would be the only one he would talk to.

After a trip to Rome, NY, we returned to New York and went to the Hygeia Hotel on Laight Street, although the doctor still kept his rooms on University Place. He took the front parlour room, and I went back to my folk, No. 300 Henry Street. Although I was not boarding with him he sent the money he would have paid for my board in a package with my salary to my people.

One day he told me he wanted to see Boston, and off we started for Boston, and then visited New Haven, and Philadelphia, when we stopped at the Girard Hotel in Philadelphia. It took us three weeks to see the sights in Philadelphia. The doctor showed me everything. We came back to New York and the doctor took it into his head to go to Glasgow. I wouldn't go with him and he went alone. He was back in a month and went to Mrs McNamara's, No. 79 East Tenth Street, to live. He telegraphed for me to come here and I lived with him for three weeks. We knocked about New York during that time and then he persuaded me to go to Queenstown with him. When we got there we went to Dublin and then after a week to Inniskillen Falls.

When we came back to New York my uncle, M. O'Brian, a produce merchant, No. 209 Washington Street, said I could not roam around any more, but I must stay at home with my sisters – I worked as a shipping clerk for my uncle, and the doctor used to come up to see me very often. While I was with the doctor I saved $1,250, and he put $780 more to it and I bought out Mr Kramer, who ran the business I am now running. All I have I owe to the doctor, and I think he is the best friend I ever had.

McGarry was, of course, asked about Tumblety's aversion to women:

He always disliked women very much. He used to say to me, 'Martin, no women for me.' He could not bear to have them near him. He thought all women were imposters, and he often said that all the trouble in this world was caused by women.

Mrs McNamara, the doctor's landlady at 79 East Tenth Street, also had some revealing memories. She said in 1888 that Tumblety had begun stopping with her years ago and had lived there ever since when he was in New York. He used to explain his long absences at night by telling her he had to go to a monastery and pray for his dear departed wife.

The ubiquitous doctor was certainly a frequent visitor to London, as claimed by Littlechild, and his presence there prior to the Whitechapel murders is confirmed in an article in the *World* of 27 November 1888, where it is stated: 'A few years ago the pimple-banishing enterprise was moved to London, where the doctor for a time is said to have made money.'

Chapter 18

The Arrest and Escape of Jack the Ripper

'. . . this destructive course . . .'

Tumblety arrived in Liverpool in 1888 aboard one of the steamers that regularly plied the transatlantic route. Outwardly, he might have looked like any other travelling professional doctor. He certainly was as bright as most of the middle-class people he would encounter in London, if not brighter. His dress was, by now, not so garish and eccentric.

It is fairly certain that in London he was involved in unusual sexual activities. His movements became irregular and he appeared and disappeared for no good reason. He was also, like many Irish-Americans, a genuine Irish sympathiser. We have seen that American newspapers of 1888 referred to him as 'Irish-American' and posing as an Irish patriot.

Donald McCormick, in *The Identity of Jack the Ripper*, notes that there was no adequate supervision of migrant doctors in England at the time of the Whitechapel murders:

Foreigners with criminal records, quacks with inadequate quali- fications could and did practise in Britain, even though this meant taking rooms in the back streets of the slums. Thus a foreign doctor, who was not registered here, or an unqualified Briton, might well have been 'Dr Jekyll' to whom the various police chiefs referred.

Although McCormick was unaware of Tumblety and his link with the murders, his description fits the Indian herb doctor perfectly.

Tumblety was very familiar with London, especially the East End. He had stayed in hotels on his previous visits to the capital, but we believe that after his return in 1888, he changed his lifestyle and took up lodgings at 22 Batty Street. By looking at the sites of the four murders, it is clear that Batty Street was an ideal refuge for

Tumblety's series of premeditated killings. It gave easy access to all the locations and allowed him to slip away unnoticed into the night. As mentioned earlier, it is possible that he also had other lodgings in London.

We know today that serial killers will go to extreme lengths to make their fantasies come true. Careful prior planning is one of the hallmarks of such killers, and in Tumblety's case we now have evidence of his bizarre, calculated moves. We believe we have shown that he engineered a safe bolt hole for himself right in the heart of the East End.

After murdering Mary Ann Nichols on 31 August 1888, he did not kill again immediately, but scoured the slums of the East End, with its many pubs and lodging houses frequented by the impoverished and wretched of Victorian London. It was during this time that the shape of his task must have crystallised in his mind. On the morning of 8 September he murdered Annie Chapman, and on 30 September Catherine Eddowes. It was on the latter occasion that Tumblety, quite uncharacteristically, was caught in a compromising position. Following the killing, he made his way back to his lodgings in Batty Street to find the police swarming around the area. Another killer had murdered Liz Stride earlier that night in Berner Street – very near his lodging house. He had been virtually ensnared completely by accident. This was to be a critical moment in the killing spree of Jack the Ripper. He was confronted by his landlady in a downstairs room whilst changing his clothes, and a sequence of events was initiated which would finally lead to his arrest.

Now he turned his back on those lodgings to take up residence elsewhere, with the police, for the first time, already on his trail. In October, Scotland Yard made contact with the San Francisco police and asked for a sample of Tumblety's handwriting. On 29 October San Fransisco Police contacted Scotland Yard saying they could send a sample of his writing, and on 22 November the Yard asked that it be sent immediately. The fact that the request was made to that city, and that the police there were able to oblige, indicates that Scotland Yard had obtained significant information on the man. Perhaps items belonging to Tumblety supplying such details had fallen into police possession, or maybe the information was gleaned from one of the hotels or lodgings where he stayed.

The *New York Times* of Monday 19 November 1888 reported the arrest of Tumblety in London on suspicion of complicity in the Whitechapel murders. This article contained an inaccuracy which may subsequently have obscured the importance of the doctor as a suspect. It stated that Tumblety 'when proved innocent of that charge was held for trial in the Central Criminal Court under the special law covering the offences disclosed in the late "Modern Babylon" scandal.'* As we will see, he was not 'proved innocent of that charge'. What the article does indicate is that the London detectives did not have enough evidence to charge Tumblety with the murders and were no doubt relying on obtaining an admission which was not forthcoming. In 1888, with no forensic science aids available, the only way to prove someone guilty of murder was for the offender to be seen or caught red-handed, or for him to make a confession.

The facts of Tumblety's detention are disclosed in an article in the *New York World* of Sunday 2 December 1888, which revealed that he was arrested

on suspicion of being concerned in the perpetration of the Whitechapel murders. The police being unable to procure the necessary evidence against him in connection therewith, decided to hold him for trial for another offence against a statute which was passed shortly after the publication in the Pall Mall Gazette of 'The Maiden Tribute' and as a direct consequence thereof Dr Tumblety was committed for trial and liberated on bail, two gentlemen coming forward to act as bondsmen in the amount of $1,500. On being hunted up by the police to-day they asserted that they had only known the doctor for a few days previous to his arrest.

Tumblety was bailed to appear at the Central Criminal Court on a charge under the Criminal Law Amendment Act, 1885, the fore-runner of the modern Sexual Offences Act (see Appendix B). This act had created several important points of law with regard to sexual offences, especially in relation to prostitution and procuring. It also raised the age of consent for girls from thirteen to sixteen years, and made illegal indecent acts between consenting male adults. Unfortunately we do not know precisely what offence Tumblety was charged with.

Once released on bail, the doctor immediately fled south for the

*This refers to an article published in the *Pall Mall Gazette* in July 1885, entitled 'The Maiden Tribute of Modern Baylon', which exposed the scandal of vice and young female prostitution in London.

Channel ports and a ferry to Boulogne. On 24 November he boarded the French steamer *La Bretagne* at Le Havre under the alias of 'Frank Townsend' and embarked on the seven-day voyage across the Atlantic. He was Scotland Yard's most wanted man and was soon to be followed to New York by a posse of Yard men headed by Inspector Andrews.

With Tumblety's escape, the Metropolitan Police investigating the murders were faced with an apparent blunder of great magnitude. In an enquiry that had from the beginning been vexed by red herrings and misleading clues, the silence over the doctor's departure graphically illustrates that it was an incident they would rather not talk about: they had lost their prime suspect.

Over one hundred policemen had flooded into the Whitechapel area. They knocked on doors and called at lodging houses and drinking dens. Others watched steamers and ferries, all to no avail. The bitter truth was that Tumblety was too clever for them, and with the phantom-like qualities he had used during the murders, he once again disappeared into the night, leaving the police humiliated and frustrated.

Tumblety's importance as a prime suspect, mysteriously neglected by the English press at the time of the murders, is illustrated in the articles which were appearing in the American papers. On 26 November the *New York World* reported:

> Among the scores of men arrested by the London police, suspected of having had something to do with the Whitechapel horrors, only one is regarded with suspicion. He is said to be an American and his name has come over the cables as Kumberty, Twumberty and Tumberty, but the description which accompanied the various names was the same all the time, and it told of a man who, once seen, was not likely to be forgotten.

The *New York Herald* also mentioned Tumblety's flight from Britain and his arrival in America, saying, 'He was admitted to bail and later came to this country, followed by Scotland Yard men.'

On 4 December the *New York World* described how Chief Inspector Thomas Byrnes, head of the New York Police Department, was deploying two men to watch Tumblety's lodgings in East Tenth Street. An English detective was also engaged in the same task. The *New York Times* of the same day reported:

'Dr' Francis Tumblety, who left his bondsmen in London in the lurch, arrived by La Bretagne of the Transatlantic Line Sunday. Chief Inspector Byrnes had no charge whatever against him, but he had him followed so as to secure his temporary address, and will keep him in view as a matter of ordinary police precaution. Mr Byrnes does not believe that he will have to interfere with Tumblety for anything he may have done in Europe, and laughs at the suggestion that he was the Whitechapel murderer or his abettor or accomplice. The man who is supposed to be Tumblety came over on the steamship as 'Frank Townsend', and kept in his stateroom, under plea of sickness.

It is possible that Byrnes may have been making light of Tumblety to deflect press interest.

The *New York Daily Tribune* described Tumblety's arrival in the States:

He wore a long English cloth ulster, without a cape, a derby hat, and carried an umbrella and two canes tied together. It was the now famous Dr Tumblety, who got into a hack after having a small, steamer trunk placed on the box. The detective jumped into a cab and followed the Doctor to East Tenth Street.

The *World* of 4 December gave more detail:

When the French line steamer La Bretagne, from Havre, came up to her dock at 1.30 Sunday afternoon two keen-looking men pushed through the crowd and stood on either side of the gangplank. They glanced impatiently at the passengers until a big, fine-looking man hurried across the deck and began to descend. He had a heavy, fierce-looking mustache, waxed at the ends; his face was pale and he looked hurried and excited. He wore a dark blue ulster, with the belt buttoned. He carried under his arm two canes and an umbrella fastened together with a strap.

He hurriedly engaged a cab, gave the directions in a low voice and was driven away. The two keen-looking men jumped into another cab and followed him. The fine-looking man was the notorious Dr Francis Twomblety, or Tumblety, and his pursuers were two of Inspector Byrnes's best men, Crowle and Hickey.

The owner of the house at 79 East Tenth Street was Mrs McNamara, an old friend of the doctor. His New York business had been located at number 77, and he had lodged with her before.

The *World*'s detailed piece on the whole Tumblety saga included a reference to the English detective watching Mrs McNamara's lodging house:

> . . . a new character arrived on the scene, and it was not long before he completely absorbed the attention of everyone. He was a little man with enormous red side whiskers and a smoothly shaven chin. He was dressed in an English tweed suit and wore an enormous pair of boots with soles an inch thick. No one could be mistaken in his mission. There was an elaborate attempt at concealment and mystery which could not possibly be misunderstood. Everything about him told his business. From his little billycock hat, alternately set jauntily on the side of his head and pulled loweringly over his eyes, down to the very bottom of his thick boots, he was the typical English detective. If he had been put on the stage just as he paraded up and down Fourth Avenue and Tenth Street yesterday afternoon he would have been called a caricature.
>
> First he would assume his heavy villain appearance. Then his hat would be pulled down over his eyes and he would walk up and down in front of No. 79, staring intensely into the windows as he passed, to the intense dismay of Mrs McNamara, who was peering out from behind the blinds at him with ever-increasing alarm. Then his mood changed. His hat was pushed back in a devil-may-care way and he marched by No. 79 with a swagger, whistling gaily, convinced that his disguise was complete and that no one could possibly recognise him.

Significantly, the article contained an interview with a barman who had talked to the detective; the only reference to the latter explaining why he was in New York:

> His headquarters was a saloon on the corner, where he held long and mysterious conversations with the barkeeper, always ending in both of them drinking together. The barkeeper explained the conversation by saying: 'He wanted to know about a feller named Tumblety, and I said I didn't know nothink at all about him, and he sez he wuz an English detective and

he told me all about them Whitechapel murders, and how he came over here to get the chap that did it.'

This mysterious detective, we believe, must have been dispatched from England by the Yard as soon as they realised that Tumblety was on the run. Leaving for the USA from Liverpool, he would probably have arrived before the fleeing Tumblety, who was forced to travel via France.

The *World* reporter commented that Tumblety must have kept himself very quiet on the *La Bretagne*, for a number of passengers who were interviewed could not remember having seen anyone answering his description.

Inspector Byrnes was asked what his object was in shadowing Tumblety, and underlined why he could not be arrested:

I simply wanted to put a tag on him so that we can tell where he is. Of course he cannot be arrested for there is no proof of his complicity in the Whitechapel murders, and the crime for which he was under bond in London is not extraditable.

The Inspector was asked whether he thought Dr Tumblety was Jack the Ripper. He replied:

I don't know anything about it, and therefore I don't care to be quoted. But if they think in London that they need him and he turns out to be guilty our men will probably have an idea where he can be found.

Byrnes' attitude with regard to the Yard's quarry, therefore, was not as light-hearted as some of his comments may have suggested.

The *Evening Star-Sayings* of St Louis reported on 3 December another interview with Byrnes:

A reporter called on Inspector Byrnes this morning and asked if there was anything for which Tumblety could be arrested in this country. The Inspector replied that although Tumblety was a fugitive from justice under $1,500 bail for a nominal offence in England, he could not be arrested here. The Inspector added that in case the doctor was wanted he knew where to lay his hands on him. Two Central Office detectives were on the dock when the steamer arrived and followed Tumblety to a boarding

house, the number of which will not be made public. The doctor
will be kept under strict surveillance.

Byrnes was obviously acting as a result of a wire from Scotland
Yard. Detective Inspector Walter Andrews, one of the three original Yard Ripper hunters, had been tasked with finding the fleeing
Tumblety. Unlike the other two inspectors, Andrews is not mentioned in any of the police reports or memos to the Home Office
about other areas of the investigation. Our conclusion is that he had
been given the task of investigating Tumblety as a suspect from an
early stage. Now he was chasing him across the globe in a last-ditch
attempt to retrieve the situation. While the press talked increasingly
about the murders, Andrews' American journey went almost
unnoticed.

Once again the doctor exhibited his great skill of disappearing
without trace, fleeing from 79 East Tenth Street on Wednesday 5
December and slipping out of sight of everyone. The *New York
World* reported on Thursday 6 December:

> It is now certain that Dr Thomas F. Tumblety, the notorious
> Whitechapel suspect, who has been stopping at 79 East Tenth
> Street since last Sunday afternoon, is no longer an inmate of
> the house. It is not known exactly when the doctor eluded
> his watchers, but a workman named Jas. Rush, living directly
> opposite No. 79, says that he saw a man answering the doctor's
> well-known description standing on the stoop of No. 79 early
> yesterday morning, and he noticed that he showed a great deal
> of nervousness, glancing over his shoulder constantly. He finally
> walked to Fourth Avenue and took an uptown car.

The *World* reporter managed to elude the vigilant landlady, Mrs
McNamara, and found his way to the doctor's room:

> The bed had not been touched and there was no evidence that
> the room had been entered since early morning. A half-open
> valise on a chair near the window and a big pair of boots of
> the English cavalry regulation pattern were all that remained to
> tell the story of Dr Tumblety's flight.

The reporter ended by saying that those who knew Tumblety thought he had left New York for some quiet country town, where he expected to live until the excitement died down.

On 22 December the *St Louis Republican* reported that a Scotland Yard detective had arrived in Montreal and was now looking for the Whitechapel murderer in America:

Inspector Andrews of Scotland Yard arrived here today from Toronto and left tonight for New York. He tried to evade newspaper men, but incautiously revealed his identity at the central office, where he had an interview with Chief of Police Hughes. He refused to answer any questions regarding his mission, but said there were 23 detectives, two clerks and one inspector employed on the Whitechapel murder cases and that the police were without a jot of evidence upon which to arrest anybody.

The article continues with a description of the verbal exchange between Andrews and the reporter:

'How many men have you working in America?'

'Half a dozen,' he replied, then hesitating, continued: 'American detective agencies have offered to find the murderer on salaries and payment of expenses. But we can do that ourselves, you know.'

'Are you one of the half a dozen?'

'No. Don't say anything about that. I meant detective agencies.'

'But what are you here for?'

'I had rather not say just at present.'

The key section of the article reads:

It was announced at police headquarters today that Andrews has a commission in connection with two other Scotland Yard men to find the murderer in America. His inaction for so long a time, and the fact that a man suspected of knowing considerable about the murders left England for this side three weeks ago, makes the London police believe 'Jack' has left that country for this.

By 31 December the English press had caught up to a degree with the *Pall Mall Gazette* reporting that the search for the Whitechapel murderer had switched to America and that detectives were on the lookout in New York. However, this is the only report about the search in America to appear in the British press.

Meanwhile, Tumblety again performed his disappearing act and by the time the Yard men arrived near the end of the month he was no-where to be found. Andrews was too late, the doctor had vanished and Andrews was set to return to England empty-handed. One theory that now arose in the American press was that the Ripper had moved to new killing fields. Is it possible that Tumblety, frustrated by the constant media interest and aware of the police surveillance, had fled to more exotic locations?

The *Pall Mall Gazette* of 18 February 1889 carried the following startling report:

> It would seem from the intelligence published this morning that 'Jack the Ripper' has transferred himself from the Old World to the New, and is practising his horrible crimes with as much impunity in the Far West as he did in the East of London. Some time ago it was reported that some unknown criminal had perpetrated several murders of the well-known Whitechapel type upon the outcast women in Jamaica. It will be seen from the paragraph which we quote from The New York Sun that a similar outbreak of crime has occurred in Nicaragua.

The article continued with a theory that a Malay ship's cook was the killer, and noted that the last Whitechapel murder had been committed on Lord Mayor's Day, 9 November. It continued:

> We now learn at the beginning of January similar atrocities were taking place in Nicaragua, and that about the end of December equally barbarous mutilations are reported from Jamaica.
>
> It would be interesting to know whether any steamer left the Thames after the 9th November, and after calling at Jamaica in December proceeded to Central America. If such a steamer exists there seems a strong possibility that the murderer will be found among her crew – at any rate, the clue is one which might well be followed up by our detectives.

The *New York Sun* reported from Managua on 25 January 1889:

Either 'Jack the Ripper' of Whitechapel has emigrated from the scene of his ghastly murders or he has found one or more imitators in this part of Central America. The people have been greatly aroused by six of the most atrocious murders ever committed within the limits of this city. The murderer or murderers have vanished as quickly as 'Jack the Ripper' and no traces have been left for identification. All of the victims were women, and of the character of those who met their fate at the hands of the London murderer. Like those women of Whitechapel, they were women who had sunk to the lowest degradation of their calling. They have been found murdered just as mysteriously, and the evidences point to almost identical methods. Two were found butchered out of all recognition. Even their faces were horribly slashed, and in the cases of all the others their persons were frightfully disfigured. There is no doubt that a sharp instrument violently but dextrously used was the weapon that sent the poor creatures out of the world. Like 'Jack the Ripper's' victims, they have been found in out-of-the-way places, three of them in the suburbs of the town and the others in dark alleys and corners. Two of the victims were in the last stage of shabbiness and besottedness. In fact in almost every detail the crimes and the characteristics are identical with the Whitechapel horrors. All of the murders occurred in less than ten days, and as yet the perpetrator or perpetrators have not been apprehended. Every effort is being made to bring him or them to justice. The authorities have been stimulated in their efforts by the statement, which seems to be generally accepted, that 'Jack the Ripper' must have emigrated to Central America and selected this city for his temporary abode.

The killing of a woman called Carrie Brown in a New York dockside hotel in April 1891 again brought the Ripper's name to people's tongues. 'Has Jack the Ripper arrived?' asked one New York newspaper. This was a good question, because the New York Police Department had smirked at the inability of Scotland Yard to capture the killer, and had said that if the notorious Ripper started his games in New York City he would be arrested in a matter of hours.

Carrie Brown, who was a familiar figure in all the waterfront dives, had been strangled and slashed with a filed-down cooking knife. Her body had been found on the floor of her room in the East River Hotel. She had been seen to arrive at the hotel with a man at about 11 p.m. on 25 April. He was described as medium-sized, stocky, blond, and having the appearance of a seaman.

A short while later the police arrested a man who filled this description in general terms, and who was known to frequent the neighbourhood. He was an Algerian-Frenchman called Ameer Ben Ali, who was subsequently tried and found guilty of murder. However, it appeared that a man who had previously been seen in Brown's company was observed in the vicinity just prior to the killing. He was never seen again after the night of the murder, but in his abandoned room the police found a bloodstained shirt and a key which fitted the door of Brown's room.

On the strength of this new evidence, Ameer Ben Ali's sentence was commuted, and he was eventually allowed back to his native Algeria. The man involved by the new evidence was never traced. As writer Robin Odell observed in his book, *Jack the Ripper in Fact and Fiction*, 'the New York police were experiencing some of the frustrations that had beset London's Metropolitan Police during those terrible months of 1888.'

Guy Logan, the only Ripper writer to identify Tumblety's involvement without naming him, mentions both the Jamaican and the Nicaraguan killings in his book *Masters of Crime*. He states that Scotland Yard contacted the chief of police in Managua, and received a report from him that strongly suggested that the Ripper had made his way to Central America.

Logan puts forward his own theory about these killings:

I think it probable that the Whitechapel fiend, finding London at last too hot to hold him, deprived of the opportunities for his blood debauches, did betake himself abroad, and that he went to America. Further, I think it likely that he had come from the States in the first place.

If this theory is correct, Dr Tumblety is possibly the first example of that most dangerous and elusive criminal – the travelling serial killer. We believe he killed four victims over a period of ten weeks in London, and then returned to America to escape the police. Perhaps, though, he could not escape his urge to kill. Nobody knows the true death toll; the doctor took that secret with him to his grave.

The hunt for Tumblety ended in total disarray. According to Littlechild, the doctor was never heard of again after leaving Boulogne and was believed to have committed suicide. It is not known why he wrote this; it may simply be how he remembered the outcome of the pursuit, as they certainly did not find him in America. One can only assume that this information on the fleeing suspect must have originated from Andrews. It provided a convenient reason for not continuing the pursuit. However, even after Andrews' unsuccessful mission to America, there were more reports pointing to an American suspect.

In his book *Scoundrels and Scallywags and Some Honest Men*, 1929, Tom Divall, the ex-Chief Inspector of CID at Scotland Yard, wrote:

The much lamented and late Commissioner of the CID, Sir Melville Macnaghten, received some information that the murderer had gone to America and died in a lunatic asylum there. This perhaps may be correct, for after this news nothing was ever heard of any similar crime being committed.

This strange and unexplained reference to America was not mentioned by Macnaghten in his report of 1894, nor his memoirs.

Tumblety himself could not remain silent about his ordeal. In his second booklet, *Dr Francis Tumblety – Sketch of the Life of the Gifted, Eccentric and World Famed Physician*, published in 1889, he attacks the press for the 'slanders' they had made against him. Without mentioning the Whitechapel incident explicitly, he riles against what he perceives as the wild injustice of his persecution:

The bitter persecution, venomous assaults and the impudent curiosity which, when balked, becomes malevolent, aimed at the writer from the reptile section of the public press, justify the assumption that the authors of these attacks can only be likened to serpents and similar crawling nuisances. These unjust and infamous slanders, amazing in their frequency and absolute lack of foundation, have almost deprived me of my wonder capacity. But far from reducing me to the other miserable level, such rascally endeavours to subvert an honest reputation have only filled my mind with contempt. I have been too much engrossed with larger themes than matters of mere personal discussion to justify myself from malignant and, I trust, palpably mendacious newspaper assaults. Yet, absurd and farcical as these are in one sense, as slightly as they appeal in general to intelligent readers, it may be that there are some who have been influenced by their iteration and the fact that their victim has remained silent.

He maintains that he has been urged by others to defend himself in writing rather than remain quiet about his arrest:

> At the urgent requests of friends, therefore, I hence concluded to offer the best refutation of them, the testimony of honest, upright and useful life, which has been cordially recognised by prominent personages [. . .]
>
> Were this my only end I should be, indeed, an object of ridicule. But my reputation as a man has been blackened by hideous malice. I need not quote the hackneyed but powerful line by Shakespeare in this connection: 'He who steals my purse steals etc.' to justify my action in defending my reputation, which is dearer to me than all else that earth can give. I have chosen to do this by plain, unvarnished details of the leading events of my life, a life entirely inconsistent with the foul indictment which has been hurled against my innocent head without warning or shadow of cause. I leave the matter to the honourable and fair-minded public, confident that there can be but one verdict. To my assailants, one and all, I leave my contempt, proud in the consciousness of my own integrity; and to each one of them I answer in the words [that] one of the most noted victims of Junius tacks to that savage and bitter writer:

> 'Cease, viper, you bite against a file.'

It is consistent with what we know about Tumblety that he should react in this way. The anger and indignation are clear to see, but he does not deal in specifics: there is no mention of his arrest or any detail about the incidents of 1888. This section is followed by a stream of tributes and eulogies written by so-called admirers and supporters. These were probably self-penned and many of the people quoted were almost certainly unaware that their names were being used to praise the doctor.

In the final chapter, 'My Vindication', Tumblety attacks his subject with his usual gusto and outrage:

> Now let me say a word about the attacks which certain American newspapers recently made on me, attacks that were

as unfounded as the onslaught made on the great Irish leader. While I was not in a position to defend myself, these papers continued their foul slanders, but my friends will readily see, from the foregoing pages and from the testimonials, how utterly base and wholly groundless these aspersions were. Like Parnell, I have emerged from the battle totally unscathed with my social and professional standing unimpaired. It is gratifying to recall the pleasure with which my friends welcomed me to my native land. I treasure these tributes among the dearest things in my possession.

As far as we know, this is the closest Tumblety ever came to actually denying that he was the Whitechapel murderer.

On Friday 10 January 1890, the *Western Morning News* reported that the police were watching the docks in Plymouth because they were expecting Jack the Ripper. This does not square with claims that the police believed the Whitechapel killer to have drowned in the Thames just after the murders, or to be 'safely caged in an asylum'. The article stated:

> During the past few days there has been an increase of vigilance on the part of the East London police owing to 'information received'. A number of the police have been watching some cattle boats which have arrived at the docks from the United States, and a very strict lookout is being kept at night in the neighbourhood where the recent tragedies were committed by Jack the Ripper.

Four days later, the *News* repeated the tidings in its columns, but admitted that the story that the Ripper was returning to London was based purely on rumour. However, there may well have been truth in assertions that Scotland Yard still feared that the Ripper might return from America: after all, as we have shown, their suspect was an American, had returned to the USA and, of course, could always come back to England.

In the weeks after the murders of Stride and Eddowes, Dr Tumblety was under police investigation. Although we have searched for the 'large dossier' kept on him at the Yard, so far it has not been found. There is also no reference to him in any police or government letter or document in the existing Public Record Office files. In fact, his name exists nowhere in the official paperwork, so far found.

Now that it is clear how strong a suspect Dr Tumblety is, the question must be raised as to why he was not mentioned by any of the senior investigating police officers, particularly by Macnaghten in his report. Nor was he referred to in the progress reports by the police to the Home Office. Does this indicate some sort of police cover-up or, at least, a suppression of the full facts?

During the Ripper investigation the police displayed a marked reluctance to share any knowledge with the press or with coroners' enquiries. The late Stephen Knight thought that this secrecy was unique to the Whitechapel killings and read into it evidence that the police were party to a government-sponsored cover-up of the affair. It was, in fact, the Yard's policy generally to withhold information from the press, especially where it might compromise their investigation of a suspect.

This was especially true of Tumblety's escape before his court appearance. Disclosure of the loss of a major suspect would have added even more weight to the growing fear that the police were ineffective, bungling and inefficient. The public anger that such an incident would have stirred up might have ruined the careers of several senior officers. The gravity of the error in bailing Tumblety cannot be overemphasised, and publicising it would have been a disaster for the Metropolitan Police.

An attempt was made to retrieve the situation by sending Andrews in hot pursuit of Tumblety. The Yard certainly would not have followed across the Atlantic a man who was wanted merely for 'unnatural offences' that had warranted only a remand on bail and were non-extraditable. The indications are that some stronger evidence against Tumblety had come to light, and this was certainly underlined by his flight.

We must next look at the thoughts, as far as they are known, of James Monro, head of CID. He stated in an interview in 1890 that he had decidedly formed a theory on the case and that 'when I do theorise it is from a practical standpoint, and not upon any visionary foundation.' He did, however, confirm that the police had nothing positive by way of clues, by which, being a policeman, he meant hard evidence. Monro stated later to his family that 'the Ripper was never caught, but he should have been'. Some papers he left on the subject were said by his son to contain a theory that was a 'very hot potato'. The fact that the police had arrested the culprit and released him, and that he had then escaped, certainly fitted the 'hot potato' description. Add to this the fact that Chief Inspector Littlechild was

Monro's immediate subordinate and it becomes probable that Monro was referring to Tumblety's escape.

Tumblety was truly invisible. The police had strong suspicions but apparently insufficient hard evidence to charge him. More importantly, they could not catch him once he escaped. The Whitechapel killer evinced no obvious motive and left no clue. In such a case orthodox police methods were almost futile.

Chapter 19
The Nature of the Beast

'Accessory to crimes of the deepest and blackest magnitude.'

Understanding of sexually motivated murder in its varying forms was in its infancy in Victorian times. In the light of modern knowledge we are better equipped to understand the nature of the Whitechapel killer. Today he would be recognised as a lust killer.

It was the Germans who invented the word *lustmord*, which means murder for pleasure and enjoyment. The definition implies the enaction of extremes of perverted sexual fantasy where the victim is totally dominated and ravished.

Of all psychiatric descriptions this is probably the most accurate when trying to describe the Ripper. For this type of killing, the act of causing death itself, rather than the anticipation of possessing dead bodies, is the passionate stimulus. The characteristic signs include mutilation of the genitals, slashing of the abdomen with exposure of the viscera, very often accompanied by evisceration, and can include biting and amputation. The killer, in a wild state of frenzy, will slash and mutilate the intestines, often cutting or pulling them out. Lust murder is normally premeditated and the killer, in the heat of his passion, may seek to gain satisfaction through inflicting physical injury and sometimes even torture.

As in the case of the Ripper, death is often caused by strangulation prior to mutilation. As a general rule such killers do not deviate from their *modus operandi*, in that those who use blunt instruments do not usually resort to a knife and the knifeman, such as the Ripper, continues to use a sharp weapon. They will follow a recognised pattern. In a legal sense the lust killer is usually sane.

The types of lust killer vary greatly and the traits they exhibit in their murders contrast accordingly, thus making them very difficult to profile. It is not uncommon for such killers to be bisexual and to have homosexual relationships. Many contract venereal diseases.

Typically they hate and resent women, this hatred sometimes leading them to turn towards men for sexual pleasure and company.

As we have seen, Tumblety liked to be in the company of young men, and had, he claimed, suffered at the hands of a woman. It has also been alleged that as the youngest of eleven children, he had been neglected by his mother, one of those who had known him as a boy in Rochester describing him as 'uncared for'. These are typical elements that are often found in the lust killer.

A more recent and extremely explicit example of the lust killer was the German murderer and sadist Peter Kurten, who was brought to trial in 1931. It is possible to draw several lessons from his pattern of behaviour which may be helpful in an interpretation of the Ripper's psychology and motives. Indeed, the German was known to read of the Ripper's exploits.

Kurten, who was only five years old at the time of the Whitechapel murders, had committed his first killing before the turn of the century. After an incestuous and unbalanced childhood, he was apparently able to get sexual gratification only while simultaneously copulating and killing. As well as his interest in Jack the Ripper, he also confessed to a love of movies depicting people falling from cliffs. When finally caught he was found guilty of nine murders and seven attempted murders. Less selective than the Ripper, he killed or badly injured men, women, children, horses, sheep and even on one occasion, when there was no other suitable victim to hand, a swan. He experienced orgasm as he seized the victim's throat or plunged in the knife.

The sexual nature of the Ripper's crimes is clearly indicated in the overt attack on the genitalia, and the later excision of Mary Kelly's breasts. The single-minded aim of this pitiless type of killer is not the achievement of an act of rape or sexual intercourse, it is the satisfaction of his urge to kill the hated object, women. Like the Ripper, many sex murderers never actually rape their victims, but use a characteristic violation as their equivalent for the sexual act.

Tumblety also fits into another part of the pattern. In cases of the most extreme control, where the desire to have power over the victim is especially intense, offenders perpetrate the most bizarre crimes: excessive mutilations, alive and dead, the keeping of body parts as mementoes, cannibalism and other practices that treat human beings as an object for fulfilling their own desires. The mutilations we have already discussed, and we also know that he removed certain organs.

There is no doubt that the Ripper took away 'trophies' from more than one of his victims, an exercise of complete power and the provision of an item to gloat over later. Both Chapman's and Eddowes' wombs and Eddowes' left kidney were taken away. It is also believed, from Bond's notes, that Kelly's heart was missing. Other trophies taken by the Ripper may have been the two cheap rings torn from Annie Chapman's hand.

Littlechild's description of Tumblety as a 'Sycopathia Sexualis' subject needs some explanation. The pioneering work on sexual deviancy and pathology is Dr Richard von Krafft-Ebing's *Psychopathia Sexualis*, which was first published in 1886, two years before the Ripper killings. It revealed the extraordinary extent of sexual deviations on the European continent. Many of these deviations were variants of sadism and masochism but the majority were forms of fetishism, in which sexual excitement is derived from some object connected with women – hair, shoes or underwear. Woman had become so forbidden and so desirable that her magic could operate just as potently at second hand. Krafft-Ebing's book has been updated many times over the years and now includes an entry on Jack the Ripper.

Thomas Neill Cream, a serial killer in 1891–2, shared startling parallels with Dr Tumblety. Born in Glasgow in 1850, he emigrated with his family to Canada in 1854. He entered McGill College, Montreal, in October 1872, to study medicine, and completed a thesis on the effects of chloroform.

After graduating from McGill in 1876, he quickly found a life of fraud, blackmail and attempted murder more appealing. At least four women, including his wife, died under his care. In 1881, the law finally caught up with him and he was sentenced to life imprisonment at Joliet Prison, Illinois, for the strychnine poisoning of Daniel Stott, with whose wife Cream had formed an association.

He was released in 1891 and arrived in England on 1 October of that year. Almost immediately, a series of prostitute murders began in London. Ellen Donworth, who worked as a prostitute in Duke Street, Westminster Bridge Road, was killed with strychnine. A week later, a twenty-six-year-old prostitute, Matilda Clover, was also poisoned. Some months later, two more young street-walkers died in agony on the same day. Emma Shrivell and Alice Marsh both lived in second-floor rooms at 118 Stamford Street, a brothel at the Elephant and Castle. They too had been poisoned.

So just four years after the Ripper killings the Metropolitan Police were seeking another serial killer of prostitutes. This time, though, they found their man. In October Cream was tried at the Old Bailey and on 15 November 1892 he went to the scaffold at Newgate Prison.

In *Prescription For Murder*, writer Angus McLaren makes the following observation:

> Cream's conviction and execution raised the police's hopes that Jack the Ripper had finally been eliminated. Cream was obviously much the same sort – a foreigner, often out of the country, who murdered prostitutes for no apparent motive. If not the Ripper himself, Cream was certainly the same 'criminal type'. The term was popularised by those who laid the basis for the new science of criminology, which in the 1890s was in the very process of emerging. In theory it promised to protect society from people like Cream; in practice it espoused the desire to eliminate in its own way the very class of poor women who Cream murdered.

Although McLaren could not have known anything about Tumblety, he has in fact described him accurately.

What is it that distinguishes a psychopath from other people? Professor Hervey Cleckley suggests the following points:

> Superficial charm and good intelligence, absence of signs of irrational thinking, absence of nervousness; unreliability, untruthfulness and insincerity; lack of remorse or shame, inadequately motivated anti-social behaviour; poor judgement and failure to learn by experience; pathological egocentricity and incapacity for love . . . specific loss of insight; suicide rarely carried out; sex life impersonal, trivial, and poorly integrated; failure to follow any life plan.

Psychopaths are emotionally 'flat' and do not respond to situations which would, in others, produce feelings of excitement, anxiety or fear. Nor do they experience the more social emotions of shame, guilt, remorse or embarrassment which are learned early on in life and go to make up the developed conscience.

Because these emotions develop in childhood, it is obvious that upbringing and early experience will affect the adult's 'conscience'. Studies of the family backgrounds of psychopaths show that a very high proportion come from broken or emotionally impoverished homes, often with alcoholic, brutal or anti-social fathers and weak, absent or rejecting mothers. Hostile psychopaths tend to come from very disturbed backgrounds, are impulsive and unpredictable, lack anxiety, and seem incapable of forming any emotional attachments, appreciating the feelings of others, or anticipating the consequences of their own behaviour. Tumblety certainly seemed to display a lack of remorse and guilt, as well as being aggressive, unfeeling, egocentric, even cold and callous.

Elliott Leyton, in *Hunting Humans – The Rise of the Modern Multiple Murderer*, explains why the likes of Albert De Salvo and David Berkowitz become killers:

> If the murders can be understood only as a personalised social protest, it must be emphasised that these killers are not radicals: they have enthusiastically embraced the established order only to discover that it offers them no place they can endure. Their rebellion is a protest against their perceived exclusion from society, not an attempt to alter it as befits a revolutionary.

Edward Haywood a boyhood acquaintance of Tumblety, said that Tumblety grew up like a 'weed' on the canal at Rochester a – 'dirty, awkward, ignorant, uncared-for, good-for-nothing boy'. A classic case of the outsider who will go to great lengths to win acceptance. In his two publications Tumblety fantasised about his influence and the famous people he professed to know. He claimed he had met Napoleon and Charles Dickens. The feeling of being an outsider in his own land was not transformed either by success or by flight.

Simply by looking at Tumblety's writings, it becomes obvious that he felt he was an outcast, forever being knocked back and singled out for humiliation despite every effort to be accepted and respected. His entire being was acutely attuned to every real or fancied social slight. He resented any kind of criticism or imagined humiliation, however small. Early in his life, he certainly embraced the established order, only to suffer several devastating setbacks. It is clear that he nursed the darkest feelings of persecution. Following his imprisonment he felt excluded and turned on those whom he perceived to have brought about his downfall.

Although it may be difficult to make direct comparisons between a modern murderer and a Victorian counterpart, some valid conclusions can be drawn by looking at the case of Arthur Shawcross. In the late 1980s and 1990 Shawcross brought notoriety to Tumblety's childhood home of Rochester by murdering eleven women. A chillingly similar catalogue of horror unfolded, with the women, most of them prostitutes, being mutilated by the killer. The escalating number of bodies sent a chill through the police department, with officers fearing that perhaps a serial killer was on the loose.

When a sixth body surfaced on 23 November 1989, police were horrified to find that the victim had been mutilated from her chest to her pubic area. Was the killer becoming more frenzied or had other victims, too decomposed to gauge, been subject to the same Ripper-like ordeal? When the next victim was found, it was discovered that the murderer had attacked her genitalia with a knife.

In an odd repeat of the Tumblety saga, Shawcross was arrested, but Rochester police did not have enough evidence to charge him and he was released under twenty-four-hour surveillance. The very next day, 4 January 1990, another body turned up. The victim had been dead for a week. At noon Shawcross was picked up by police, who told him they believed he was the serial killer. He vehemently denied it. After officers brought in his mistress and allowed him to speak to his wife, Shawcross confessed to eleven murders.

Several serial killers have led some part of their lives quite normally and without menace. Peter Sutcliffe, the Yorkshire Ripper, was so apparently benign that he avoided police suspicion in five separate interviews before eventually being charged with thirteen murders. In the United States one of the most notorious of all killers, Ted Bundy, was recommended by a senator for law school. Albert Fish, who killed and possibly ate his child victims in New York in the mid-1930s, was seen as a kind old man who took people's children for walks.

What is particularly relevant to Tumblety is the capacity of these men to exist, often for long periods, as normal, law-abiding citizens. They could cope with the vicissitudes of daily life without the need to reveal anger or rage. Their violent outbursts were only a part of their life story. It was in their secret lives that they unmasked the evil part of their nature.

Tumblety's intelligence and opportunities had taught him how to present a sociable face to the world. He mixed effortlessly with politicians and high-ranking military leaders, who found him charismatic. Historian Michael Kauffman, while warning that caution should be used when reading Tumblety's own accounts of knowing the President and moving freely at the White House, in no way dismisses the doctor's claim. He says that it would have been possible for a person like Tumblety to be given access to the best circles.

It is easy to lose track of a serial killer, because he develops an uncanny knack of becoming invisible and fading into the background. As we have already seen, Tumblety had the ability to vanish like a phantom and reappear again, to move from one hotel or lodging to another with the minimum of fuss, hardly noticed. Apparent normality was one of his major assets.

The likes of John Wayne Gacy, Ted Bundy and Peter Sutcliffe illustrate how a serial killer can be amongst us, unseen and unsuspected. They use the same shops and pubs, and appear in every sense normal. But they have a dark side. Their hidden lives are an expression of their evil. People who met Tumblety would never have suspected that beneath the eloquent, confident, bombastic, highly intelligent exterior beat the calculating heart of a killer.

Cold and aloof, Tumblety killed for no apparent motive other than enjoyment. His ability to be embroiled in all manner of controversy, no matter how innocent he professed to be, is a recurring theme. This man would wax indignant about other men who were egotistical and betrayers. He would preach to others about morality, while he himself murdered women and disfigured their lifeless bodies.

He had a disproportionate desire for power and superiority. He might have been safe if he could have attained high power or recognition, but when this aggression could not be channelled into some creative activity he became dangerous. Feeling defeated and humiliated, and unwilling to blame himself for his misfortunes, resentment grew within Tumblety, and others would pay the price.

Chapter 20

The Death of the Ripper

'I trust the reader will not deem me an egoist.'

'Of late years he lived quietly here, spending his winters in the south.' So read the obituary of Dr Francis Tumblety which appeared in the *New York Herald* on Friday 26 June 1903.

For the last ten years of his life the mysterious doctor lived with his elderly niece, Alice FitzSimons, at 569 Plymouth Avenue, Rochester, New York, using her house as both home and office. By this time he was ageing rapidly and his health appears to have declined accordingly. A valvular heart condition developed and in his latter days he was treated for a 'long and painful illness' at a hospital in St Louis.

Whether or not the demons that drove him were still there, we do not know, but it would seem that his last years were certainly quieter, his days of amazing travel were over. He had many relatives, the offspring of his eight sisters and one brother.

At the time of his final illness Tumblety appears to have been wintering in St Louis, where he seemed to realise that age had finally caught up with him. He decided that the St John's Hospital, a charitable institution run by the Sisters of Mercy, an order of nuns established in Dublin, was 'a good place to die'. The hospital was situated at 307 South Euclid Avenue, St Louis, and was a six-storey building with 358 beds. It had been founded in 1871 by Mother M. de Pazzi Bentley.

He engaged a room at the hospital on Sunday 26 April 1903, booking in under the assumed name of Townsend, the same that he had used on his frantic flight from England in 1888.

By Monday 25 May he had become very weak, and realised that he did not have long to live, owing to his serious heart condition. Notwithstanding, he insisted on dressing for a walk and, showing his strength of will and independence, forbade attendants to accompany him. He walked for some time, tiring himself greatly, and on his return to the hospital sat down on the steps. His weakness overcame him and he fell forward, breaking his nose and sustaining shock from which he did not recover.

He was returned to his bed and lingered for three days, finally expiring on Thursday 28 May 1903. So ended a colourful and deadly career, spanning seventy years and many oceans. Jack the Ripper died the moment that Dr Francis Tumblety's heart stopped.

The inventory from the hospital shows that Dr Tumblety had few possessions with him when he died. However, his personal property indicates his wealth and flamboyance. In addition to $432.70 in cash and a $1,000 West Shore railway bond, there was also a seventeen-diamond cluster ring valued at $75, a second five-diamond ring valued at $60, a gold pocket watch valued at $10 and two imitation rings worth $3.

The Sisters of Mercy applied for the $432.70 to pay his bill. A certain Sister Mary Theresa stated that the money was to pay for furniture, rugs, carpets and bedclothes which had been partially destroyed by fire, and by the dropping of acids and medicines. Could it be that the dying doctor continued to experiment during his last days? The money was also to be in recognition of the care and attention he had received from the nuns through 'his long and painful illness'.

His remains were transported from St Louis back to Rochester, where they were laid to rest. The removal of the body was handled by National Express at a cost of $37.60. Undertakers Cullinan Brothers provided services at St Louis, whilst Irish undertakers B. O'Reilly and Sons handled the arrangements and funeral at Rochester, at a cost of $68.50.

Dr Tumblety was interred on Lot 73, Section 13, of the Holy Sepulchre Cemetery, 2461 Lake Avenue, Rochester, in a family grave. The memorial reads:

REQUIESCAT IN PACE
DR FRANCIS TUMUELTY
DIED
MAY 28, 1903
AGED 70 YEARS

Thus a final irony is added to the story of the doctor: in death his name is again spelt differently.

The *St Louis Post Dispatch* of 29 May 1903 featured news of his death on page seven, with the headline: 'Big Bequests of Aged Physician – Large Sums Named in Will Left by Itinerant Practitioner.'

The subsequent article referred to him as Dr Francis Tumbleton, and incorrectly gave his age as eighty-two. This mistake also appeared on his death certificate, with his date of birth shown as 1820. This, as we know, is incorrect and may have been a mistake by the hospital staff reporting the death. Interestingly, the certificate also shows him as widowed and the cause of death as 'Disease of heart – Nephritis' (nephritis is inflammation of the kidneys).

The *Post Dispatch* article stated that he had not completed his will and that $10,000 was left to Cardinal Gibbons, and $10,000 to Archbishop Ireland for charitable purposes, with the rest going to relatives and former servants.

The *New York Herald* of 26 June began his obituary thus:

After a life which included in its multitude of exciting incidents an arrest on suspicion that he was London's Jack the Ripper and another arrest on a charge that he was implicated in a plot to infect the north with yellow fever during the Civil War, Dr Tumblety died several months [*sic*] ago in St John's Hospital, St Louis.

St John's Hospital is a charitable institution maintained by the city, but that Dr Tumblety had no need of charity is shown by the recent announcement that at the time of his death he had on deposit with the banking firm of Henry Clews and Co. $138,000 cash.

The piece elaborated on his 1888 exploits:

In 1888 he went to England. This was in the period of the mysterious Whitechapel murders, and for some reason, probably because of his outspoken hatred of women, he was arrested. He was admitted to bail and later came to this country, followed by Scotland Yard men.

Henry Clews, with whom a considerable part of Tumblety's fortune had been made by investments, were informed that his will bequeathed $45,000 to various relatives, but that no provision had been made for the residue. The Public Administrator at St Louis was duly appointed to carry out the provisions of the will, and later appeared in New York before Surrogate Thomas and had ancillary papers granted to him. He then made a demand upon Henry Clews and Co. for the funds, but the bankers refused to turn over the property until they had made their own investigation.

Tumblety had left money to a number of relatives who lived in various places, including Rochester, California and Liverpool. The Rochester legatees, upon learning the facts of the case from Clews, appeared immediately, through their attorneys, before Surrogate Thomas and asked for a revocation of the ancillary letters granted to the Public Administrator of St Louis. In the meantime they applied to the Surrogate of Monroe County, New York, for administration papers on the grounds that Tumblety was a resident of Rochester. On this application Michael H. FitzSimons, a nephew of the doctor's, was appointed temporary administrator, and he, in turn, made a demand to Clews for the money. The bankers declined to pay until a decision was rendered.

The cause of this contention seems to have been the fact that Tumblety's will failed to mention one particular section of his large family – the children of his nephews and nieces. At the time of his death all his brothers and sisters, with the sole exception of Jane Hayes, were already deceased, and by the time the will was read, Mrs Hayes too was dead. His brother Lawrence had died without issue or a wife, which left his sister Jane and the children of his other brother and sisters making claim on the will. The various branches of the family included his brother Patrick's son, James Tumilty, of Rochester; his sister Alice's children, Charles FitzSimons of Chicago, and Mary and Michael FitzSimons of Rochester (though Charles and Michael also died before the reading of the will); his sister Julia's children, Catherine Way of Bath, England, and Annie Barrett and Jane Moore of Rochester; his sister Margaret's children, Agnes Lynch and John and Patrick Kelly of Rochester, Charles of Geneva, New York, James of Waterloo, New York, Mary McSorley of Vallejo, California, and Margaret J. Valeer of Rochester, who died shortly after the doctor; his sister Elizabeth's children, Joseph Powderly and Mary Farrell of Waterloo, New York, and Thomas Powderly of Indianapolis; his sister Ann's children, William and Frank Mahoney, William also dying shortly afterwards; his youngest sister Mary's children, Mary Ann, John and Bartholomew of Ireland (the latter two also died shortly after the doctor); the five children of Mary's deceased son, Thomas Kavanagh; and lastly the daughter of his sister Bridget, Mrs Margaret Brady, of 20 Frederick Street, Widnes, near Liverpool.

The doctor's final will went to the St Louis Probate Court, and his considerable fortune was distributed among the extended family. The most unusual and significant part of the probate proceedings, however, was a claim received from an attorney for petitioners in Maryland: Joseph R. Kemp of Baltimore, and the Home for Fallen Women in Baltimore City. It was claimed that by a will of 3 October 1901, Tumblety, an inhabitant or citizen of the State of Maryland, had left all his jewellery, consisting of one diamond breastpin, three diamond rings, and one watch and chain, to Kemp, and the sum of $1,000 to the Home for Fallen Women. Although the application was denied, perhaps Tumblety's bitter hatred of women had finally died, and it was time to atone and make peace with his maker.

Afterword

'Of present fame I think little, and of the future less.'

This book is important because we have departed from the old formula. Here we have presented a genuine suspect and a factual account of the events. There is a possibility that the 'large dossier' mentioned by Littlechild is still in existence, hidden amongst hundreds of other long-forgotten files and papers, perhaps uncatalogued in the depths of the Public Record Office. And that dossier may hold the full answer to the century-old mystery.

We are not discussing here an unlikely candidate for the mantle of the Ripper, nor one whose name has no tangible link with the murders. For no less a person than one of the chiefs of Scotland Yard, a man privy to many secrets, has revealed that he was not only a police suspect, but a very likely one. This lifts him out of the category of merely another suspect to add to the long list. Indeed, his name should have been at the top of that list many years ago, and would have been had the Yard not maintained its silence about him.

At last a genuine primary source document on which valid future research can be based has been produced. We have also been able to put a new interpretation on contemporary reports which have, until now, seemed meaningless or unconnected. Many of the niggling mysteries that have dogged the Jack the Ripper story have been resolved and canards have been swept aside. We have avoided wild guesswork, and there are no lies or prevarication presented here, only reasoned deductions from the facts.

The gravity of the police 'error' in bailing Tumblety cannot be overemphasised. Several careers could have been ruined and the already slandered name of Scotland Yard totally discredited. It is not too unrealistic to suggest that the repercussions would have reached the Government itself. What is clear through the fog that has descended around Tumblety is that the detectives investigating his movements considered him dangerous enough to pursue to New York. Official details of this investigation have not, apparently, survived. It is worth remembering that one senior officer, Inspector Andrews, was apparently assigned to deal solely with this suspect. Not a single official reference to his investigation can be found. This police cover-up or silence is evidenced by the lack of publicity about the American end of the chase, and the fact that no result of these enquiries was ever published.

Documents did exist, and the explosive nature of the enquiry might well suggest a fear of such evidence becoming publicly known and a desire to ensure it would never see the light of day. If that was the case, it appears to have succeeded.

We cannot be precise as to how many women Tumblety killed, for he never made a confession. Was he the forerunner of the travelling series killer, who murdered unknown numbers of victims upon whom he happened, randomly, silently, thereby escaping not only detection, but also notice, for years?

Here we must look at the sort of objections that may be raised against Tumblety being Jack the Ripper. At fifty-five, he was older than perhaps has been earlier imagined for this killer, and at 5ft.10in. was a little too tall.

As we have shown in the preceding chapters, there is no reliable description of the killer, but of the two valid ones, Mrs Long's is the closest. Height is relative and very often miscalculated by witnesses. A mistake of a mere two inches is the difference between 5ft.8in., the generally accepted height of the killer, and Tumblety's 5ft.10in. Logic dictates that whilst the killer was with his victim he would not be raising himself to his full stature and making himself conspicuous. On the contrary, he would slouch and lean over her whilst talking, in order to lessen his profile to any witness. In the same way age cannot be held as a deciding factor. With a large moustache and a hat pulled over his eyes, the killer would be impossible to describe accurately. It is here that we should perhaps point out the similarity between Tumblety and the suspect seen with Kelly by George Hutchinson. Both the facial and dress aspects match very well, the only discrepancies being the age and height, points we have disposed of above.

If Littlechild thought Tumblety 'a very likely suspect' in 1888, then we must bow to his superior knowledge and accept the fact. Thus we can enumerate as follows the factors pointing to this man being the killer:

1. He fits many of the psychological requirements; he was a 'psychopathia sexualis' subject, and hated women, especially prostitutes, with a vengeance.

2. He was in London at the relevant time, and, we believe we have shown, had a good knowledge of the slums of the East End.

3. He had the necessary anatomical knowledge evinced by the murderer, and owned an anatomical collection that included wombs 'from all classes of women'.

4. He was arrested within days of the Kelly murder on suspicion of being the Whitechapel murderer.

5. The murders ceased upon his arrest and subsequent flight, a very strong indicator.

6. A top Yard man felt that he was the killer, and he was not alone in this belief.

7. He used aliases, was always turning up and disappearing again, and was the subject of police enquiry before his arrest.

8. Scotland Yard was in touch with the American police about him both before and after his arrest.

9. One of the three detective inspectors assigned to the Ripper hunt, Walter Andrews, was sent with other officers to pursue him to New York.

10. He was not located and Andrews' mission was a failure; he had successfully evaded the police again.

11. He was wealthy enough to move about as he pleased, and if our suggestions are correct he had more than one lodging-house retreat in London. He also changed his clothing in order to disguise himself. These factors have never before been considered but are indicated in the contemporary reports.

12. He was eccentric, but shrewd.

13. His bloody career probably included offences abroad which, as yet, have not been recognised as his work.

14. Several of the people who knew him in the USA thought it likely that he was the Ripper.

15. We believe that it is beyond reasonable doubt that Tumblety and the Batty Street lodger, an American, were one and the same, thus providing further evidence of his identification as 'Jack the Ripper', and explaining the police belief in his guilt.

It is a dream of many researchers and historians to put a name to Jack the Ripper. We believe we have.

Appendix A
The Littlechild Letter

8, The Chase,

Clapham Common.S.W.

23rd September 1913.

Dear Sir.,

      I was pleased to receive your letter which I shall put away in "good company" to read again perhaps some day when old age overtakes me and to revive memories of the past may be a solace.

      Knowing the great interest you take in all matters criminal, and abnormal, I am just going to inflict one more letter on you on the "Ripper" subject. Letters as a rule are a nuisance when they call fo a reply but this does not need one. I will try and be brief.

      I never heard of a Dr. D. in connection with the Whitechapel murders but amongst the suspects, and to my mind a very likely one, was a Dr. T. (which sounds much like D.) He was an American quack named Tumblety and was at one time a frequent visitor to London and on these occasions constantly brought under the notice of police, there being a large dossier concerning him at Scotland Yard. Although a "Sycopathia Sexualis" he was not known as a "Sadist" (which the murderer unquestionably was) but his feelings towards women were remarkable and bitter in the extreme, a fact on record. Tumblety was arrested in connection with unnatural offences and charged at Marlborough Street, remanded on bail, jumped his bail, and got away to Boulogne. He shortly left Boulogne and was never heard of afterwards. it was believed he committed suicide but certain it is that from this time the "Ripper" murders came to an end.

      With regard to the term "Jack the Ripper" it was generally believed at the Yard that Tom Bullen of the Central News was the

the originator but it is probable Moore, who was his chief, was the inventor. It was a smart piece of journalistic work. No journal of my time got such privileges from Scotland Yard as Bullen. Mr James Munro when Assistant Commissioner, and afterwards Commissioner, relied on his integrity. Poor Bullen occasionally took too much to drink, and I fail to see how he could help it knocking about so many hours and seeking favours from so many people to procure copy. One night when Bullen had taken a "few too many" he got early information of the death of Prince Bismarck and instead of going to the office to report it sent a laconic telegram "Bloody Bismarck is dead" On this I believe Mr Charles Moore fired him out.

It is very strange how those given to "Contrary sexual instinct and degeneration" are given to cruelty, even Wilde used to like to be punched about. It may interest you if I give you an example of this cruelty in the case of the man Harry Thaw and this is authentic as I have the boys statement. Thaw was staying at the Carlton Hotel, and one day laid out a lot of sovereigns on his dressing table, then rang for a call boy on pretence of sending out a telegram. He made some excuse and went out of the room and left the boy there and watched through the chink of the door. The unfortunate boy was tempted and took a sovereign from the pile and Thaw returning to the room charged him with stealing. The boy confessed when Thaw asked him whether he should send for the police or whether he should punish him himself. The boy scared to death consented to take his punishment from Thaw who then made him undress, strapped him to the foot of the bedstead, and thrashed him with a cane drawing blood. He then made the boy get into a bath in which he placed a quantity of salt. It seems incredible that such a thing could take place in any hotel but it is a fact. *This was in 1906*

Now pardon me— It is finished.— *Except that I knew Major Griffiths for many years. He probably got his information from Anderson who only "thought he knew"* Faithfully yours.,

J. G. Littlechild

George R. Sims Esq.,
   12, Clarence Terrace,
      Regents Park. N.W.

Appendix B

The Criminal Law Amendment Act 1885
[Sections to Offences only]

Offences
Section 2 Any person who –
(1) Procures or attempts to procure any girl or woman under 21 years of age not being a common prostitute or of known immoral character to have unlawful carnal connection either within or without the Queen's dominions with any other person or persons; or
(2) Procures or attempts to procure any woman or girl to become either within or without the Queen's dominions a common prostitute; or
(3) Procures or attempts to procure any woman or girl to leave the United Kingdom with intent that she may become an inmate of a brothel elsewhere; or
(4) Procures or attempts to procure any woman or girl to leave her usual place of abode in the United Kingdom (such place not being a brothel) with intent that she may for the purposes of prostitution become an inmate of a brothel within or without the Queen's dominions,
shall be guilty of a misdemeanour, and being convicted thereof shall be liable at the discretion of the court to be imprisoned for any term not exceeding two years, with or without hard labour:
   Provided that no person shall be convicted of any offence under this section upon the evidence of one witness, unless such witness be corroborated in some material particular by evidence implicating the accused.

Section 3 Any person who –
(1) By threats or intimidation procures or attempts to procure any woman or girl to have any unlawful carnal connection whether within or without the Queen's dominions; or
(2) By false pretences or false representations procures any woman or girl, not being a common prostitute or of known immoral charac-

ter, to have any unlawful carnal connection, either within or without the Queen's dominions; or

(3) Applies, administers to, or causes to be taken by any woman or girl any drug, matter, or thing, with intent to stupefy or overpower so as thereby to enable any person to have unlawful carnal connection with such woman or girl, shall be guilty of misdemeanour, and being convicted thereof shall be liable at the discretion of the court to be imprisoned for any term not exceeding two years, with or without hard labour.

Provided that no person shall be convicted of an offence under this section upon the evidence of one witness only, unless such witness be corroborated in some material particular by evidence implicating the accused.

Section 4 Any person who –
unlawfully and carnally knows any girl under the age of 13 years shall be guilty of felony, and being convicted thereof shall be liable . . . to be kept in penal servitude for life . . .

Any person who attempts to have unlawful carnal knowledge of any girl under the age of 13 years shall be guilty of misdemeanour, and being convicted thereof shall be liable at the discretion of the court to be imprisoned for any term not exceeding two years, with or without hard labour.

Provided that in the case of an offender whose age does not exceed 16 years, the court may, instead of sentencing him to any term of imprisonment, order him to be whipped, as prescribed by the Whipping Act, 1862, and the said Act shall apply, so far as circumstances admit, as if the offender had been convicted in manner in that Act mentioned . . .

Whereas doubts have been entertained whether a man who induces a married woman to permit him to have connection with her by personating her husband is or is not guilty of rape, it is hereby enacted and declared that every such offender shall be deemed guilty of rape.

Section 5 Any person who –
(1) Unlawfully and carnally knows or attempts to have unlawful carnal knowledge of any girl being of or above the age of 13 years and under the age of 16 years; or
(2) Unlawfully and carnally knows or attempts to have unlawful carnal knowledge of any female idiot or imbecile woman or girl,

under circumstances which do not amount to rape, but which prove the offender knew at the time of the commission of the offence that the woman or girl was an idiot or imbecile, shall be guilty of a misdemeanour, and being convicted thereof shall be liable at the discretion of the court to be imprisoned for any term not exceeding two years, with or without hard labour.

Provided also that no prosecution shall be commenced for an offence under subsection (1) of this section more than twelve months after the commission of the offence.

Section 6 Any person who, being the owner or occupier of any premises, or having or acting or assisting in the management or control thereof –

induces or knowingly suffers any girl of such age as is in this section mentioned to resort to or be in or upon such premises for the purpose of being unlawfully and carnally known by any man, whether such carnal knowledge is intended to be with any particular man or generally,
(1) shall, if such girl is under the age of 13 years, be guilty of felony, and being convicted thereof shall be liable . . . to be kept in penal servitude for life . . .
(2) If such girl is of or above the age of 13 and under the age of 16 years, shall be guilty of a misdemeanour, and being convicted thereof, shall be liable at the discretion of the court to be imprisoned for any term not exceeding two years, with or without hard labour.

Section 7 Any person who –
with intent that any unmarried girl under the age of 18 years should be unlawfully and carnally known by any man, whether such carnal knowledge is intended to be with any particular man, or generally –

takes or causes to be taken such girl out of the possession and against the will of her father or mother, or any other person having the lawful charge of her,

shall be guilty of a misdemeanour, and being convicted thereof shall be liable at the discretion of the court to be imprisoned for any term not exceeding two years, with or without hard labour:
Provided that it shall be a sufficient defence to any charge under

this section if it shall be made to appear to the court or jury that the person so charged had reasonable cause to believe that the girl was above the age of 18 years.

Section 8 Any person who detains any woman or girl against her will –
(1) In or upon any premises with intent that she may be unlawfully and carnally known by any man, whether any particular man, or generally; or
(2) In any brothel,
shall be guilty of a misdemeanour, and being convicted thereof shall be liable at the discretion of the court to be imprisoned for any term not exceeding two years, with or without hard labour.

Where a woman or girl is in or upon any premises for the purpose of having any unlawful carnal connection, or is in any brothel, a person shall be deemed to detain such woman or girl in or upon such premises or in such brothel, if, with intent to compel or induce her to remain in or upon such premises or in such brothel, such person withhold from such woman or girl any wearing apparel or other property belonging to her, or, where wearing apparel has been lent or other wise supplied to such woman or girl by or by the direction of such person, such person threatens such woman or girl with legal proceedings if she takes away with her the wearing apparel so lent or supplied.

No legal proceedings, whether criminal or civil, shall be taken against such woman or girl for taking away or being found in possession of any such wearing apparel as was necessary to enable her to leave such premises or brothel.

Section 11 Any male person who, in public or private, commits, or is a party to the commission of, or procures, or attempts to procure the commission by any male person of any act of gross indecency with another male person, shall be guilty of a misdemeanour, and being convicted thereof shall be liable at the discretion of the court to be imprisoned for any term not exceeding two years, with or without hard labour.

Part II
Section 13 Any person who –
(1) keeps or manages or acts or assists in the management of a brothel; or

(2) being the tenant, lessee, or occupier of any premises, or the agent of such lessor or landlord, lets the same or any part thereof with the knowledge that such premises or some part thereof are or is to be used as a brothel, or is wilfully a party to the continued use of such premises or any part thereof as a brothel,

shall on summary conviction in manner provided by the Summary Jurisdiction Acts be liable –

(a) to a fine not exceeding one hundred pounds or imprisonment with or without hard labour for a term not exceeding three months; and

(b) on a second or subsequent conviction, to a fine not exceeding two hundred and fifty pounds or to imprisonment with or without hard labour for a term not exceeding six months;

or, in any case, to both fine and imprisonment.

Appendix C
The Whitechapel Murders 1888–91

The series of murders in the East End of London that became commonly known as the Whitechapel murders are filed in the surviving Metropolitan Police files under that heading. However, not all these murders were the work of one man, and the notorious murderer, later known to history as Jack the Ripper, was almost certainly at work for only three months – August to November 1888. To assist the reader, we here list the complete series, with dates and locations:

1. 3 April 1888, Emma Elizabeth Smith, Osborn Street
2. 7 August 1888, Martha Tabram, George Yard Buildings
3. 31 August 1888, Mary Ann Nichols, Buck's Row
4. 8 September 1888, Annie Chapman, 29 Hanbury Street
5. 30 September 1888, Elizabeth Stride, Berner Street
6. 30 September 1888, Catherine Eddowes, Mitre Square
7. 9 November 1888, Mary Jane Kelly, Miller's Court
8. 20 December 1888, Rose Mylett, Clarke's Yard, Poplar
9. 17 July 1889, Alice McKenzie, Castle Alley
10. 10 September 1889, female torso, Pinchin Street
11. 13 February 1891, Frances Coles, Swallow Gardens

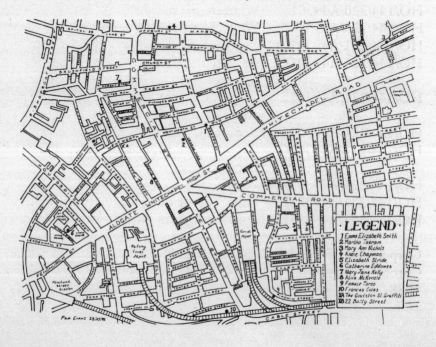

Sources

Many of the source references are mentioned individually in the text. The main sources used throughout the book are as follows:

Official Documents, Public Record Office

MEPO 1/48	Commissioner's letters, 1867–91
MEPO 1/55	Letters to Home Office, 1883–1904
MEPO 3/140	Metropolitan Police files on murders.
MEPO 3/141	Whitechapel murders, miscellaneous correspondence and suspects
MEPO 3/142	'Jack the Ripper' letters
MEPO 3/3153	Miscellaneous documents relating to the Whitechapel murders, returned to Scotland Yard in 1987
MEPO 3/3155	Photographs of Whitechapel murder victims
HO/144/220/A49301	Whitechapel murder suspects
HO/144/220/A49301B	Whitechapel murders, rewards
HO/144/221/A49301C	Report on endeavours to trace criminal
HO/144/221/A49301D	Despatches from foreign countries re suspects
HO/144/221/A49301E	Suggestion that dogs be used to track criminal
HO/144/221/A49301F	Report on Miller's Court murder
HO/144/221/A49301G	Report on allowances to police on special duty granted
HO/144/221/A49301H	Poplar murder, statement
HO/144/221/A49301I	Police report on Castle Alley murder
HO/144/221/A49301K	Police report on Pinchin Street murder

Corporation of London Records Office
Coroner's inquest (L), 1888, No. 135, Catherine Eddowes inquest, 1888

Greater London Record Office
MJ/SPC, NE 1888 Box 3 Case Paper 19, Mary Jane Kelly inquest,
1888

British Newspapers
*Daily Telegraph, Daily Graphic, East Anglian Daily Times, Eastern
Post, East London Advertiser, East London Observer, Evening
News, The Globe, Manchester Evening News, Pall Mall Gazette,
The Star, Star of the East, Suffolk Chronicle, The Times, Western
Morning News*

American and Canadian Newspapers
The Democrat (St Louis), *Evening Star-Sayings, Missouri Republican*
(St Louis), *New York Daily Tribune, New York Sun, New York
Times, New York World, St Johns Albion* (NB), *St Louis Dispatch,
St Louis Post, St Louis Post Dispatch, St Louis Republican, Sunday
Mercury* (New York), *Washington Intelligencer, Washington Star,
Quebec Mercury, The Union* (Ottawa)

Magazines and Journals
*Lloyd's Weekly News, The Police Review and Parade Gossip, Rip-
perana, Blue and Gray Magazine, Civil War Times Illustrated, Medicine Science and the Law*

Select Bibliography

Books About Jack the Ripper

Matters, Leonard, *The Mystery of Jack the Ripper*, Hutchinson, 1929 (reprinted W.H. Allen, 1948)

Stewart, William, *Jack the Ripper – A New Theory*, Quality Press, 1939

Barnard, Allan (ed.), *The Harlot Killer Jack the Ripper*, Dodd, Mead & Co. (New York), 1953

McCormick, Donald, *The Identity of Jack the Ripper*, Jarrolds, 1959 (reprinted, revised, John Long, 1970)

Cullen, Tom, *Autumn of Terror – Jack the Ripper His Crimes & Times*, Bodley Head, 1965

Odell, Robin, *Jack the Ripper in Fact and Fiction*, Harrap, 1965

Farson, Daniel, *Jack the Ripper*, Michael Joseph, 1972

Harrison, Michael, *Clarence – Was He Jack the Ripper?* W.H. Allen, 1972

Whittington-Egan, Richard, *The Identity of Jack the Ripper*, reprinted from the *Contemporary Review*, 1973 (limited to 100 copies)

Kelly, Alexander, *Jack the Ripper – A Bibliography and Review of the Literature*, Association of Assistant Librarians SED, 1973 (reprinted and revised, 1984, 1995)

Raper, Michell, *Who Was Jack the Ripper?*, Tabaret Press, 1974 (limited to 100 copies)

Rumbelow, Donald, *The Complete Jack the Ripper*, W.H. Allen, 1975 (revised 1987)

Jones, Elwyn and Lloyd, John, *The Ripper File*, Arthur Barker, 1975

Whittington-Egan, Richard, *A Casebook on Jack the Ripper*, Wildy & Sons, 1975

Knight, Stephen, *Jack the Ripper: The Final Solution*, Harrap, 1976 (revised reprint Treasure Press, 1984)

Spiering, Frank, *Prince Jack*, Doubleday (New York), 1978

Douglas, Arthur, *Will The Real Jack the Ripper*, Countryside, 1979

Fido, Martin, *The Crimes, Detection and Death of Jack the Ripper*, Weidenfeld & Nicolson, 1987

Harris, Melvin, *Jack the Ripper – The Bloody Truth*, Columbus Books, 1987

Howells, Martin and Skinner, Keith, *The Ripper Legacy*, Sidgwick & Jackson, 1987

Sharkey, Terence, *Jack the Ripper – 100 Years of Investigation*, Ward Lock, 1987

Underwood, Peter, *Jack the Ripper – One Hundred Years of Mystery*, Blandford Press, 1987

Wilson, Colin and Odell, Robin, *Jack the Ripper – Summing Up and Verdict*, Bantam Press, 1987

Begg, Paul, *Jack the Ripper – The Uncensored Facts*, Robson Books, 1988

Harris, Melvin, *The Ripper File*, W.H. Allen, 1989

Fuller, Jean Overton, *Sickert and the Ripper Crimes*, Mandrake, 1990

Begg, Paul, Skinner, Keith and Fido, Martin, *The Jack the Ripper A to Z*, Headline, 1991

Fairclough, Melvyn, *The Ripper and the Royals*, Duckworth, 1991

Harrison, Paul, *Jack the Ripper – The Mystery Solved*, Hale, 1991

Abrahamsen, David, *Murder & Madness*, Robson Books, 1992

Wolf, A. P., *Jack the Myth*, Hale, 1993

Wilding, John, *Jack the Ripper Revealed*, Constable, 1993

Harrison, Shirley, *The Diary of Jack the Ripper*, Smith Gryphon, 1993

Harris, Melvin, *The True Face of Jack the Ripper*, Michael O'Mara, 1994

Sugden, Philip, *The Complete History of Jack the Ripper*, Robinson, 1994

Wolff, Camille (compiled by), *Who Was Jack the Ripper?*, Grey House Books, 1995

Biographies and Memoirs Containing References

Le Caron, Henri, *Twenty-Five Years in the Secret Service*, Heinemann, 1892

Littlechild, John, *The Reminiscences of Chief-Inspector Littlechild*, Leadenhall Press, 1894

Anderson, Sir Robert, *The Lighter Side of My Official life*, Hodder & Stoughton, 1910

Smith, Sir Henry, *From Constable to Commissioner*, Chatto & Windus, 1910

Collins, L. C., *Life and Memoirs of John Churton Collins*, The Bodley Head, 1911

Macnaghten, Sir Melville, *Days of My Years* Edward Arnold, 1914

Sims, George R., *My Life*, Eveleigh Nash, 1917

Barnett, Henrietta, *Canon Barnett, His Life, Work and Friends*, John Murray, 1918

Le Queux, William, *Things I Know*, Nash & Grayson, 1923

Leeson, Benjamin, *Lost London – The Memoirs of an East End Detective*, Stanley Paul, 1934

Pemberton, Sir Max, *Sixty Years Ago and After*, Hutchinson, 1936

Dew, Walter, *I Caught Crippen*, Blackie, 1938

Oddie, S. Ingleby, *Inquest – A Coroner Looks Back*, Hutchinson, 1941

Books About the Police and Scotland Yard

Griffiths, Major Arthur, *Mysteries of Police and Crime*, Cassell, 1904

Dilnot George, *Scotland Yard*, Geoffrey Bles, 1929

Divall, Tom, *Scoundrels and Scallywags and Some Honest Men*, Ernest Benn, 1929

Moylan, J.F., *Scotland Yard – And The Metropolitan Police*, Putnam, 1929

Wensley, Frederick Porter, *40 Years of Scotland Yard*, Garden City (New York), 1931

Thomson, Sir Basil, *The Story of Scotland Yard*, The Literary Guild (New York), 1936

Woodhall, Edwin T., *Secrets of Scotland Yard*, The Bodley Head, 1936

Browne, Douglas G., *The Rise of Scotland Yard*, Harrap, 1956

Cobb, Belton, *Critical Years at the Yard*, Faber & Faber, 1956

Allason, Rupert, *The Branch: A History of the Metropolitan Police Special Branch 1883–1983*, Secker & Warburg, 1983

Begg, Paul and Skinner, Keith, *The Scotland Yard Files*, Headline, 1992

Lock, Joan, *Scotland Yard Casebook*, Hale, 1993

Books and Booklets With References to Jack the Ripper

Anon, 'Jack the Ripper: The Story of the Whitechapel Murders', in *Famous Crimes Past and Present*, Harold Furniss, 1903

Sims, George R., *Mysteries of Modern London*, C. Arthur Pearson, 1906

Douthwaite, Louis, *Mass Murder*, Long, 1928

Logan, Guy B.H., 'The "Ripper" Murders', in *Masters of Crime*, Stanley Paul, 1928

Walbrook, H.M., *Murders and Murder Trials 1812–1912*, Constable, 1932

Hopkins, R. Thurston, 'Shadowing the Shadow of a Murderer', in *Life and Death at the Old Bailey*, Herbert Jenkins, 1935

Woodhall, Edwin T., *Crime and the Supernatural*, John Long, 1935

Dearden, Harold, 'Who Was Jack the Ripper?', in *Great Unsolved Crimes*, Hutchinson, 1935

Beaumont, F.A., 'The Fiend of East London', in *The Fifty Most Amazing Crimes of the Last 100 Years*, Odhams, 1936

Pearson, Edmund, *More Studies in Murder*, Random House (New York), 1936

West, D. J., 'The Identity of "Jack the Ripper", an Examination of an Alleged Psychic Solution', in *Journal of the Society for Psychical Research*, July–August 1949, Vol.XXXV, No. 653

Shew, Edward Spencer, *A Companion to Murder*, Cassell, 1960

Ambler, Eric, *The Ability to Kill and Other Pieces*, The Bodley Head, 1963

Cargill, David and Holland, Julian, *Scenes of Murder: A London Guide*, Heinemann, 1964

Camps, Francis E., 'A New Look At Jack the Ripper', in *The Investigation of Murder*, Michael Joseph, 1966

Camps, Francis E., 'More About Jack the Ripper', in *The Criminologist*, No. 7, February 1968

MacLeod, C. M., 'A "Ripper" Handwriting Analysis', in *The Criminologist*, No. 9, August 1968

Stowell, T.E.A., ' "Jack the Ripper": A Solution', in *The Criminologist*, No. 18, November 1970

Morland, Nigel, 'Jack the Ripper', in *The Criminologist*, No. 22, autumn 1971

Butler, Ivan, *Murderers' London*, Robert Hale, 1973

Camps, Francis E., 'More About Jack the Ripper', in *Camps on Crime*, David & Charles, 1973

Downie, Robert A., *Murder in London – A Topographical Guide to Famous Crimes*, Barker, 1973

Bell, Donald, ' "Jack the Ripper": The Final Solution' in *The Criminologist*, No. 33, summer 1974

Davis, Derek, ' "Jack the Ripper": The Handwriting Analysis', in *The Criminologist*, No. 33, summer 1974

Friedland, Martin L., *The Trials of Israel Lipski*, Macmillan, 1984

Ogan, Jon, 'Martha Tabram – The Forgotten Ripper Victim', in *Journal of the Police History Society*, No. 5, 1990

Walkowitz, Judith R., *City of Dreadful Delight*, Virago Press, 1992

Stotter, Mike, 'Jack the Ripper – A Look at the Non-Fiction Works', in *Book and Magazine Collector*, No. 108, March 1993

McLaren, Angus, *A Prescription For Murder*, Chicago University Press, 1993

Other Books Consulted

Wertham, Frederic, *Dark Legend – A Study in Murder*, Victor Gollancz, 1947

DeRiver, J. Paul, *The Sexual Criminal*, Blackwell Scientific Publications, 1949

Krafft-Ebing, Richard von, *Psychopathia Sexualis*, G. P. Putnam's Sons (New York), 1965

Nicholson, Michael, *The Yorkshire Ripper*, W.H. Allen, 1979

Larsen, Richard, *Bundy – Deliberate Stranger*, Englewood Cliffs: Prentice Hall, 1980

Yallop, David, *Deliver Us From Evil*, Macdonald Futura, 1981

Michaud, Stephen and Aynesworth, Hugh, *The Only Living Witness*, Simon & Schuster, 1983

Masters, Brian, *Killing For Company*, Jonathan Cape, 1985

Ressler, Robert K., Burgess, Ann W. and Douglas, John E., *Sexual Homicide*, Lexington Books, 1988

Leyton, Elliott, *Compulsive Killers*, New York University Press, 1986

Ressler, Robert K. and Shachtman, Tom, *Whoever Fights Monsters*, Simon & Schuster, 1992

Clark, Steve and Morley, Mike, *Murder in Mind*, Boxtree, 1993

Books on President Lincoln and the Civil War

Bryan, George S., *The Great American Myth*, Chicago Americana House, 1940

Hanchett, William, *Lincoln Murder Conspiracies*, University of Illinois Press, 1983

Peterson, M.D., *Lincoln in American Memory*, Oxford University Press, 1989

Oates, Stephen B., *With Malice Toward None*, Allen & Unwin, 1990
McPherson, J.M., *Abraham Lincoln and the Second American Revolution*, Oxford University Press, 1991

Index